New Dimensions of Politics in India

Following India's general election in May 2009, this book undertakes a critical evaluation of the performance of the United Progressive Alliance (UPA). It presents a thorough evaluation of the UPA coalition government's policies and, by providing an understanding of the new innovations, evaluates the effectiveness of these policies against their aims and objectives.

This book suggests that there is an analytical framework for assessing the political consequences of the policies and the UPA's success, both at the national and state levels, with particular reference to new developments in governance, secularism and security. These three areas constitute important fault lines between the main national political parties in India, and provide an interesting point of departure to explore the new emerging trends, as well as the strong underlying continuities between the UPA administration and its predecessors. The book offers fresh insights into the structure of Indian politics, and is a useful contribution to studies in South Asian Politics, governance and political parties.

Lawrence Sáez is Senior Lecturer (Associate Professor) in Comparative and International Politics at the School of Oriental and African Studies (SOAS), UK. He is also Director of the Centre for South Asian Studies at SOAS and an Associate Fellow in the International Economics programme at Chatham House.

Gurharpal Singh is Dean of the Faculty of Arts and Humanities and Chair in Inter-Religious Relations and Development in the Department for the study of Religion at SOAS.

Routledge Advances in South Asian Studies
Edited by Subrata K. Mitra
South Asia Institute, University of Heidelberg, Germany

South Asia, with its burgeoning, ethnically diverse population, soaring economies, and nuclear weapons, is an increasingly important region in the global context. This series, which builds on this complex, dynamic and volatile area, features innovative and original research on the region as a whole or on the individual countries. Its scope extends to scholarly works drawing on the history, politics, development studies, sociology and economics of individual countries from the region, as well as those that take an interdisciplinary and comparative approach to the area as a whole or draw a comparison between two or more countries from the region. In terms of theory and method, rather than basing itself on any one orthodoxy, the series draws broadly on the insights germane to area studies, as well as the toolkit of the social sciences in general, emphasizing comparison, the analysis of the structure and processes, and the application of qualitative and quantitative methods. The series welcomes submissions from established authors in the field, as well as from young authors who have recently completed their doctoral dissertations.

1   **Perception, Politics and Security in South Asia**
    The compound crisis of 1990
    P. R. Chari, Pervaiz Iqbal Cheema and Stephen Philip Cohen

2   **Coalition Politics and Hindu Nationalism**
    Edited by Katharine Adeney and Lawrence Sáez

3   **The Puzzle of India's Governance**
    Culture, context and comparative theory
    Subrata K. Mitra

4   **India's Nuclear Bomb and National Security**
    Karsten Frey

5   **Starvation and India's Democracy**
    Dan Banik

6   **Parliamentary Control and Government Accountability in South Asia**
    A comparative analysis of Bangladesh, India and Sri Lanka
    Taiabur Rahman

7 **Political Mobilisation and Democracy in India**
   States of emergency
   Vernon Hewitt

8 **Military Control in Pakistan**
   The parallel state
   Mazhar Aziz

9 **Sikh Nationalism and Identity in a Global Age**
   Giorgio Shani

10 **The Tibetan Government-in-Exile**
   Politics at large
   Stephanie Roemer

11 **Trade Policy, Inequality and Performance in Indian Manufacturing**
   Kunal Sen

12 **Democracy and Party Systems in Developing Countries**
   A comparative study
   Clemens Spiess

13 **War and Nationalism in South Asia**
   The Indian state and the Nagas
   Marcus Franke

14 **The Politics of Social Exclusion in India**
   Democracy at the crossroads
   Edited by Harihar Bhattacharyya, Partha Sarka and Angshuman Kar

15 **Party System Change in South India**
   Political entrepreneurs, patterns and processes
   Andrew Wyatt

16 **Dispossession and Resistance in India**
   The river and the rage
   Alf Gunvald Nilsen

17 **The Construction of History and Nationalism in India**
   Textbooks, controversies and politics
   Sylvie Guichard

18 **Political Survival in Pakistan**
   Beyond ideology
   Anas Malik

19 **New Cultural Identitarian Political Movements in Developing Societies**
   The Bharatiya Janata party
   Sebastian Schwecke

20 **Sufism and Saint Veneration in Contemporary Bangladesh**
   The Maijbhandaris of Chittagong
   Hans Harder

21 **New Dimensions of Politics in India**
   The United Progressive Alliance in power
   Lawrence Sáez and Gurharpal Singh

22 **Vision and Strategy in Indian Politics**
   Jawaharlal Nehru's policy choices and the designing of political institutions
   Jivanta Schoettli

New Dimensions of Politics in India

The United Progressive Alliance in power

Edited by
Lawrence Sáez and
Gurharpal Singh

LONDON AND NEW YORK

First published 2012
by Routledge
2 Park Square, Milton Park, Abingdon, Oxfordshire OX14 4RN

Simultaneously published in the USA and Canada
by Routledge
711 Third Avenue, New York, NY 10017

First issued in paperback 2016

Routledge is an imprint of the Taylor & Francis Group, an informa business

© 2012 Lawrence Sáez and Gurharpal Singh

The right of the editors to be identified as the authors of the editorial material, and of the contributors for their individual chapters, has been asserted by them in accordance with sections 77 and 78 of the Copyright, Designs and Patents Act 1988.

All rights reserved. No part of this book may be reprinted or reproduced or utilised in any form or by any electronic, mechanical, or other means, now known or hereafter invented, including photocopying and recording, or in any information storage or retrieval system, without permission in writing from the publishers.

Trademark notice: Product or corporate names may be trademarks or registered trademarks, and are used only for identification and explanation without intent to infringe.

British Library Cataloguing in Publication Data
A catalogue record for this book is available from the British Library

Library of Congress Cataloging in Publication Data
New dimensions of politics in India : the United Progressive Alliance in power / edited by Lawrence Sáez and Gurharpal Singh.
  p. cm. -- (Routledge advances in South Asian studies ; 21)
  Includes bibliographical references and index.
  1. United Progressive Alliance (India) 2. Political parties--India.
  3. India--Politics and government--21st century. I. Sáez, Lawrence, 1965- II. Singh, Gurharpal. III. Series: Routledge advances in South Asian studies ; 21.
  JQ298.A1N48 2011   954.05'32--dc22
  2011012237

ISBN 13: 978-1-138-63565-4 (pbk)
ISBN 13: 978-0-415-66897-2 (hbk)

Typeset in Times New Roman
by Bookcraft Ltd, Stroud, Gloucestershire

Contents

List of figures and tables ix
List of contributors x
Acknowledgements xi
List of abbreviations xii

1 **Introduction** 1
  LAWRENCE SÁEZ AND GURHARPAL SINGH

PART 1
Governance 11

2 **Did the central government's poverty initiatives help to re-elect it?** 13
  JAMES MANOR

3 **UPA (2004–) and Indian federalism** 26
  HARIHAR BHATTACHARYYA

4 **Educational exclusion and inclusive development in India** 39
  SHAILAJA FENNELL

PART 2
Secularism 53

5 **UPA and secularism** 55
  GURHARPAL SINGH

6 **The UPA and Muslims** 68
  STEVE WILKINSON

7 **Beyond identity? UPA rhetoric on social justice and affirmative action** 79
  ROCHANA BAJPAI

PART 3
Security 97

8 The UPA's foreign policy, 2004–9 99
KANTI BAJPAI

9 India's energy security during the UPA government 113
LAWRENCE SÁEZ

10 Anti-terrorism and security policy 131
RAHUL ROY-CHAUDHURY

11 Conclusion 149
GURHARPAL SINGH AND LAWRENCE SÁEZ

Notes 154
Bibliography 170
Index 186

List of figures and tables

Figures

1.1	Comparative electoral performance of the principal parliamentary groupings (2004 and 2009)	4
4.1	India's public expenditure on education 2006–7	40
9.1	India's energy consumption by sector (2007)	118
9.2	Projected electricity generated by nuclear sources	126

Tables

1.1	UPA performances in 2009 and 2004	3
1.2	List of state assemblies controlled by either the INC or the BJP in 2004 and 2009	5
2.1	Spending on poverty-reducing programmes (2004–2009)	16
2.2	All-India voting preferences by economic class (assets and income)	20
2.3	Voting preferences of those who had heard (or not) of poverty initiatives	21
2.4	Voting preferences of beneficiaries and non-beneficiaries	21
2.5	States governed by various parties/alliances	22
2.6	Satisfaction with Central and State Governments	24
5.1	UPA's policies and secularism	59
9.1	Comparison between India and the world's primary energy consumption, 1990–2030 (in Quadrillion BTUs)	114
9.2	India's energy profile and projected outlook (2006 and 2030)	115
9.3	India's indigenous production of primary energy (2004)	116
9.4	Proportion of total assets owned by the state in India's leading energy firms	128
9.5	ONGC international holdings	129
10.1	Selected major terror attacks during the first UPA government (22 May 2004 – 21 May 2009)	135
10.2	Selected major attacks by Naxalites during the first UPA government (22 May 2004 – 21 May 2009	138

List of contributors

Kanti Bajpai is visiting Professor, Lee Kuan Yew School of Public Policy, National University of Singapore.

Rochana Bajpai is Lecturer in Politics, Department of Politics, School of Oriental and African Studies (SOAS).

Harihar Bhattacharyya is Professor of Political Science, University of Burdwan, India.

Shailaja Fennell is Lecturer in Development Studies, Department of Land Economy, University of Cambridge.

James Manor is Emeka Anyaoku Professor of Commonwealth Studies, Institute of Commonwealth Studies, London.

Rahul Roy-Chaudhury is Senior Fellow for South Asia, International Institute for Strategic Studies (IISS), London.

Lawrence Sáez is Senior Lecturer (Associate Professor) in Comparative and International Politics, Department of Politics, School of Oriental and African Studies (SOAS).

Gurharpal Singh is Dean of the Faculty of Arts and Humanities and Chair in Inter-Religious Relations and Development at SOAS.

Steve Wilkinson is Nilekani Professor of India and South Asian Studies and Professor of Political Science and International Affairs, Yale University.

Acknowledgements

This book could not have been written without the collaboration and patience of a great number of people. We thank Dorothea Schaefter of Routledge for showing interest in our project during its inception. We would also like to acknowledge our thanks to Professor Subrata Kumar Mitra for his encouragement and support as editor of Routledge's *Advances in South Asian Studies* series. We further acknowledge the support of the School of Oriental and African Studies (SOAS) for hosting an international workshop in September 2009, which was made possible as result of financial support from its Faculty Research Committee. Additional support was provided by the University of Birmingham College and Arts Research Committee. The editors would also like to thank Jane Savory and Ed Quipp for their invaluable administrative assistance. The Centre of South Asian Studies and the Department of Politics at SOAS, as always, provided priceless publicity and logistical backup. We are also extremely indebted to our contributors who responded enthusiastically to our initial call. Editing a book can be a thankless task but fortunately our contributors as leading experts in their field helped to make this exercise less exacting. The September 2009 workshop at SOAS was, indeed, a memorable occasion and we thank all those who took part in the event. Last but not least, at a personal level, we should thank our respective families. This work is dedicated to Joy, Jackson, Raghu, Sukhmani and Harman.

List of abbreviations

AB	*Abhinav Bharat*
ACD	Asian Cooperation Dialogue
AG&SP	accelerated generation and supply program
AIMIM	All India Majlis-e-Ittehadul Muslimeen
AITC	All India Trinamool Congress
APDP	accelerated power development program
APDRP	accelerated power development and reform program
ARC	Arunachal Congress
ARF	ASEAN Regional Forum
AREP	accelerated rural electrification program
ASEAN	Association for South East Asian Nations
ASEM	Asia–Europe Meeting
ASSOCHAM	Associated Chambers of Commerce and Industry of India
BBC	British Broadcasting Company
BCM	billion cubic metres
BIMSTEC	Bay of Bengal Initiative for Multisectoral Technical and Economic Cooperation
BJD	Biju Janata Dal
BJP	Bharatiya Janata Party
BkWh	billion kilowatt hours
BRGF	Backward Regions Grant Fund
BRIC	Brazil, Russia, India, China
BSP	Bahujan Samaj Party
BTU	British thermal unit
CABE	Central Advisory Board for Education
CAD	Constituent Assembly debates
CBI	Central Bureau of Investigation
CBM	confidence-building measure
CCS	Cabinet Committee on Security
CDS	chief of defense staff
CERM	coordinated emergency response measure
CII	Confederation of Indian Industry
CM	Chief Minister
CMP	Common Minimum Programme

CNPC	China National Petroleum Corporation
CO_2	carbon dioxide
CoBRA	Commando Battalion for Resolute Action
CoS	Committee of Secretaries
CPI	Communist Party of India
CPI (M)	Communist Party of India (Marxist)
CPM	Communist Party of India (Marxist)
CRPF	Central Reserve Police Force
CSDS	Centre for the Study of Developing Societies
CSS	Common School System
DAE	Department of Atomic Energy
DIA	Defense Intelligence Agency
DMK	Dravida Munnetra Kazhagam
DPEP	District Primary Education Programme
EEZ	exclusive economic zone
EFA	Education for All
EGoM	empowered group of ministers
EU	European Union
FDI	foreign direct investment
FICCI	Federation of Indian Chambers of Commerce and Industry
FIR	first information report
GDP	gross domestic product
GNP	gross national product
GoM	group of ministers
GPI	Gender Parity Index
HM	*Hizbul Mujahideen*
HUM	*Harkat-ul-Mujahidin*
IAEA	International Atomic Energy Agency
IB	Intelligence Bureau
IBSA	India, Brazil, South Africa
ICDS	Integrated Child Development Services
ICSSR	Indian Council for Social Science Research
IEA	International Energy Agency
IED	improvised explosive device
IFI	international financial institution
IM	Indian Mujahideen
IMG	Inter-Ministerial Group
INC	Indian National Congress
IND	Independent
IOC	Indian Oil Corporation
IOR-ARC	Indian Ocean Rim Association for Regional Cooperation
IPI	Iran–Pakistan–India
IPS	Indian Police Service
ISC	Inter State Council
ISI	Inter-Services Intelligence
ISPRL	Indian Strategic Petroleum Reserve Limited

IUML	Indian Union Muslim League
JD (S)	Janata Dal (Secular)
JD (U)	Janata Dal (United)
JeM	*Jaish-e-Mohamed*
JIC	Joint Intelligence Committee
JKNC	Jammu and Kashmir National Conference
JKPDP	Jammu and Kashmir People's Democratic Party
JMM	Jharkhand Mukti Morcha
JOC	Joint Operation Centre
JPRGY	*Jai Prakash Rozgar Guarantee Yojana*
JWG	Joint Working Group
KC (I)	Kerala Congress (Issac)
KEC (M)	Kerala Congress (Mani)
LAC	Line of Actual Control
LeT	*Lashkar-e-Taiba*
LJNSP	Lok Jan Shakti Party
LOC	Lines of Control
LPG	liquefied petroleum gas
LSD	Lok Sabha debates
LTTE	Liberation Tigers of Tamil Eelam
MAC	Multi-Agency Center
mbd	million barrels a day
MCD	Minority Concentration District
MDMK	Marumalarchi Dravida Munnetra Kazhagam
MDG	Millennium Development Goal
MDM	Mid-Day Meal scheme
MGC	Mekong-Ganga Cooperation
MHRD	Ministry of Human Resource Development
mmt	million metric ton
MNF	Mizo National Front
MoMA	Ministry of Minority Affairs
MoU	memorandum of understanding
MP	Member of Parliament
MSDP	multi-sector development program
MT	million tons
Mtoe	metric tons of oil equivalent
MUL	Muslim League
MW	megawatt
NAFRE	National Association for the Fundamental Right to Education
NAM	Non-Aligned Movement
NATGRID	National Intelligence Grid
NCAER	National Council for Applied Economic Research
NCERT	National Council for Educational Research and Training
NCF	National Curriculum Framework
NCP	Nationalist Congress Party
NCTC	National Counter Terrorism Center

NDA	National Democratic Alliance
NELP	New Exploration Licensing Policy
NGO	non-governmental organization
NREGS	National Rural Employment Guarantee Scheme
NIA	National Investigative Agency
NSA	national security advisor
NSCS	National Security Council Secretariat
NSG	Nuclear Suppliers' Group
NSG	National Security Guard
NSSP	Next Steps in Strategic Partnership
OBCs	Other Backward Classes
OECD	Organisation of Economic Co-operation and Development
OIDB	Oil Industry Directorate Board
OIL	Oil India Limited
ONGC	Oil and Gas Corporation
PDR	People's Democratic Party
PDS	Party for Democratic Socialism
PMGY	*Pradhan Mantri Gramodaya Yojana*
PMK	Pattali Makkal Katchi
POTA	Prevention of Terrorism Act
PPP	Pakistan People's Party
PROBE	Public Report on Basic Education in India
PSG	Public Study Group
R&AW	Research & Analysis Wing
RECOUP	Research Consortium on Educational Outcomes and Poverty
REST	Rural Electricity Supply Technology
RJD	Rashtriya Janata Dal
RJM	Rashtriya Jagran Manch
RPI	Republican Party of India
RPI (A)	Republican Party of India (Athwale)
RPI (G)	Republican Party of India (Gavai)
RSD	Rajya Sabha debates
RSS	Rashtriya Swayamsevak Sangh
RSVY	*Rashtriya Sama Vikas Yogna*
SAARC	South Asian Association for Regional Cooperation
SAP	Structural Adjustment Programs
SC	scheduled caste
SCO	Shanghai Cooperation Organization
SDF	Sikkim Democratic Front
SEB	state electricity board
SIB	State Intelligence Bureau
SGRY	*Sampoorna Grameen Rozgar Yojana*
SGSY	*Swarnjayanti Gram Swarozgar Yojana*
SIMI	Students' Islamic Movement of India
SMAC	Subsidiary Multi-Agency Center
SP	Samajwadi Party

SPR	strategic petroleum reserve
SSA	*Sarva Shiksha Abhiyan*
ST	scheduled tribe
STU	state transmission utility
TADA	Terrorist and Disruptive Activities (Prevention) Act
tcf	trillion cubic feet
TDP	Telugu Desam Party
TFC	total final consumption
TPES	total primary energy supply
TRS	Telangana Rashtra Samithi
UAPA	Unlawful Activities (Prevention) Act
UEE	universal elementary education
UGC	Universities Grants Commission
UIC	unique identity card
ULFA	United Liberation Front of Asom
UN	United Nations
UPA	United Progressive Alliance
UPE	universal primary education
VCK	Viduthalai Chiruthaigal Katchi
VHP	Vishwa Hindu Parishad
WTO	World Trade Organization

1 Introduction

Lawrence Sáez and Gurharpal Singh

Introduction

The 2009 general election in India revealed that, contrary to conventional wisdom, a governing coalition can complete a full term of office and be re-elected. This landmark development, after almost 20 years of coalition governments, suggests that India's transition to an era of minority governing coalitions has reached a degree of systemic stability. The concept of systemic stability under conditions of coalition governance in democratic parliamentary systems has an extensive pedigree in political science. For instance, William Riker's seminal work (Riker 1962) on the theory of coalitions has generated a rich tradition of analysis into the dynamics behind cabinet formation and government durability that has subsequently been extended by others (see Taylor and Herman 1971; Dodd 1974; Brass 1977; Mitra 1980; Lijphart 1984). Game-theoretic and institutionalist approaches to the subject of systemic stability also share a common perspective that the size and the policy distance between coalition actors have specific expected outcomes in terms of cabinet size and government durability. Moreover, analytical perspectives that focus on ideology (Strom 1985, 1988) predict that ideological cohesiveness and the potential conflict levels among coalition partners can affect the expected duration of a coalition government.

In the literature on the transformation of India's political system from a dominant one-party system to coalition politics, a great deal of attention is paid to the institutional mechanisms in the functioning of party systems. Since 1989, India has had six minority governing coalitions, some of them short-lived. Scholarly analyses of these governments has focused on the features of minority coalition governments at the national level (Manor 1994; Sridharan 2003) or changes in the party system at the sub-national level (Sáez 2002; Heath 2005; Wilkinson 2005). Other authors have also attempted to evaluate the impact of coalition politics on public policy formulation against the backdrop of the rise of Hindu nationalism, (Adeney and Sáez 2005), increasing corruption (Singh 2005) and minority, gender and affirmative action rights (Mitra 2005; Rao 2005).

Ideological difference between the parties, as we shall see below, and in the papers presented in this volume, are significant in determining the policies pursued, but in India these cannot be easily framed or understood within the existing political science literature. For example, Downsian models of democracy (Adams *et al.* 2004; Adams and Somer-Topcu 2009; Ezrow 2005, 2008) postulate that in plurality elections there should be a party convergence towards the views of the median voter. While this is no doubt the case in that successful winning coalitions in the last 20 years are those that have sought to appeal to middle ground – the traditional center occupied by Congress – the implicit assumption about rational utility-maximizing voters in Downsian models can be difficult to apply in India because of the different arenas under which party competition takes place.

Arenas of political competition

A minority coalition government in India normally faces two challenges. At a national level it must stave off potential threats from the non-governing opposition coalition. More importantly, it must engage with the components of the coalition itself. Such coalitions can be unstable if there is a high degree of internal fractionalization; that is, division of support among the constituent parties. For this reason, minority governing coalitions must be able to maintain stability by ensuring a minimum number of parliamentary seats to secure a simple majority. In India's case this means securing more than 272 parliamentary seats. As Table 1.1 shows, in 2004 the United Progressive Alliance (UPA) obtained 248 seats and in addition had the support from four parties (the Samajwadi Party (SP), the Rashtriya Janata Dal (RJD), the Sikkim Democratic Front (SDF) and the Lok Jan Shakti Party (LJNSP)). In 2009, the UPA coalition increased its seat share to 262 parliamentary seats (nearly 96.3 per cent of the seats needed to obtain a simple majority). Its external allies in the 2004 general election suffered a substantial decline in total seats (a net loss of 45 seats). However, with the enhanced position of the Indian National Congress (INC, henceforth Congress/Congress Party), the UPA coalition was in a firmer parliamentary position in 2009.

Nonetheless, as Duverger (1951: 324) has noted, alliances between parties 'can vary greatly in form and degree. Some are ephemeral and unorganized … others are lasting and are strongly organized, so that sometimes they are like super-parties.' The UPA's coalition governments in 2004 and 2009 have features of growing organization and strength, but it is worth remembering that India's minority governing coalitions in 2004 and 2009 necessitated more than 11 parties to secure a simple parliamentary majority.

Figure 1.1 shows that there has been a significant shift in parliamentary strength of the core group of UPA coalition allies, relative to the National Democratic Alliance (NDA), from 2004 to the 2009 general election. Figure 1.1 also shows that the parliamentary strength of the leftist parties has diminished considerably between 2004 and 2009.

India's federal system represents a secondary arena of political competition. Individual national parties, like the Congress or the Bharatiya Janata Party (BJP), must also compete at a provincial level. Although the national electoral cycle is five years, Indian political parties must contest a plethora of state assembly elections every year. This ongoing system of sub-national electoral competition forces the main national political parties to pursue national policies that will not alienate its allies in regional electoral contests.

Table 1.1 UPA performances in 2009 and 2004

	UPA (2009)	UPA (2004)	Seat change
INC	206	145	+61
AITC	19	2	+17
DMK	18	16	+2
NCP	9	9	–
JKNC	3	2	+1
MUL	2	1	+1
JMM	2	–	+2
IND (Congress)	1	1	–
KEC (M)	1	–	+1
VCK	1	–	–
RPI	–	–	–
PDS	–	–	–
ARC	–	–	–
RPI (A)	–	1	–
TRS	n.a.	5	–5
JKPDP	–	1	–1
Total	262	183	+79
External allies			
SP	22	36	–14
BSP	21	19	+2
RJD	4	24	–20
JD (S)	3	3	–
SDF	1	1	–
LJNSP	–	4	–4
MDMK	1	4	–3
PMK	–	–	–6
Total	314	280	+34

Sources: Electoral Commission of India; Lok Sabha website

Abbreviations: INC: Indian National Congress; AITC: All India Trinamool Congress; DMK: Dravida Munnetra Kazhagam; NCP: Nationalist Congress Party; JKNC: Jammu and Kashmir National Conference; MUL: Muslim League; JMM: Jharkhand Mukti Morcha; IND: Independent; KEC (M): Kerala Congress (Mani); VCK: Viduthalai Chiruthaigal Katchi; RPI: Republican Party of India; PDS: Party for Democratic Socialism; ARC: Arunachal Congress; RPI (A): Republican Party of India (Athwale); TRS: Telangana Rashtra Samithi; JKPDP: Jammu and Kashmir People's Democratic Party; SP: Samajwadi Party; BSP: Bahujan Samaj Party; RJD: Rashtriya Janata Dal; JD (S): Janata Dal (Secular); SDF: Sikkim Democratic Front; LJNSP: Lok Jan Shakti Party; MDMK: Marumalarchi Dravida Munnetra Kazhagam; PMK: Pattali Makkal Katchi.

Notes
1 UPA coalition allies in 2004 included the INC, TRS, RJD, LJNSP, NCP, JMM, JKPDP, MUL, KEC (M), JD (S), RPI, RPI (A), DMK, MDMK, PMK, PDS, ARC and IND (Congress). Many of these parties were not UPA allies in 2009.
2 Political party acronyms correspond to those used by the Electoral Commission of India.

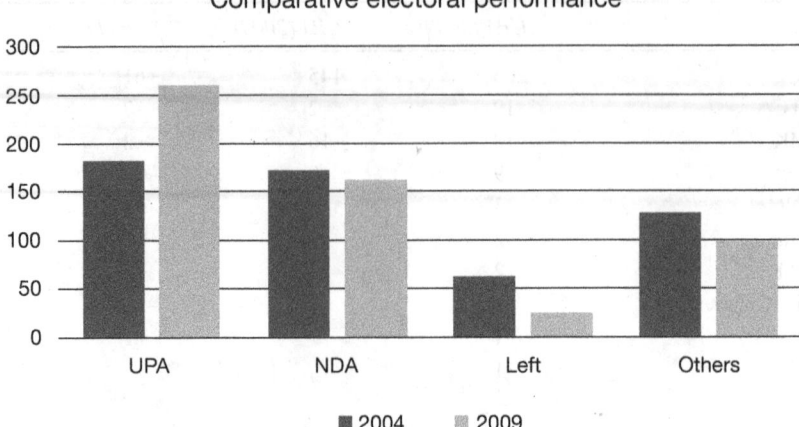

Source: Electoral Commission of India; Lok Sabha website

Note
Figures represent number of parliamentary seats obtained by each parliamentary group. Figures for the UPA and the NDA exclude external coalition supporters.

Figure 1.1 Comparative electoral performance of the principal parliamentary groupings (2004 and 2009)

During the last two national electoral cycles (2004 and 2009), the INC and the BJP have been competitive in about half of India's state assemblies. For instance, Table 1.2 shows the comparative level of strength of the INC and the BJP in 14 state assemblies in India in 2004 and 2009.

As Table 1.2 shows, between 2004 and 2009, there has been some alternation in six of these states. Three states (Himachal Pradesh, Karnataka, and Uttarakhand) switched from the INC in 2004 to the BJP in 2009. In turn, two states (Goa and Rajasthan) switched from the BJP to the INC during the same time period. One state (Jharkhand) switched from the BJP to a regional party (the JMM) from 2004 to 2009, one state (Mizoram) switched from a regional party (the MNF) to the INC. The state of Kerala switched from the INC in 2004 to the CPM in 2009. Outside these 16 states, the level of penetration by the two largest national parties in India's state legislatures is severely constrained.

To complicate matters, some political parties (e.g. DMK, Telugu Desam Party (TDP), CPM) are essentially provincial parties that often compete against and form alliances with the two main national parties (Congress and BJP). Since the de-linking of national and state elections in 1967, political competition in the states has produced a variety of party systems ranging from the dominant to multiparty systems (Rudolph and Rudolph 1987; Nikolenyi 1998; Sáez 2002). In some ways, though, the most significant change has come about as result of the

Table 1.2 List of state assemblies controlled by either the INC or the BJP in 2004 and 2009

State assembly	2004	2009
Andhra Pradesh	INC	INC
Assam	INC	INC
Chhattisgarh	BJP	BJP
Goa	BJP	INC
Gujarat	BJP	BJP
Himachal Pradesh	INC	BJP
Jharkhand*	BJP	JMM
Karnataka	INC	BJP
Kerala	INC	CPM
Madhya Pradesh	BJP	BJP
Maharashtra	INC	INC
Manipur	INC	INC
Meghalaya	INC	INC
Mizoram	MNF	INC
Rajasthan	BJP	INC
Uttarakhand	INC	BJP

Source: INC and BJP websites

Abbreviations: CPM: Communist Party of India; MNF: Mizo National Front.

Note
* Jharkhand was under President's Rule from 19 January 2009 until 29 December 2009.
The list does not include union territories.

rise of *dalit* parties in north India (SP, RJD and the Bahujan Samaj Party (BSP)) that have effectively eroded Congress party support, especially in its northern heartland (Chandra 1999, 2000; Jaffrelot 2000). For instance, the Congress party has not governed the state of Bihar since 1990 and Uttar Pradesh since 1998. In these conditions, national coalition building requires not only that ideological and policy differences are accommodated, but it also necessitates that the coalition building and maintenance process is able to reconcile the demands of these regional parties, which often can be idiosyncratic, designed to outbid their main political rival in the state (e.g. DMK) or, still, determined by their pragmatic relationship with either the Congress or the BJP.

The UPA as a political phenomenon

To date there has been no serious analysis of the UPA in power. The literature on the Congress party, both from an overarching historical perspective as well as its role in Indian politics, is quite extensive (Franda 1962; Kothari 1964, 1974; Morris-Jones 1967; Kochanek 1969; Mendelsohn 1978; Rudolph and Rudolph 1980; Chand 1985; Gehlot 1991). Some scholars, however, have tried to develop our understanding of the changing role of the Congress party within an era of coalition governments in India (Vanderbok 1990; Singh 1992; Pai 1996; Candland 1997). It is only in recent years that there has been a renewed interest in the Congress party as a leading force in a governing coalition. For example, Johari (2006) provides a useful example of the analysis of the party's development, including a chapter on the UPA. More narrowly, Bijukumar (2006) aims to evaluate Congress's economic policies, but only offers a cursory treatment of the subject. Although useful in their own right, these works do not really offer a comprehensive assessment of the UPA's performance across a broad range of policies. Nor for that matter do they evaluate the performance of the UPA coalition once it was in power.

The issue of the challenges faced by minority governing coalitions has sparked an intense debate among Indian politics specialists. For instance, Chakravarti (2006) offers a sound analysis of the historical structure of national governing coalitions in India. However, the book takes an aggregate look at the phenomenon of coalition politics over time (focusing on three coalitions) and its focus is strongest on the Janata Party coalition (1977–1979), and does not assess the importance of the UPA victory beyond its electoral performance in the 2004. Similarly, Roy and Wallace (2007) provide a comprehensive analysis of the performance of different political parties leading to the formation of the UPA coalition after the 2004 general election, but offer no insights into the post-election period. Similarly, Bhambhri (2007) is a useful overview of the historical development of capitalism and the maturing of the Indian state, but only devotes the closing chapters to the phenomenon of the UPA.

A final strand of literature compares the performance of the NDA with that of the UPA. This particular approach, however, is framed mainly around the personality clashes between Sonia Gandhi, the president of the Congress Party, and her BJP opponents. Thus Sharma (2004) is a leading example of this genre. Likewise, Bhambhri (2006) provides a polemical account of the Congress Party's president during the first two years in office. However, these works offer only fragmentary insights into the UPA government while overlooking some of the more important challenges and developments (e.g. the US–India nuclear deal, the November 2008 terrorist attacks in Mumbai).

In contrast to the publications outlined above, this study offers a thorough and timely analysis of the UPA coalition government. Our primary focus is to understand the new innovations in UPA's policies, especially towards poverty reduction, minorities, secularism, education, security, and foreign policy. At the same time we are also interested in evaluating the effectiveness of these policies as measured against their proclaimed aim and objectives. In this volume we argue for a critical evaluation of discreet areas of public policy against their aims and objectives as well as impact and effectiveness. We suggest that there is an analytical framework for assessing the political consequences of these policies and the UPA's success – both at the national and state levels – with particular reference to new policies in governance, secularism, and security. These areas provide new opportunities for fresh reflections on policy innovation and policy implementation largely because they have been the source of intense competition between the UPA and NDA. At the same time, though, we recognize the need to understand the underlying continuities between the UPA's policies and those of its predecessors.

We also highlight the importance of drawing attention to some of the discontinuities, notably the impact of UPA's policies in reconfiguring the political formations that support it (both nationally and at the state level), the changing nature of governance in Indian politics in which 'development' and 'good governance' appear to trump fiscal or communal populism and the apparent 'reinvention' of the Congress as a neo-social democratic, distributionist party that aims to manage growth alongside poverty.

Critical areas of policy contestation

The aim of this volume is to evaluate these dimensions of contemporary Indian politics more comprehensively, especially in light of the durability of the UPA. Using the UPA as an analytical centerpiece, we aim to advance our understanding of the relationship between the state and politics in three critical areas: *governance*, *secularism*, and *security*. In our view these three features constitute important fault lines between the two main national political parties in India (Congress and BJP) and provide an interesting point of departure to explore the new emerging new trends as well as the strong underlying continuities between the UPA administration and its predecessors.

This volume follows, in many respects, the approach adopted in Adeney and Sáez (2005), which explored the challenges to policy-making by the NDA. However, our approach goes further in offering new insights into the structure of Indian politics because we concentrate on those policy areas on which there is some distance between the Hindu nationalist BJP-led NDA and the center-left Congress-led UPA – namely, governance, secularism, and security and how they provided the battleground for the critical election of 2004 that led to the UPA's victory.

Governance

During its first term of office, the UPA initiated a plethora of anti-poverty schemes that are generally accredited with its success in the 2009 general election. Using data from the National Election Study at the Centre for the Study of Developing Societies (CSDS), James Manor (Chapter 2) tests this claim empirically. According to Manor, UPA's poverty-reducing initiatives did, indeed, win votes for Congress and its allies, but that they fell well short of determining the outcome. Manor also demonstrates that that the capacity of the Congress and its allies to reap electoral benefits from the central government's poverty initiatives was diluted somewhat by the ability of some anti-Congress state governments to claim popular credit for these schemes themselves. The 2009 general election verdict, Manor suggests, was the result of an extremely complex array of factors, and it would be foolhardy to attribute these only to poverty reduction measures. But perhaps more significantly, however, Manor offers a pessimistic assessment of these measures as instruments of governance: for him they represent a transition to post-clientelistic politics that, in the absence of party organization (primarily the Congress), has led the UPA and Congress to pursue mass, populist policies to remain in power.

Another dimension of governance that differentiated the UPA from the NDA was federalism. Harihar Bhattacharya (Chapter 3) argues that UPA's approach to federalism was characterized by efforts to restore the idea of 'unity in diversity' in preference to NDA's emphasis on unitarism. It also marked an unmistakable shift towards market forces in restructuring state economies with states given more regulatory powers. Many of these changes were only implemented some time into the UPA administration. However, for Bhattacharya the policy measures and the institutional steps initiated by the UPA were indicative of a desire for long-term reforms of the federal structure in favour of the states. This shift, Bhattacharya notes, retains sensitivity to cultural linguistic identities of the people of India and a pluralist conception of Indian nationhood.

Like federalism, educational exclusion and inclusive development has been one of the most divisive facets of India's political life. Shailaja Fennell (Chapter 4) addresses the UPA's record in this field by focusing on whether there was any distinctive shift under the UPA. The starting point of her analysis is the Common Minimum Programme (CMP) in which the UPA pledged to raise public spending on education to 6 per cent of GDP, with at least half this amount being spent in the primary and secondary sectors. Following an initial examination of the financial outlays that were actually undertaken by the UPA government, Fennell then proceeds to examine the specific educational programs that were introduced by the UPA – such as the Mid-day Meals (MDM) scheme and the Integrated Child Development Services (ICDS) scheme in relation to existing schemes, such as the *Sarva Shiksha Abhiyan* (SSA), that were initiated by the NDA government. This chapter critically reviews the milestones achieved during the first term of the UPA in office against its stated objectives and finds that there have been more legislative and administrative changes than genuine advances in program achievements. This conclusion, suggests Fennell, indicates that while there was a strong policy commitment to improve educational access, the reality is that marginal groups continue to be excluded. The shortfall is especially worrying as it appears to suggest that the financial and policy promises of the CMP have yet to be realized and will remain a tantalizing possibility only, unless there is a far greater emphasis on institutional delivery.

Secularism

One of the major policy divides between the NDA and UPA before the 2004 national elections centered on commitment to state secularism. Following the Gujarat riots of 2002, in which the ruling NDA and regional BJP were implicated, this division became even more pronounced. Although Congress's commitment to principles of state secularism has been far from consistent in the past, the 2004 election marked something of clear blue water between the policies of the NDA and the UPA. Indeed, the UPA's commitment to reinvigorating faith in Indian state secularism was a central plank of the CMP.

In Chapter 5, Gurharpal Singh evaluates the legislative and administrative measures taken by the UPA to better promote communal and social harmony and addresses the concerns of religious minorities. This chapter reviews the efforts to 'de-saffronize' textbooks and the range of policy initiatives emanating from the findings of the Sachar Committee report into the social, economic and educational status of Muslims in India as well as the efforts to better promote minority affairs and make incentives for communal conflict much more difficult. It also critically assesses the reality behind the UPA's rhetoric by examining the extent to which the new policies in their design and implementation have consolidated the Congress's (and UPA's) traditional political support. Finally, in introducing the subsequent contributions by Wilkinson and Bajpai, the chapter reflects on whether UPA's experience marks a radical departure in our understanding of Indian state secularism or merely a continuity in its practices that dates from Independence.

As noted above, in recent years there has been an alarming increase in episodes of violence against Muslims (e.g. Gujarat in 2002). The UPA in its manifesto and on the campaign trail promised to do two main things to arrest such acts in the future: first, that it would prevent a Gujarat-type massacre from taking place while it was at the center and, second, it would respond to religious minorities' concerns about economic underdevelopment. In Chapter 6 Steve Wilkinson observes that the UPA's stance on these issues reflected the very robust support the Congress and its allies secured from the minority communities in the 2004 election. Paradoxically, while the pragmatic electoral considerations on the part of the Congress and its allies give the UPA a powerful incentive to attend to minority concerns, observes Wilkinson, a too great a focus on these issues could potentially undermine their support among the non-minorities.

The UPA is also sometimes distinguished from the NDA in terms of its ideology, notably social justice. Rochana Bajpai (Chapter 7) probes this dimension of the ideological distinctiveness of the UPA by focusing on official rhetoric on social justice and reservations. Making a case for a conceptual analysis of political rhetoric for understanding political explanations, Bajpai offers an account of the UPA's rhetoric through a close reading of party manifestos, government reports, interviews and, most importantly, parliamentary debates. Significantly, the chapter contrasts the Congress's rhetoric on reservations and social justice with that of the NDA (1999–2004) and Janata Dal (1990) coalitions, as well as the Congress's positions during the Constituent Assembly (1946–1950) and Mandal Commission debates (1990). What emerges, according to Bajpai, is that as part of the UPA, Congress's rhetoric has differed substantially from its own earlier positions on social justice and reservations. An egalitarian conception of social justice is now the key legitimating trope in political argument for the extension of identity-based reservations. While marking a significant departure from earlier Congress positions, these features represent a *polity-wide shift* that can be traced back at the national level to at least to the Mandal debate. Overall, concludes Bajpai, both the UPA and NDA supported the expansion of identity-based reservations, *but because* of their ideological differences they favoured different social groups (NDA – SCs and STs; UPA – religious minorities).

Security

The conduct of foreign policy is generally thought to have much greater continuity between governments and is normally held to be above partisanship. However, for Kanti Bajpai (Chapter 8) the UPA's foreign policy was noticeably different – even though there were some continuities with the NDA's approach – and these differences are to be found in the realm of ideology. Bajpai evaluates the transformation in India's foreign policy between 2004 and 2009 by focusing on the UPA's dealings with three key states – the US, Pakistan, and China – that dominate India's external relations. The author argues that during these years the realist, 'coercive diplomacy' of the NDA was replaced by the more liberal, negotiatory approach of the UPA. This change reflected, in large measure, the ideological difference between the two coalitions with the latter placing a greater emphasis on sustained negotiations, accommodation and a cautionary approach to intractable difficulties (e.g. Pakistan). This outlook, according to Bajpai, has resulted in some major breakthroughs (e.g. US and energy policy) that will probably remain one of the most enduring achievements of the administration.

Like external security, energy security has been portrayed by Indian policy makers as a core security concern. Energy security can be narrowly defined as a condition whereby a country and its citizens have access to energy resources free from serious physical disruption of service. In recent years this concern is being recognized as one of the most important challenges for the sustainability of India's domestic economic development. Given the importance of the subject, it has featured prominently in the political parties' manifestos. In Chapter 9, Lawrence Sáez argues that because of critical bureaucratic and institutional constraints, the UPA government struggled to establish an energy security policy that was substantively different from its NDA predecessor. Nevertheless, specific policies were pursued relating to national coordination, sustainability, and international collaboration that marked a noticeable new departure. The author contends, however, that these innovations are far too timid to address the real challenges to India's energy security needs in the long run.

Finally, this volume reviews the issue of India's anti-terrorism and security policy. The UPA coalition government that took office in May 2004 had to cope with a spurt in terror and violent attacks during its five-year term. As Rahul Roy-Chaudhury (Chapter 10) notes, this included an intensification of attacks in India's major cities (including the attack on Mumbai in November 2008), the rise in home-grown Indian *jihadi* terrorism, violent attacks by Hindu extremists and, for the first time, an attack on an Indian diplomatic mission abroad (Afghanistan). Simultaneously there were high levels of violence in Jammu and Kashmir, the North-east, eastern, and central India (Maoist Naxalites). In order to address these challenges the UPA took some major initiatives that included amending anti-terror legislation as well as efforts to define and implement the institutional capabilities of the National Investigative Agency and strengthened the intelligence establishment. For Roy-Chaudhury some of these changes are ambitious and remain to be implemented during UPA's second term of office. Although these reforms, Roy-Chaudhury concludes, represent a major renewal of India's national security and management and anti-terror policies, their ability to stem India's internal and external security challenges remains to be demonstrated.

Part 1
Governance

2 Did the central government's poverty initiatives help to re-elect it?[1]

James Manor

Introduction

Some readers will recall a widely touted explanation for the result of India's general election in 2004. We were told repeatedly that the Congress Party and its allies had won thanks to a revolt by the rural poor against globalization and the economic liberalization undertaken by the previous government. That was demonstrably false. Congress and its allies did better in urban areas than in rural parts. And several pairs of similar and contiguous states produced radically different results. In, for example, Haryana and Punjab, the rural poor were in roughly similar situations – and yet Congress triumphed in the former and was humbled in the latter. Such marked differences would not have emerged if the rural poor all across India had staged a revolt and turned to Congress and its allies.

The 2009 parliamentary election produced new myths. Numerous commentators (some of whom should have known better[2]) claimed that Rahul Gandhi had rejuvenated Congress and Parliament, attracted the youth vote, and rebuilt his party's organization. All three claims are false (Manor 2010). Younger people actually voted *less* often for Congress and its allies than did their elders.[3] The new Parliament was the fifth oldest of the 15 that have been elected since 1952.[4] And Congress strategists at state and national levels – including Rahul Gandhi himself – agreed that organizational reconstruction had not yet occurred.[5]

Other explanations deserve more serious consideration. Several panelists discussing the election outcome on Indian television made a further claim – and as we shall see, they were echoed in numerous press reports. They argued that a remarkable array of initiatives with poverty-reducing impact mainly in rural areas, undertaken since 2004 by the Congress-led United Progressive Alliance (UPA) government in New Delhi, had persuaded large numbers of voters to support it.[6] Some considered this to be a decisive factor, while others described it as an important element in the explanation.

This chapter examines that issue. It argues that those poverty-reducing initiatives did indeed win votes for Congress and its allies, but that they fell well short of determining the outcome. The Congress vote in rural areas rose by only two per cent. And as Yogendra Yadav, who headed the formidable National Election Study at the Centre for the Study of Developing Societies (CSDS) noted in television discussions, when one moves from villages to towns to cities, support for

Congress and its allies increases (as in 2004). We shall also see here that the capacity of Congress and its allies to reap electoral benefits from the central government's poverty initiatives was undermined somewhat by the capacity of some anti-Congress state governments to claim credit for those schemes. The election outcome was the result of a very complex set of processes, of which this was only one. The evidence presented here will shed light not just of the topic of this chapter, but also on some of the other important processes that were at work.

The complex, ambiguous picture that emerges here will come as no surprise to students of Indian politics, but it will disappoint some who are eager to see poverty reduced. This writer shares that eagerness, but it is important that we not overstate the government's achievements. If we do so, we create unrealistic expectations that cannot be fulfilled by this or any government. And when such inflated hopes become unavoidably entangled in ambiguity, then disillusionment with efforts to tackle poverty will ensue. We therefore need to set out the complexities in a realistic manner in order to *sustain* such efforts.

The central government's poverty initiatives

After its victory in 2004, senior Congress election strategists knew that the alleged revolt of the rural poor was a myth. Three of them made it very plain in private to this writer that they saw the election result as 'state-led' – that is, determined by voters' responses not so much to events at the national level, but at the state level in India's federal system.[7] That was the only way to account for the marked contrasts in voting patterns between similar, neighbouring states like Haryana and Punjab. But Congress leaders did not say this openly – they did not challenge the myth of the rural revolt.

The myth was politically useful because it made Congress appear to be more caring than its rivals. Partly to lend credence to that notion, the party and the central government set about developing a formidable array of anti-poverty initiatives. But image-building was not the only reason for these programs, although it was quite important. Key leaders, including Prime Minister Manmohan Singh and Congress President Sonia Gandhi were also acting out of social democratic conviction. They genuinely wanted their ruling coalition, called the United Progressive Alliance, to *be* 'progressive'. They wanted to redistribute wealth and provide poor people with new opportunities and resources.

This comment will sound dubious to some readers, and their skepticism is understandable. Under Indira Gandhi between 1971 and 1984, Congress promised to 'abolish poverty' but then did little of substance to make that happen. And Rajiv Gandhi's spell as Prime Minister between 1984 and 1989 was notable mainly for inconsistency and confusion – he reversed himself in midstream on most of the important policies that he had adopted at the outset (Manor 1994). In the minds of many people –including this writer – this sorry record inspired cynicism about the commitment of Congress, in that era, to poor people. This chapter does not depart from that view. But it argues that times – and the Congress leadership – have changed.

The change began in 1991 when a minority Congress government took power in New Delhi. That statement will also sound dubious to some readers. It was in

1991 that the liberalization of the Indian economy began under Prime Minister P.V. Narasimha Rao and Finance Minister Manmohan Singh. How can those liberalizers be seen as friends of the poor? Were they not neo-liberals?

No. Economic liberalizers need not be neo-liberals. They were social democrats. This was made entirely plain, in private,[8] by Narasimha Rao. He had a subtle command of language and chose his words very carefully, and he said flatly, 'I do not believe in trickle-down economics.' He added that his model was 'not Margaret Thatcher but Willy Brandt', a social democrat. He went on to explain that Brandt believed in encouraging market forces in order to generate wealth, *so that* government revenues would increase, *so that* the state could provide things for poorer groups that the private sector would never provide. He did not throw the economy open to market forces. In his time – and since – India's economic liberalization has been cautious and limited by comparison to many other countries in and beyond Asia. When we compare India today with its old self before 1991, significant changes have occurred. But when we compare it with the 'big bangs' in many other liberalizing countries, we find great caution and restraint (an early indication of this was provided in Manor 1995).

Was Narasimha Rao's social democratic vision of growing government revenues a naive pipe dream? For many years, this seemed to be so. Government revenues fell for a period after 1991. But since 2003, revenues have surged. The precise scale of the surge is a matter of debate among economists. A discussion of that issue must wait until another occasion. But there is broad agreement that the increase in revenues has been very substantial. Politicians (of all parties) who held power at state and national levels before 2004 consistently stress the difference that this can make. Before economic liberalization began in earnest in 1991, the central government had spent only 30 per cent of the plan budget on social sectors and rural development. But since 2004, that figure has been roughly 70 per cent – partly because the government no longer spends heavily on setting up industries.[9] Narasimha Rao's social democratic vision has begun to become a reality.[10]

This is true not just because massive funds have become available to the central government, but because of how the Congress-led coalition has deployed them. Since taking office in mid-2004, it has created a number of major new poverty initiatives and poured substantial additional funds into pre-existing programs.

The list in Table 2.1 underestimates expenditure on poverty initiatives. The figures for three of the programs included in it are only available up to 2008. And it is important to stress that the 'total' set out does not include several other initiatives that entailed hefty outlays. The waiver on agricultural loans, much of which benefited small and marginal farmers, cost Rs 60,000–70,000 crores (US$12.7–14.7 billion). The Congress-led government increased payments under the national old age pension scheme after it was elected in 2004. The Aam Bima Yojana scheme, launched in October 2007 (and to be augmented in October 2009) has provided insurance for landless families to cover the death or disability of heads of households and one earning member. The Rashtriya Swashtya Bima Yojana program, which is separate from the National Rural Health Mission, provides families below the poverty line with up to Rs 30,000 per year in hospitalization coverage – and tackles one of the main reasons that poor families turn to moneylenders, since medical emergencies crop up unexpectedly and urgently require large amounts of cash.[11]

It is of course true that problems attend the implementation of these programs, and that not all of the funds disbursed under them reach the poor.[12] Also, Santhosh Mathew's research indicates that not all the money listed as 'expenditures' in many government programs is actually spent.[13] But even when we note these caveats, US$57.40 billion – plus much of a further US$12.7–14.7 billion committed to the loan waiver, and the sums disbursed on other initiatives not listed in Table 2.1 – is a massive amount of money.

Table 2.1 Spending on poverty-reducing programs (2004–2009)

Program	Expenditure in billions	
	crores[1]	US$
Bharat Nirman (a cluster of six infrastructure programmes)	114,257	24.12
Sarva Shiksa Abhiyan[2] (figures only to 2008)	37,500	7.92
Mid-day Meals Scheme[3] (figures only to 2008)	20,625	4.35
National Rural Employment Guarantee Scheme (NREGS)[4]	44,480	9.40
Total Sanitation Campaign[5]	2,550	0.54
National Rural Health Mission[6]	20,000	4.22
Integrated Child Development Services (figures only to 2008)	16,000	3.38
Jawaharlal Nehru National Urban Renewal Mission[7]	7,428	1.57
Polio Eradication	9,000	1.90
Total	271,840	57.40[8]

Notes
1 A crore is ten million rupees.
2 This program, which was executed in partnership with state governments, sought to ensure that children up to the age of 14 received eight years of schooling by 2010. It stressed the need to bridge gender and social gaps, and to draw local communities into efforts to see that it worked effectively.
3 This program provided cooked meals to pupils in schools and permitted them to take some food home, a far from trivial feature for families in severe need. It had originated under a regional party in Tamil Nadu in the 1980s and had been copied by several other state governments, but the UPA government turned it into a major national initiative.
4 This huge program provided every rural household the right to demand 100 days of employment per year on public works sites as a hedge against destitution. It introduced extremely formidable transparency mechanisms in an attempt to minimize corruption. These were partially successful, and vast numbers of poor people in rural areas benefited from the Scheme, as a major study by this writer and Rob Jenkins will demonstrate.
5 This initiative provided modest subsidies to poor households for the construction of toilets, and included a significant drive to disseminate information about the need to end the practice of open defecation. In order to promote sanitation and to combat the spread of illnesses, and to foster an awareness of the need for these things, the programme also focused on the provision of toilets and water supplies to schools where the need for hand washing was emphasized.
6 This program, which began in 2006, has enhanced the provision of the health service by hiring doctors on contracts in order to avoid the slow, cumbersome, bureaucratic procedures of recruitment through the Public Service Commission. In many areas of the country it has made a major difference – so that consultations with doctors have increased by ten times. Interview with a member of the National Advisory Council, New Delhi, 3 June 2009.
7 This program funded cities to improve infrastructure and service delivery. It sought (among other things) to expand social housing with particular attention to the needs of slum dwellers, and to provide universal access to services for the urban poor.
8 These sums were initially set out in the *Times of India*, 3 June 2009, and have since been checked with the Planning Commission.

Some further comments are in order here. Several of the programs noted above were demand driven, in order to draw poorer people more fully into the public sphere as actors – in part to enhance their political capacity (which this writer defines as political awareness, confidence, skills and connections). Several of the programs either barred the non-poor from participation or offered opportunities that would be taken up almost entirely by the poor. The Congress-led government in New Delhi also reinforced its spending on poverty initiatives with several new laws that sought – in part or entirely – to benefit poorer groups. They do not require heavy spending, but they have made some impact. These included the Right to Information Act 2005 (which reinforced the demand-driven character of some other programs), the Protection of Women from Domestic Violence Act 2005, and the Forest Rights Act 2006.[14] The first and third of those initiatives resonated with the demand-driven character of some of the expensive poverty programs. The Domestic Violence Act may not at first glance appear to merit inclusion here, but civil society organizations operating in over 300 parliamentary constituencies as the election approached found that it resonated strongly with voters – even though Congress did not stress it during its campaign (John 2009).

These initiatives were broadly in line with the CMP set out by the UPA at the parliamentary election of 2004 (UPA 2004). A brief summary of the main points in that program that were relevant to poor people (most of which were substantially addressed in practice) will indicate the thrust of the Congress-led government in this vein.

- *Employment*: The main undertaking in this sphere was the massive NREGS, but efforts were also made to sustain and develop sectors in which artisans worked, and to expand credit for small-scale industries and the self-employed.
- *Agriculture*: The government sought to address the crisis in agriculture, with emphases on rural credit (for both prosperous and marginal farmers), on protections for agricultural labor, and on farmers in the least developed states and districts of India.
- *Education*: A commitment was made to spend at least six per cent of the gross domestic product (GDP) on education with at least half of that amount being devoted to primary and secondary education. A special tax was later imposed to help to fund basic education. A national mid-day meals scheme was introduced to encourage poor families to send their children to schools and keep them there.
- *Health*: Spending on health was to be raised to at least two to three per cent of GDP, with special emphasis on public health. Subsidies on life-saving drugs were expanded and a health insurance program for poor families was created.
- *Women's welfare*: Legislation was promised and later delivered to address the problem of domestic violence against women. Programs to assist women's self-help groups were expanded, and an effort was made to persuade state governments to ensure that at least one third of funds flowing to *panchayats* would be devoted to the welfare of women.
- *Labor in the informal sector*: Legislation was promised and later passed to provide protections to workers in the informal sector – a difficult thing to implement.

- *Scheduled Castes and Scheduled Tribes*: Efforts were made to promote minor irrigation works on lands owned by both of these groups. A Forest Rights Act was later passed that was intended to benefit poor people – mainly *Adivasis* – who inhabit forested areas, and an attempt was made to tackle the alienation of *Adivasis* from their lands, by minimizing the practice and by rehabilitating those who had suffered from it.

The UPA government in New Delhi did not spend heavily *only* on initiatives to assist poorer groups. It also provided funds that benefited various prosperous interests. It is beyond the scope of this paper to enumerate these, but since 2004, the Congress has maintained its tradition of providing something for everyone.[15] By committing substantial sums to initiatives for prosperous groups, the Congress-led government sought (with some success) to mute their resistance to poverty programs, by persuading them that initiatives for the poor did not occur at the expense of assistance to the non-poor.

It is extremely important to note that national leaders in the Congress have sought to make an impact through *government programs rather than through their party's organization*.[16] They know that the organization suffers from such severe problems that it is incapable of playing a constructive role. One senior advisor to Congress recently said in private that the only thing most of the party's members knew how to do is to shout 'Sonia Gandhi Zindabad'. A leading Congress strategist toured India in 2007 and found that the condition of the organization was 'terrible, terrible'. When a political scientist visited various party offices across Uttar Pradesh during the 2007 election campaign there, he found Bahujan Samaj Party activists brimming with ardor. He saw that at least half of the BJP activists were working flat out because 'in their guts' they were burning with spite towards the minorities. But in Congress offices, he found 'only listlessness – cronies and relatives of candidates, and what I would call political pimps'. When he told Congress leaders in New Delhi of this, they agreed that this was an accurate description.[17] It is thus logical that India's current leaders should rely not on the party – the regeneration of which is only beginning and is a daunting challenge – but on government programs.

In stressing such programs, Congress leaders were conforming to an immensely important trend that had been especially evident in many Indian states at least since the early 1990s. They had recognized that the old politics of patronage distribution through patron–client networks – the politics of clientelism – was insufficient to ensure a government's re-election. This was true partly because the organization of the Congress Party had decayed and partly because the organizations of nearly all other parties (including the BJP) lacked the capacity to make their influence penetrate effectively down to the local level. But it owed more to a political awakening over that last four decades that made ordinary (and poor) people politically aware and quite demanding. Clientelism was a patently inadequate response to the demand overload that afflicted all governments, state and central.

Senior politicians found it impossible to abandon clientelism, since their subordinates insisted that they must be permitted to continue distributing patronage in order to maintain support in their bailiwicks. But if governments were to have any hope of re-election, they had to supplement patronage distribution with programs like those discussed above. Such programs, when taken together, comprise *post-clientelistic* strategies that had developed (especially at the state level) across much of India during the 1990s. In many parts of the country, well before 2009, such strategies had come to outweigh patronage distribution in political importance. The increase in revenues after 2003 enabled the central and many state governments to carry that process further. Thus, descriptions of India as a patronage democracy are out of date and misleading.

Voters' responses to poverty initiatives

Let us now consider evidence on voters' responses to these poverty initiatives. Leaders of the Congress and its allies naturally claimed that these programs had helped to ensure their re-election. That should perhaps be dismissed as 'just politics'. But similar official statements by the Communist Party of India (Marxist) carry more weight – although the attendant claim that those initiatives 'were pushed through under Left pressure' (Manoj 2009) is open to serious doubt.[18]

Several media reports from people who had little or no hard evidence also made this claim. But let us set these aside and instead consider only the testimony of commentators who were actually in close touch with the grassroots. A small number of reporters who had had extensive ground-level exposure to rural areas during the election campaign made similar statements. They tended to stress that the NREGS and the loan waiver – which Yogendra Yadav regards as arguably the best known poverty-reducing initiatives since independence[19] – had persuaded poorer voters (and others who were sympathetic) that the central government cared and had made serious efforts to ease poverty.[20] Further solid evidence came from the national campaign coordinator of the aforementioned network of progressive civil society organizations (the *Wada Na Todo Abhiyan*) that had been active in over 300 parliamentary constituencies. It found that the New Delhi government's poverty initiatives were widely recognized and appreciated in rural areas. The NREGS had 'the greatest recall value', but the National Rural Health Mission, *Sarva Shiksa Abhiyan* (an education program) and, to their surprise, the Domestic Violence Act also resonated powerfully (John 2009).

For a fuller understanding, we must consider polling data. Let us begin with Table 2.2, from the National Election Study at CSDS, which breaks down voting preferences by 'class' – that is, by assets and incomes. It offers only limited insight into the question at hand, but readers may find it helpful as a rough guide to the overall character of the result.

The implications of the data in Table 2.2 are complicated. The figures indicate that both Congress and its allies gained more than half of their votes from people in the 'lower' and 'poor' categories. But that was also true of every other party or group of parties. Congress received more support than the BJP from every 'class', and the same can be said when we compare Congress and its allies (the UPA) versus the BJP and its allies (the NDA). The figures also show that as we move up the economic ladder, the Congress share of the vote increases slightly. That

Table 2.2 All-India voting preferences by economic class (assets and income)

	Congress (%)	Congress allies (%)	BJP (%)	BJP allies (%)	Left (%)	BSP (%)	Others (%)	Total (%)
Upper	30.1	7.1	23.1	6.6	3.6	5.4	24.1	100.0
	15.1	12.9	17.6	17.7	6.6	12.5	13.4	14.3
Middle	29.2	7.8	7.8	4.7	5.6	4.9	26.8	100.0
	27.7	27.1	27.1	24.1	19.7	21.5	28.2	29.7
Lower	29.5	6.3	17.9	5.1	7.0	5.5	28.7	100.0
	30.6	24.0	28.3	28.1	27.1	26.5	33.1	29.7
Poor	26.2	9.7	15.4	5.4	12.3	8.5	22.4	100.0
	26.5	36.0	23.8	29.6	46.6	39.5	25.3	28.9
Total	28.5	7.8	18.8	5.3	7.6	6.2	25.7	100.0
	100.0	100.0	100.0	100.0	100.0	100.0	100.0	100.0

Source: CSDS post-poll. (I am grateful to Sanjay Kumar for providing this material.)

suggests that its victory is not explained by inordinate electoral support from less prosperous groups.

Despite all of that, however, when we compare the support from either the 'lower' or the 'poor' category for Congress and the BJP on their own, Congress had a slightly greater edge than it did among the entire electorate. The same can again be said when we consider Congress and its allies with the BJP and its allies. More importantly, when we compare only the lead that Congress had over the BJP or the lead that the UPA had over the NDA among voters in the 'lower' and the 'poor' categories, the differences are not at all trivial. That leaves open the possibility that the central government's poverty initiatives since 2004 earned Congress and its UPA allies an important, though not spectacular, advantage.

Other polling data enable us to focus more closely on the impact of poverty initiatives. Table 2.3 has also been extrapolated from the all-India post-poll data collected by the National Election Study. It indicates the electoral support for Congress and the BJP from people who had heard, and not heard, of various anti-poverty initiatives.

The implications of these figures are ambiguous. Those who had heard of four of the five initiatives were slightly more likely to vote for Congress than those who had not heard, but the same is true among BJP voters – and in any case, the differences are very small. It therefore appears that the mere awareness of these various schemes played, at best, only a marginal role in the election victory.

Table 2.4, developed out of the same all-India post-poll survey, shows the proportions of beneficiaries and non-beneficiaries of five poverty-reducing initiatives who voted for the Congress and for the BJP. Here we see somewhat more significant differences.

Beneficiaries were more likely than non-beneficiaries to vote for Congress under all programs apart from mid-day meals – an unexplained exception. Non-beneficiaries of those same four programs were more likely to vote for the

Table 2.3 Voting preferences of those who had heard (or not) of poverty initiatives

	NREGS (%)	Pensions (%)	Mid-day meals (%)	Health insurance (%)	Loan waiver (%)
Congress voters					
Heard of scheme	28.5	28.9	29.0	29.8	29.2
Not heard	29.0	28.2	27.6	27.8	27.6
BJP voters					
Heard of scheme	18.6	16.7	18.7	18.4	18.6
Not heard	17.4	20.9	16.6	18.1	17.5

Note
The total shares of the vote in the 2009 general election were 29.67 per cent for Congress and 19.29 per cent for the BJP.

Table 2.4 Voting preferences of beneficiaries and non-beneficiaries

	NREGS (%)	Pensions (%)	Mid-day meals (%)	Health insurance (%)	Loan waiver (%)
Congress voters					
Benefited	33.2	31.6	27.9	32.8	30.0
Didn't benefit	25.4	27.4	30.7	28.2	28.9
BJP voters					
Benefited	16.2	11.7	19.3	14.4	17.2
Didn't benefit	20.4	19.2	17.8	20.8	19.0

Note
The total shares of the vote in the 2009 general election were 29.67 per cent for Congress and 19.29 per cent for the BJP.

BJP than were beneficiaries. Even if we include the mid-day meals scheme, the gaps between the figures for beneficiaries of all programs who voted for Congress and those who voted for the BJP give Congress a significantly greater edge than was seen in Table 2.3, which focused on those who had only heard of these initiatives. So among beneficiaries, these programs clearly helped Congress. It is also worth stressing that the Congress edge over the BJP in Table 2.4 – among beneficiaries – is significantly greater than its overall edge among 'poor' people shown in Table 2.2, which set out aggregate data based on 'class'.

It is impossible to say with confidence how many seats Congress and its allies gained as a result of the various poverty initiatives. But as Yogendra Yadav has stressed, in close races, an advantage of (say) three per cent among voters in the 'lower' and 'poor' categories can prove decisive. This appears to have happened in at least a modest number of rural constituencies. It did not decide to overall result, but it almost certainly produced at least a small increase in the proportion of seats won by Congress and its allies.

The relative influence of state and central governments on voters

All central government initiatives are filtered through state governments in India's federal system, many of which are controlled by parties that are not part of the ruling coalition in New Delhi. Were those parties able to take part of the credit for central initiatives from New Delhi and reap some of the electoral benefits that ensued?

The available evidence does not yield a precise answer to the question, but useful insights emerge. Several of the points set out below also enrich our understanding not just of the impact of central government initiatives, but also of the overall process at the 2009 general election.

Let us first see how much of India was governed at the state level by parties that were – and were not – part of the Congress-led alliance in New Delhi during April and May 2009, when people were voting (see Table 2.5).

Across nearly two thirds of India, state governments headed by non-Congress (and mostly anti-Congress) parties were in a position to poach the credit for the central government's poverty-reducing initiatives – or at least to poach enough of it to prevent Congress from reaping sizeable electoral rewards. When we consider the vast sums committed to these programs that flowed down through state governments, it is hardly surprising that many anti-Congress parties holding power at that level should seize upon them.

Not all did so. For example, the politicians heading the BJP government in Karnataka responded with characteristic ineptitude.[21] But that should not be taken to imply that the BJP was universally lukewarm to these initiatives. The largest single poverty-reducing program, the NREGS, was more enthusiastically implemented in two BJP-ruled states – Rajasthan and Madhya Pradesh – than anywhere else. At the time of writing in August 2009, Rajasthan has provided 2,000.47 lakhs (just over 200 million) person days of employment to poor rural dwellers, and Madhya Pradesh has provided 1,020.33 lakhs. By contrast, Karnataka has provided 135.8 lakhs, even though its population is only slightly smaller than those of the other two states, and it contains numerous underdeveloped districts where the scheme could have yielded significant benefits. Indeed, Karnataka as a whole has provided fewer person days than either Banswara District (165.63 lakhs) or Dungarpur District (160.54 lakhs) in Rajasthan (Ministry of Rural Development, Government of India 2010).

Table 2.5 States governed by various parties/alliances

	Population of states governed (millions)	Total population (%)
Congress and/or allies	370.2	36.1
BJP and/or allies	308.7	30.1
Other parties, alliances or formations	345.6	33.7

Note
Meghalaya, population 2.3 million, was under President's Rule.

The other state governments headed by non-Congress parties fall between these two extremes – when we consider both the NREGS and other central government initiatives. But most stand closer to the zealous governments in Rajasthan and Madhya Pradesh than to their drowsy counterparts in Karnataka.

It is worth noting that the architects of the NREGS took great care to avoid attaching a partisan name to it – such as the 'Jawaharlal Nehru Urban Renewal Mission'. They did so because they wanted other parties to embrace it so that it would not be scrapped if Congress and its allies were ousted from power.[22] The eagerness with which the BJP has taken it up in Rajasthan and Madhya Pradesh indicates that this has largely happened. When confronted with programs that *do* have partisan names, non-Congress state governments have often attached new labels of their own, in the hope that they can take the political benefit from implementing them.

How much success did these governments have in poaching the credit for these initiatives? The evidence on this indicates that their record has been mixed. Opinion surveys by CSDS in 2007 asked respondents in numerous states whether they gave credit for the NREGS to the central government or their state government. No consistent pattern emerged. For example, in Madhya Pradesh and Chhattisgarh – two contiguous states where the NREGS had been implemented with similar vigor by the same ruling party (the BJP) – the survey found that the state government got most of the credit in one while the Congress-led central government got most of it in the other, in both cases by somewhat modest margins.[23]

Yogendra Yadav and Suhas Palshikar (2009a) provide further insight into this issue. They have developed what they call a *centre–state ratio*: that is, 'the proportion of voters who mention the central government as the main consideration for voting (at parliamentary elections) divided by the proportion of those who mention their state government as the main consideration'. The CSDS post-poll survey at the 2004 general election found that the ratio was 1.0 – which is to say that the proportions 'perfectly balanced each other'.[24] They followed this in January 2009 with a pre-poll survey about voting intentions in the Lok Sabha election that was still a few months away. They found that the centre–state ratio had slipped to 0.8 – which indicated that respondents were more preoccupied with their state governments than with the central government (Yadav and Palshikar 2009a: 406–7). We might logically expect the ratio to move back towards 1.0 as the parliamentary election campaign unfolded, since it stressed national issues. But in fact, the opposite happened. A post-poll survey a few months later found that the ratio had fallen still further, to 0.63.[25] State-level preoccupations counted for a good deal more in 2009 than five years earlier.

So in 2009, after five years of unprecedentedly heavy spending by the central government on a broad array of programs – not just the poverty-reducing programs discussed above, but also a number of others that were intended to spur development and/or to benefit prosperous groups – people's preoccupations had shifted *away* from the central government to the state level. This strongly suggests that it was indeed possible for some non-Congress state governments to take part of the credit for those poverty programs.

Finally, it is worth considering telling evidence from the CSDS post-poll survey in 2009. It indicates that the anti-incumbency sentiments towards central and state governments that had loomed large in India's politics for a generation had largely vanished at this election – in part as a result of the surge in revenues for both types of governments, and the tendency of many of them to commit their more abundant resources to post-clientelistic programs. The data presented in Table 2.6 show that in 2009, pervasive *pro*-incumbency sentiments existed towards *both* state *and* central governments.

Respondents were asked whether they were 'fully satisfied', 'somewhat satisfied', 'somewhat dissatisfied' or 'very dissatisfied' – first with the performance of the Congress-led UPA government in New Delhi, and then with that of their state government. Table 2.6 aggregates responses by 'fully' and 'somewhat' satisfied voters into one figure – for states that elected at least four Lok Sabha members.

Every state government (except Jharkhand, which has witnessed serious political disarray) enjoys a better than 50 per cent satisfaction rating – and 17 out of

Table 2.6 Satisfaction with Central and State Governments

State	Satisfaction with central government (%)	Satisfaction with state government (%)
Andhra Pradesh	58.0	63.2
Assam	66.9	63.7
Bihar*	75.6	87.9
Chhattisgarh*	60.4	72.4
Delhi	73.6	71.3
Gujarat*	67.8	64.9
Haryana	63.3	64.1
Himachal Pradesh*	73.9	71.6
Jammu & Kashmir	64.9	61.4
Jharkhand*	42.6	43.1
Karnataka*	76.5	61.6
Kerala*	66.3	61.1
Madhya Pradesh*	74.6	82.3
Maharashtra	62.1	61.5
Orissa*	55.4	73.7
Punjab*	63.9	56.7
Rajasthan	66.9	63.2
Tamil Nadu	73.8	71.7
Uttar Pradesh*	66.5	57.9
Uttarakhand	67.5	62.8
West Bengal*	61.2	57.9

Source: CSDS post-poll. (I am grateful to Sanjay Kumar for providing this material.)
Note
* States in which Congress or its allies did not govern.

21 achieved over 60 per cent. It is therefore not surprising that pro-incumbency sentiments should have manifested themselves at the 2009 election. This lends substantial credence to the idea that many non-Congress state governments were indeed able to capture at least some of the credit for central government initiatives.

But the Congress-led UPA government in New Delhi can also take comfort from this evidence. It not only enjoys a better than 50 per cent satisfaction rating in every state except Jharkhand but, in 18 out of 21, it scores more than 60 per cent. And in seven of the 12 states governed by anti-Congress parties, the central government inspires more satisfaction that does the state government.

Note also that in six states where anti-Congress parties did badly in the Lok Sabha election, their state governments still achieved reasonably good satisfaction levels: Himachal Pradesh, Kerala, Punjab, Uttar Pradesh, Uttarakhand and West Bengal. By the same token, in another five states where Congress and its allies did badly, the central government that they head achieved reassuring satisfaction ratings: Bihar, Chhattisgarh, Karnataka, Madhya Pradesh and Orissa. Thus, with few exceptions, this election witnessed contests between parties whose performances in office, whether at state or national levels, were seen quite positively by voters.[26]

These high satisfaction ratings for both central and state governments strongly suggest that incumbent governments at both levels gained electoral support at this election as a result of the central government's poverty initiatives that were largely post-clientelistic in character. It is impossible to say with precision how much of the credit for these programs went to the central and to various state governments – although the evidence set out in Table 2.4 suggests that Congress and its allies made at least modest electoral gains as a result. It is also impossible to say with any precision how great those gains were. They were clearly not decisive determinants of the election outcome. A great many other things, not discussed in this chapter, mattered. But those influential people, including leaders of some opposition parties, who have said that Congress and its allies reaped some electoral reward from the central government's poverty initiatives, are almost certainly correct. And the mere fact that they believe this, and say it openly, suggests that efforts to tackle poverty will be sustained.

3 UPA (2004–) and Indian federalism

A paradigm shift?

Harihar Bhattacharyya

The problem

Thomas Kuhn (1962) has used the term 'paradigm' in scientific discourse to refer to, amongst other things, a conceptual, or theoretical, framework, a model, or a problematic. In the ongoing theoretical literature on federalism, the term 'paradigm' has acquired a specific meaning, which should be explained for our purpose here. When looked at historically, federalism has so far been conjoined to liberalism, social welfarism and socialism. At origin though, federalism flourished in liberal conditions because individual liberty was the *sine qua non* of federalism too. Remarkably, federalism has adapted itself to social welfarism. There is apparently no conflict between federalism and the welfare state because 'in multi-ethnic federations, social policy may serve as the cement for reducing the depths of political cleavages' (Obinger *et al.* 2005: 6). This means that a certain degree of functionality of the social interventionist state in maintaining federalism in multi-ethnic countries is to be recognized. However, the consensus today is that there is a paradigmatic shift for federalism. Watts (2008: 4) expresses this shift when he says that 'we appear to be moving from a world of sovereign nation-states to a world of diminished state sovereignty and increased interstate linkages of a constitutionally federal character'.

Today's resurgence of federalism with Europe as the 'epicenter of federalist tendency' (Galligan 2009: 262) is caused mostly by the forces of globalization, and is manifested in major institutional reconfigurations: cosmopolitanism, multiple spheres of government, shifting allegiances, new forms of identity, and overlapping jurisdiction. Federalism is increasingly seen to be the form of governance in a world marked, on the one hand, by the decline of Keynesianism in favour of neo-liberal economics, and, on the other hand, the decline of socialism in favour of market solutions in most domestic economies. Federalism appears to be reorienting itself to the requirements of the market. Within the nation-state these changes are reflected in the gradual withdrawal of the social welfare state, increasing shrinkage of public expenditure, and opening up the social and economic space for the market forces. Rudolph and Rudolph (2001: 161) would term the shift, in the light of the developments in India since the late 1980s, as the one from an interventionist state giving way to a regulatory state suited to India's emerging reality of liberalization, multi-party coalition governments at the centre and so on. There is of course a caution in the Rudolphs' (2001: 162) understanding of the shift when they say that in India 'a relatively centralized and interventionist state ... is being replaced by a relatively decentralized regulatory state willing to rely on, but not to surrender, to a market economy...' Thus India defines its own course of change conditioned by a complex set of factors generally relating to the federal structure of the state as a whole, a change that is neither wholly pro-market nor anti-state. Yet despite this general outlook, the Congress-led UPA's approach to federalism marks an unmistakable shift towards economic liberalization and the market forces, in particular through a greater emphasis on the States that are seen as the most important actors in making reforms work.

Argument

It will be argued here that the policies and measures adopted and implemented by the Congress-led UPA between 2004 and 2009 on federalism indicate a shift in approach. Several caveats are in order here, however. First, the changes that necessitated a shift have been path-dependent so that there was no going back to the old days of centralization and concentration of powers at the Centre, most notably under the late Mrs Indira Gandhi (Dua 1979, 1985).[1] Second, the liberalization of the Indian economy since the early 1990s has had a profound impact. While India has been benefiting from the economy's resurgence, it has also opened up the need to implement Structural Adjustment Programs (SAPs), in which the strategic role of the States, as defined by the provisions of the Indian Constitution, is indispensable. Third, there is also some continuity in approach between the National Democratic Alliance (NDA) and the UPA, even though both follow diametrically opposed approaches to federalism determined by their opposing conceptions of nationhood (Adeney 2005). Finally, the logic of coalition politics at the centre – the UPA being a 14-party alliance of mostly State-based and regional parties – has necessitated a shift in approach to federalism so that the rights of the States are adequately recognized and protected, and that the States are allowed to play an active role in development rather than being simply treated as 'glorified municipalities'.

A brief history

Since 1950 federalism in India has been subject to many shifts and turns marked by centralization, assertion of States' rights and a return to the status quo (Bhattacharyya 2001, 2005). Post-1967, buoyed by the loss of Congress dominance, the States began to assert themselves against centralization and for more autonomy. In the post-Emergency period (1975–7), the renewed drive for centralization after the rise to power of the Congress again in 1980 (1980–4) (Dua 1985) brought forth vociferous demands from the States for more autonomy (Kurian and Varugheese 1981). Since then some of the more notable changes have included the increasing acknowledgement by the Centre for more state autonomy (Sarkaria Commission 1988; Ministry of Law, Justice and Company Affairs, Department of Legal Affairs, Government of India 2002); sub-state level decentralization since the early 1990s; and the States' reluctance to devolve powers down the sub-State level bodies (Bagchi 2003).

There is little disagreement among scholars that the Indian federation was designed to be highly centralized. For a variety of reasons, both operationally and strategically, the States remain critical actors in executing their own – and more importantly – the federally sponsored welfare programs (Watts 1966, 1999, 2008; Morris-Jones 1967, 1987). In 2000–4 India's federal government expenditure, after intergovernmental transfers, was 44.6 per cent of the total public expenditure,[2] a figure that is second only to the US, and lower than that of Malaysia, Brazil, Nigeria, Australia, Mexico, Austria, Spain, and South Africa (Watts 2008: 103). This means India's States together are responsible for more than half of the public expenditure. It must, however, be mentioned that during the heyday of one-party Congress dominance, and the so-called license-permit raj, Indian federalism suffered additionally from the high doses of political centralization. The extent of political interference in formal aspects of relations between the Centre and the States during this phase is a subject of some dispute among scholars (Brass 1989; Austin 1999; Rao and Singh 2005; Bhattacharyya 2009), but the States suffered from the problem of fiscal imbalances resulting from rising expenditure and declining revenues. For example, during 1990–2002, central transfers to the States stayed mostly at around 38 per cent (Rao and Singh 2005: 192).

New context

More recent assessment of Indian federalism, more particularly since the 1990s (Arora and Verney 1995; Manor 1998, 2001; Bhattacharyya 2001, 2009; Rudolph and Rudolph 2001; Das Gupta 2001; Sáez 2002; Dua and Singh 2003; Arora 2004; Rao and Singh 2005; Majeed 2009), highlight a vastly changed context shaped by economic liberalization as well as the growing importance of coalition politics with State-based parties at the centre. Elsewhere (Bhattacharyya 2009) I have discussed the issues involved, which I will briefly summarize here. Following failed experiments (1977–80, 1989–91, and 1996–8) of non-Congress coalition governments at the Centre, since the early 1990s India has witnessed the rise of stable multi-party coalition governments. This has coincided with India's path to economic liberalization too. The rise of multi-party coalition at the Centre has increased the prominence of the regional, State-based parties and appears to offer the States more autonomy of action. This process also became inevitably linked with India's economic liberalization. Rudolph and Rudolph (2001: 129) remarked that in the 1990s, 'a multi-party system with strong regional parties displaced a dominant party system; and market forces and practices displaced the planning and the "license-permit raj"'. They further argue that the 'federal system has had a new lease of life, with the States gaining ground at the expense of the centre' (Rudolph and Rudolph 2001: 129). This may, indeed, be painting too optimistic a scenario because not all States in India are able to reap equally the benefits of the emergent reality. There was, and still is, a lot of disparity among the States. For example, in the first decade of India's economic liberalization, foreign direct investment (FDI) per capita in India's major States was as follows: Bihar (Rs 102.27 crore); Karnataka (Rs 4,628.06 crore);

Maharashtra (Rs 5,780.38 crore); West Bengal (Rs 1,237.32 crore); Uttar Pradesh (Rs 311.29 crore); and Madhya Pradesh (Rs 1,476.39 crore) (Rao and Singh 2005: 382). However, the direction of change was unmistakable.

Until the mid-1990s, Guhan (1995) believes that the Centre was 'unwilling and unable' to involve the States in the process of economic liberation because of the external agencies' preference for policy dialogue with the national government alone; the Centre's responsibility for macro-economic stabilization; and the variegated nature of states governments, politically speaking (Bhattacharyya 2009: 112). Since then the situation has changed, and the States have become much more active partners in the reforms process though, of course, this is determined by the nature of governance in the States and the location of inward flow of capital accruing from economic liberalization. Also, the State governments in India, placed as they are in a specific socio-political complex, have different mandates from their populace, which are often at variance with more pro-market demands of economic liberalization.

Constitutional position of the states

The Indian federation distributes powers and responsibilities between the Centre (Union) and the States in terms of three lists: Union, State and Concurrent. The Union List contains 97 items that are nationally important and give the Union Government overriding powers. The State List contains 66 items, and the Concurrent List 47 items, on which the Union Government has supremacy in case of conflict. Legislatively, the union government has overriding powers of legislation on the Concurrent List and also on some items in the State List in certain circumstances. However, a narrow reading of the constitutional provisions would of course give a wrong picture of the working of the federation, which has remained, operationally speaking, decentralized (Watts 1966; Watts 2008).

Constitutionally, too, the States in India occupy a strategic space. Administratively speaking, the Union government is 'all staff and no line' (Appleby 1953). The States are thus responsible for implementation of their own legislations as well as all the central government's welfare and developmental legislations and programs. As Guhan (1995: 241) has rightly pointed out, the key sectors in this respect fall within the competence of the States: industrial infrastructure; power development; agriculture, its allied sectors, and irrigation; roads (other than highways), health, education, medical services; nutrition and water supply; urban development, and so on. Therefore, it was imperative on the part of the central government to involve the States in the reforms process, and hence the States have become more important to the centre.

UPA's approach to federalism

The Congress-led UPA as a 14-party[3] coalition government,[4] supported from outside by the left parties, naturally had to accommodate the States' interests represented by its new partners. Some of these trade-offs were unusual to say the least. For example, although the Left Front supported the UPA government for most its period from outside, Buddhadev Bhattacharya, the chief minister of the Left Front-run of West Bengal, did not complain of the Centre's economic neglect of the State even though the Communist Party of India (Marxist) (CPI (M)) had withdrawn support to the UPA over the Indo–US nuclear policy issue. This silence should be compared with the periods from the 1990s to 2000s when the Marxists were in the forefront of the struggle against the Centre's, 'step-motherly attitude' to the States. Indeed since 1964 the issue of more powers for the States and a revision of the Centre–State relations has been one of the main demands of the CPI(M). The party's famous 1977 Memorandum on the Centre–States Relations is known for its advocacy for both a strong Centre and strong States (Bhattacharyya 2009: 110–11).[5]

In another case the DMK (based on Tamil ethno-regional interests), an ally of two successive UPA governments (2004 onwards), remains avowedly regionalist and federalist. Its 2004 election manifesto for the Lok Sabha elections it defined itself as a

> democratic movement to preserve and protect the rights of Tamil People and to achieve the ideals of Periyar. DMK has been working towards an egalitarian, secular society free of caste–communal conflicts. It is also working tirelessly to uphold the culture, language, arts and civilization of the Tamils.
>
> DMK Manifesto 2009

In a separate section in the manifesto titled 'Federalism', the party stated its position:

> It is DMK's consistent stand that the Constitution should be amended for the creation of a wholesome and genuine Federalism with fuller autonomy for the states. A resolution ... [on] ... State Autonomy was passed in the Tamil Nadu Legislative Assembly way back in 1974 itself by the DMK. DMK will continue to insist on the abolition of Article 356 which empowers the dismissal of state governments. It will continue to strive for the suitable Constitutional amendments that will empower the states to function freely and effectively in the changed new world order.
>
> DMK Manifesto 2009

It is beyond doubt that such regional and States' rights-centric views, demands and programs as maintained by the UPA's partners would have impacted upon the tenor of UPA's approach to federalism, and Centre–State relations.

Regional development, Centre–State relations

This heading echoes the UPA's CMP (UPA 2004) and is indicative of the perspective from which the issue of 'Centre–State relations' was viewed. The main focus of the UPA CMP on federalism was regional imbalances in development and the unfair treatment of some States in the past in respect of financial devolution and planned expenditure. The CMP was very candid on this point:

> The UPA government is committed to redressing growing regional imbalances both among states as well as within states, through fiscal administrative, investment and other means. It is a matter of concern that regional imbalances have been accentuated by not only historical neglect but also by distortions in Plan allocations and central government assistance. Even in the Tenth Five Year Plan, states like Bihar, Assam and UP have received per capita allocations that are much below the national average.
>
> The CMP proposed several measures for arresting these imbalances: the creation of a Backward States Grant Fund for creating productive assets in these states; ('proactive measures') rapid industrialization in the eastern and northeastern states; alleviation of debt burden of the states; provision for non-statutory grants from the Centre to the states to be weighted in favour of poor and backward states; emphasis on social and physical infrastructure development in the states; payment of mineral royalties to the states; speedy implementation of special economic packages of previous governments for the states in North-East, Bihar and Jammu and Kashmir; and so on. These can be seen as designed to enhance the capacity of the States, and to remove the long-drawn anti-Centre attitudes and orientations among many states, particularly the backward ones in social and economic terms.
>
> UPA 2008

The States-specific yet long-standing schemes (having 'national significance') also found a place in the CMP. Thus the CMP committed the UPA government to the Sethu Samuthuriam project (Tamil Nadu), flood control and drainage in North Bihar, the Prevention of Erosion in Padmna-Ganga and Bhagirathi rivers in West Bengal – all pet projects of Congress's regional allies like the DMK, RJD and the left parties of West Bengal respectively. The special status of Jammu and Kashmir was widely accepted as part of India's federal structure and committed the government 'to respecting the letter and spirit of Article 370',[6] and to sustain 'the healing touch policy pursued by the State government' – a partner of the UPA. Finally, the pressing problems of India's North-east (comprising seven federal units, which are all recognized as 'special category states'), such as terrorism, militancy and insurgency, were considered as 'a matter of urgent national priority'. The CMP stated that all the States in this region would be given 'special assistance' to upgrade their infrastructure. The CMP has frequently highlighted the need for the development of infrastructure.

As well as these proposals the Congress-led UPA government, very significantly, pledged itself to relatively long-term institutional reforms of Indian federalism. It was argued that about two decades had elapsed since the last governmental commission (i.e. the Sarkaria Commission, 1983–7) had reviewed Centre–State relations. So, the UPA committed itself to setting up a new commission 'keeping in view the sea-changes that have taken place in the polity and economy of India since then'.

Official language

The UPA government's commitment to 'official language[s]' had important federal bearing. The CMP declared that the 'UPA government will set up a committee to examine the question of declaring all languages in the Eighth Schedule of the Constitution as official languages'. 'In addition', it was further stated, '*Tamil* will be declared as a classical language.' While the latter was directly in DMK's manifesto, the former is broadly in line with strengthening federalism in the sense that most of the major States of India were linguistically so created and hence the recognition of the Eighth Schedule languages as 'official languages' of India would enhance their sense of ethno-regional-linguistic identity.

Performance

It is true indeed that five years may not be long enough for the effects of policy to be visible. This is particularly so in cases of redress of imbalances in regional development, infrastructural development, investment, and so on. But the UPA government in its public document *Report to the People, 2004–2008* recorded many of its achievements in matters benefiting the States (UPA 2008). To begin with, several measures are said to have been taken to alleviate the debt burden of the States: permission to refinance loans through market borrowings, if needed; retention of grant to loan ratio of 90:10 for 'special category states'; introduction of a new debt relief scheme for rescheduling all central loans contracted until 31 March 2004 and outstanding as on 31 March 2005 into fresh loans for 20 years carrying 7.5 per cent interest.[7]

The States' share of tax devolution is stated to have increased by 81 per cent, due to the new formula devised by the Eleventh Union Finance Commission[8] and accepted by the government, increasing the transfers from Rs 78,595 crore in 2004–5 to Rs 142,450 crore in 2007–8. The mineral royalty receipts to the States have been increased by 11.16 per cent over 2005.

The UPA government seems to have taken up the issue of security and development in India's North-east very seriously. Large-scale alienation, especially of the youth, leading to insurgency and militancy has remained a major problem for peace and security in the region. In response to these conditions the government introduced an improved scheme for the surrender and rehabilitation of the militants by increasing the number of constables in the Border Security Forces by 20 per cent in areas affected by militancy. One hundred per cent central funding, additionally, has been provided for modernization of the State police forces. To encourage peace efforts talks have been initiated with a host of militant groups, and the situation is said to have improved to some extent, in some States, most notably in Tripura (UPA 2008). While the usual governing practices of the Centre – releasing large financial-development packages for the North-east has also been maintained – a rehabilitation package, known as 'Operation Sadbhavana' Program, which was quite effective in Jammu and Kashmir, has also been extended to the North-east.[9]

Institutional revival and reforms

It is widely recognized that India's ongoing economic liberalization processes necessitate 'multiple interactions' (Rao and Singh 2005) and coordinated governmental actions at many levels. In a highly complex and diverse country like India, a centralized policy regime, a centralized planning, and a centralized bureaucratic hierarchy are simply inadequate. This is particularly so when the central government does not have the administrative/bureaucratic machinery to implement its own laws. The need for multiple interactions was recognized by the UPA government, which adopted, on the one hand, measures to revive existing channels of interactions that had fallen into disuse over the last few years.[10] In the aptly phrased subheading 'Collective Deliberations', the UPA government in its *Report to the People* (2008) observed:

> In order to collectively deliberate upon and arrive at a common understanding and strategies concerning critical issues requiring coordinated action by the Centre and the States, attempts have been made to activate the forums such as the National Development Council, the National Integration Council, the Inter-State Council, the Conferences on Internal Security and Law and Order, the Zonal Councils etc for facilitating frequent discussions with the Chief Ministers.

On the other hand, the second Commission on Centre–State Relations, known as the Punchhi Commission, was established (on 27 April 2007 as per the Resolution of the Government of India dated 30 April 2005). The terms of reference of the Commission included the task of taking a fresh look at and recommend the relative roles and responsibilities of each level of government and their inter-relations in the context of the 'profound changes' that the polity and economy had undergone over the last two decades. They also included: the way in which the existing arrangements between the Union and the States work, the best practices followed, judicial pronouncements on federalism in India, the role of the governors, emergency provisions, Panchayati Raj institutions, and inter-state river waters disputes. But the Commission has been particularly reminded of the need to take into account the 'social and economic developments that have taken place over the last two decades', and to avail itself of the 'emerging opportunities for sustained and rapid growth for alleviating poverty and illiteracy'.

Additionally there are some other areas in which the Commission is mandated to review. They include the responsibility and jurisdiction of the Union vis-à-vis the States: 'during major and prolonged outbreaks of communal violence, caste violence or any other social conflict'; 'in the planning and implementation of the mega projects like the inter-linking of rivers, that would normally take 15–20 years for completion and hinge vitally on the support of the States'; 'in promoting effective devolution of powers and autonomy to Panchayati Raj institutions and local bodies including the autonomous bodies under the 6th Schedule of the Constitution within a specified period of time'; 'in promoting the concept and practice of independent planning and budgeting at the district level'; 'the need for freeing inter-State trade in order to establish a unified and integrated domestic market'; and 'the feasibility of a supporting legislation under Article 355 for the purpose of *suo moto* deployment of Central forces in the States if and when the situation so demands'.[11]

The Punchhi commission

The Commission in its *Introductory* to a Questionnaire that has been sent out to all concerned parties interested in Centre–State relations (Government of India 2010) has taken cognizance of the highly centralized nature of the Indian federation until now, and emphasized two interlinked contexts that are of particular relevance to its work. First, the onset of economic liberalization since the early 1990s is highlighted, including the removal of the so-called 'license-permit raj', and the restoration of the market in its place. The same context necessitated 'more space in economic policy making' to be provided to the States. The Commission also indicated its preference for more autonomy for the States when it noted that although 'the States were expected to perform functions on a scale larger than before, their access to tax powers and borrowing remained limited' (Government of India 2010: 10). In addition, the Commission has also taken note of the inadequate powers and resources of rural and urban local bodies.

Second, the Commission has also taken note of the very significant political change in India in recent years: the rise of regional parties and coalition governments. Coupled with this, the rulings of the Supreme Court have increasingly circumscribed the Centre's powers of intervention (namely the application of President's Rule in accordance with Article 356) in the States.

As the commission is still working, we are not in a position to ascertain its eventual recommendation, or assess the nature of the federation that is eventually envisaged. But the public statement of the chairman in one of the commissioned workshops gives us some indication of the likely outcome. Here Justice Punchhi defended the case for 'stronger States' and for a strong Centre in which the aspirations of the regions are recognized: 'The accommodation of regional aspirations' within the overarching framework of country's unity', he noted, 'is the very foundation of a successful federal structure.' He also noted the impact of liberalization and the need for managing the transition successfully (*Tribune News Service* 10 December 2008).

Local government reforms

Since the passage of the 73rd and 74th Constitution Amendment Acts (1992), local governing bodies, rural and urban, have increasingly emerged as another tier of India's federal system, though still subject to many limitations.[12] Until 1992, institutionalization of rural self-governing bodies (known as *panchayats*) and urban bodies (municipalities, municipal corporations, and *nagar panchayats*) was a matter of the sweet will of the State governments because the States had no constitutional obligation to organize them, and the all-India picture was pretty dismal. The Acts made it constitutionally obligatory on the part of the States to regularly form such bodies and endow them with powers and responsibilities so that they function as units of self-government. The picture since has improved a lot and these sub-state-level local government bodies are today recognized as a distinct tier of Indian federalism.

The subject has received – and is still receiving – a lot of academic attention.[13] Both the Acts were, incidentally, passed during the Congress government at the Centre headed by the Prime Minister, the late Narasimha Rao. The rural local government known as Panchayati Raj in particular has figured in the CMP (UPA 2004). Four aspects are of important consideration here. First, it is said that the UPA government would ensure that 'all funds to States for implementation of poverty alleviation and rural development schemes by Panchayats are neither delayed nor diverted.' Second, the UPA government would consider sending funds directly to the *panchayats* after consultations with the States. Third, *panchayats* would be elected regularly. Fourth, Gram Sabha would be the foundation of *panchayati raj*.

On the performance side, the UPA government is said to have taken a few measures: the formation of a group of ministers under the Ministry of Panchayati Raj for strengthening *panchayats* and financing their devolution; the funds for Backward Regions Grant Fund (newly instituted) (for 250 designated districts) are being implemented through *panchayats*; and *panchayats* have been assigned the central role in implementing and monitoring the NREGS (CMP 2004).

The NREGS of the central government committing to providing 100 days' work for the rural poor has remained one of the most successful governmental interventions in favour of the rural poor in recent times though the success rates of the States implementing it have varied a lot. How far the Gram Sabha (comprising the total electorate of a village *panchayat*) develops into the real foundation of *panchayati raj*, as a self-governing institution, as defined as such by the 73rd Constitution Amendment Act (1992), is a moot question. Also, the real effectiveness of the local government bodies in India apparently pales into insignificance when they are found to be responsible for only 4.39 per cent of the combined central and state expenditures in India (2002–3). The expenditure to gross national product (GNP) ratio for these bodies during the same period was 1.71 per cent in contrast with that of the advanced countries where the figures range between 20 and 35 per cent normally, and, in some cases, is as high as 45 per cent (Denmark) and 41 per cent (Finland).[14]

Continuity between the NDA and the UPA

In the above, I have indicated areas of discontinuity as well as continuity between the NDA and the UPA. In this section, I shall concentrate on the performance side of the UPA with reference to two issues, and show the continuity between the two regimes.

Backward Regions Grant Fund

The Congress-led UPA's approach to Indian federalism does not represent a complete break with that of the NDA, its predecessor (1999–2004). On some core issues, such as the understanding of Indian nationhood, which have significant bearing on Indian federalism, the UPA and the NDA are poles apart. However, in the ongoing and practical aspects of governance, there is some degree of continuity. This is so because first of all the policies are long term, and, second, a sudden withdrawal of the previous administration's policies is not cost-effective, and might well be counterproductive. The Backward Regions Grant Fund (BRGF) program under the UPA is such an instance of continuity as well as a break with the NDA. The program was begun during the NDA government during the Tenth Plan period as *Rashtriya Sama Vikas Yogna* (RSVY) in 2003–4. Its purpose was to ensure the development of the backward States by helping to create productive assets.

The RSVY has not been discontinued, but is subsumed under the UPA's BRGF with the wider coverage of districts, and far greater amount of funds. In terms of the objectives, there is very little difference though. The program, 'aims to catalyze development in backward areas by providing infrastructure, promoting good governance and agrarian reforms, covering, through supplementary infrastructure and capacity building, the substantial development inflows into these district'.[15] In terms of coverage, while the RSVY had 147 districts in 27 States, the BRGF covers 250 districts in 27 States. Interestingly, both the NDA and the UPA have included 27 of 28 States of India under the above program. The BRGF placed under the Ministry of Rural Development has two funding windows: a Capability Building Fund, and an untied grant fund that takes the population into account.

However, the program was launched as late as 19 February 2007, that is, after about two years in office during the UPA's first term of office. While launching the program from Barpeta district in Assam, a backward district in a backward state on 19 February 2007, Prime Minister Manmohan Singh said that a sum of Rs 3,750 crore were available for 250 backward districts of India (each district getting about Rs 10–15 crore) for developing their infrastructure and for filling gaps in development. He also pointed out that the entire program would be implemented through the Panchayati Raj institutions and other local self-governing bodies. That way, it would give a great fillip to the Panchayati Raj as well as States (i.e. the Prime Minister's Office). Data available on the implementation side of the program up to September 2009 is very encouraging: there has been nearly 100 per cent implementation of the sum allocated and released for the purpose (Press Information Bureau 2009) The official assessment of the success of the program has highlighted the tremendous participatory, decentralizing and capacity building effects of the program at the grassroots of the polity.

Operation Sadhbhavna *(Operation Goodwill)*

This is another area of continuity between the NDA and the UPA. This program of extending welfare and development activities to the border areas was a post-Kargil initiative of the Indian army, and a brainchild of Lt General Arjun Roy who was the leader of the 14th Corps of the Northern Command of the Indian Army, and who initiated it as part of the service that the military can deliver to the border areas, a service that will pave the way for the ideal military of the future (Aggarwal and Bhan 2009). It is a goodwill gesture on the part of the army, started with funds from the Central Government Border Area Development Fund and the Ministry of Defense, in which the army engages in various welfare and developmental activities in the border areas of Ladakh to redress the credibility of the government and its institutions, as an 'aid to civil government' (Aggarwal and Bhan 2009: 520). The funds received for this program since 2001 from various sources are very large indeed: Rs 603 million (Aggarwal and Bhan 2009: 527). Operation *Sadhbhavna* has many limitations and contradictions, too, but, on the whole, social scientific assessment of the program has identified many positive achievements (Aggarwal and Bhan 2009: 539).

Conclusion

Scholars of comparative federalism have agreed that there is no optimal level of relations between the Centre and the constituent units in a federation because both structural arrangements as well as operational dynamics vary a lot among federations. Structurally, as we have seen above, Indian federation remains centralized, but operationally the federation has been decentralized. The central concern among scholars of federalism is whether a dynamic political equilibrium is created and maintained or not. If the States are neglected in the developmental process, if they do not get their due shares, if they suffer as a result of certain central policies, and if the democratically elected state government is unlawfully dismissed by the Centre, then the basis is laid for dissension in the relation between the Centre and the States that will disturb political equilibrium.

If we take a slightly long-term view then we can suggest that because of constitutional safeguards (e.g. various limitations imposed on the use of the Article 356 of the Constitution after the Supreme Court judgment in the S. R. Bommai case in 1994), the balance of relations in Indian federalism has, since the 1990s, shifted in favour of the States, which have been active participants in India's reform process, too. The rise of a multi-party (and that, too, state-based) coalition government at the Centre, the compulsion of implementing increasingly social welfarist and developmental programs, and of economic liberalization, in particular, have meant inevitably the increased role of the States in Indian federalism. This is the unmistakable shift that Indian federalism has, since the 1990s, been experiencing. The successive coalition governments at the Centre have added value to it, more or less. The UPA seems to have added more value to it thereby further contributing to the shifts in Indian federalism without, however, giving up certain long-term consensus in matters of ethno-national identity.

This aspect is clearly in need of more analysis. Despite the similar coalition partners, the BJP had had its own distinctive approach to federalism, informed as it was by its own notion of Indian nationhood (unitary but committed to smaller states). However, this commitment, as Hansen (quoted in Adeney 2005: 99) argued, is informed by 'a desire to limit the considerable power of the States, the regional sentiments, and vernacular public arenas' in order 'to strengthen the Union Government'. The 'ethnic criteria' are thus underplayed in the BJP's scheme of things on the grounds that they are potentially destabilizing and undermining the territorial integrity of the country (Adeney 2005: 99). The NDA's efforts in creating, in 2000, the three news states of Jharkhand (out of Bihar), Chhattisgarh (out of Madhya Pradesh) and Uttaranchal (later Uttarakhand) (out of Uttar Pradesh) were not inspired by any ethnic considerations, but for 'administrative' reasons, and is cited as an illustration of the Hindutva approach to Indian federalism. Jaffrelot (1996, cited in Adeney 2005: 99) notes that the BJP 'advocated the creation of 100 *janapadas* [administrative divisions grouping together several districts]. These divisions are deliberately intended to divide the linguistic zones and ensure ... that they did not become "mini-nations".'[16]

The Congress-led UPA's approach is different in this respect. It maintains the country's time-honored sensitivity to the cultural linguistic identity of the people of India, and its pluralist concept of Indian nationhood. Three points in the CMP (UPA 2004) are worthy of mention here. First, the UPA committed itself to the formation of a Telengana State by carving up Andhra Pradesh, India's first linguistic state after independence – a demand for which has been long-standing, and is based on the ethno-regional identity of the people of the area. It must, however, be mentioned that this commitment by the UPA was directly linked to the inclusion of the TRS, as its ally, a party that had been campaigning for a Telengana State since the 1970s. The TRS withdrew from the UPA subsequently, though, on the grounds that the UPA was not taking up the Telengana issue seriously.[17] Second, the UPA committed itself to the issue of 'declaring all languages in the Eighth Schedule of the Constitution as official languages'. The provisions for the Eighth Schedule of the Constitution, as any student of Indian federalism knows, were designed to accord recognition to the linguistic identity of the people in the regions of India. As the history of Indian federalism shows, in many cases, this linguistic recognition has served to prepare the basis of statehood within the federation if the particular language group has been found to be territorially rooted. Third, the UPA committed itself to declare Tamil as a classical language of India. Tamil has already been declared a *classical language* of India. It is beyond doubt that this was a price that the UPA had to pay for its Tamil partner, the DMK. All in all, ethno-culturally, the UPA's approach to federalism in India does not deviate from the country's old approach of multiculturalism and the goal of unity in diversity. However, one must not forget that the Indian States are hugely unequally positioned to reap the benefit of economic reforms. Hence, the newly created disparity among the so-called 'Forward States' and the 'Backward States' (Sáez 2002; Dua and Singh 2003) may not augur well for mitigating ethnic conflicts in the States. Thus it can be concluded that the new found State autonomy following India's economic liberalization may, if not accompanied by adequate and enduring Central State support for developmental activities in the relatively less advanced States, serve in the long run not federal but anti-federal purposes.

Acknowledgements

The author is grateful to Lawrence Sáez for his detailed comments and suggestions, which were helpful. Gurharpal deserves special thanks for his incisive comments, suggestions and the efficient editorial work rendered. The author wishes also to record his sincere gratitude to Professor Subrata K. Mitra for kindly reading the draft and for his comments.

4 Educational exclusion and inclusive development in India

Shailaja Fennell

Introduction

Educational achievements in India remain wanting after sixty odd years of independence. While the Indian constitution has deemed education to be a fundamental right the reality on the ground is that only 81.1 per cent of youth and 62.8 per cent of adults are deemed to be literate (UNESCO 2008b).

The lacklustre educational profile of India provided by national statistics is further emphasized when placed in relation to the global goals endorsed at the end of the twentieth century. The commitment to Education for All (EFA), first enunciated at the Jomtien Declaration 1990, and the achievement of universal primary education (UPE) set out as a Millennium Development Goal (MDG) to be achieved by 2015, appear to be unattainable within the context of the educational policies adopted by the Indian state (Government of India 2005).

Achieving education policy can be analysed in terms of both the consistency of the stated objectives as well as in relation to the financial outlays and administrative resources allocated to ensure the successful implementation of educational policy.[1] In this regard, the educational policies of the UPA government, comprising the Congress party and its alliance with the Left parties, the Samajvadi Party, and the Bahuhan Samaj Party, after the general elections of 2004, were set out in the Common Minimum Programme (CMP) adopted on 29 May 2004.

The main plank of the CMP was a political promise to reverse the communalization of the Indian education system that had been brought in by the previous government, the NDA, led by the BJP (see Chapter 5). This objective was to be met by ensuring that all institutions of higher learning were able to 'retain their autonomy' as this was seen to be under threat during the previous regime. The reversal was also to be brought about through the appointment of a review committee of experts to ensure a removal of communalized aspects of the school syllabus that had been brought in by the NDA government. In relation to the school system the CMP identified the Mid-Day Meals (MDM) scheme as the major programme to be introduced into primary and secondary schools as a way to improve the performance of the educational sector. It also announced that it would work to universalize education in the primary sector and ensure full coverage of education for early years under the Integrated Child Development Services (ICDS) scheme. On the financial side, the CMP underlined that it would spend at least the recommended 6 per cent of public spending on education and that at the very minimum half of this expenditure would be on the primary and secondary sectors. Additionally, there was to be the introduction of a cess on all central taxes to finance the commitment to ensure *universal basic education*.

These key components of the UPA's commitment need to be analysed in relation to both the relative success in implementing educational policy in furthering the agenda of *education for all* as well as with regard to the ability of such an educational policy to ensure a socially transformative development process.

Financing education

There has been a longstanding demand for the provision of six per cent of the national budget for education going back to the recommendations of the Kothari Commission Report of 1964. The percentage of India's GNP allocated to education in 2005–6 was 3.7 per cent. This increase is a marginal improvement on the amount allocated to elementary education in 2003–4 of 1.8 per cent (Tilak 2009). The latest statistics indicate that 10.7 per cent of government spending went to education in 2007 and of this 36 per cent went to the primary sector. It is clear that government expenditure is a far smaller amount than the GNP, and while the former figure shows that the share of spending is moving closer to five per cent, the latter figure remains close to two per cent. Figure 4.1 shows that the share of public expenditure going to education was 10.7 per cent and not significantly different from the percentages spent under the NDA (Fennell 2006).

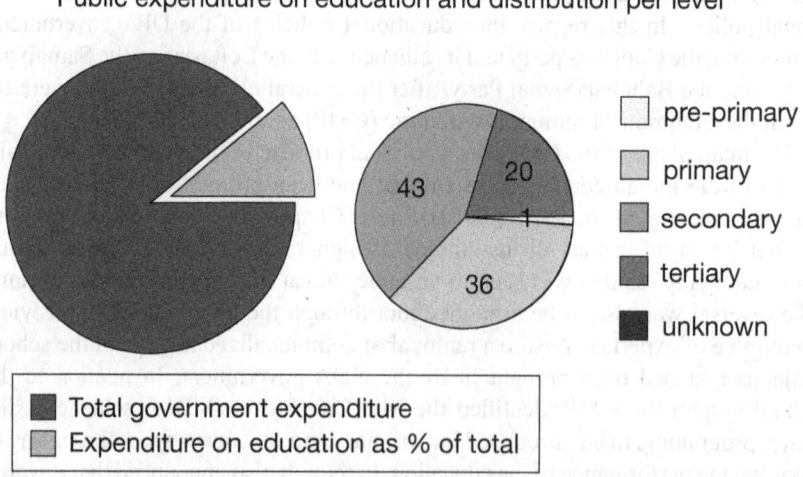

Source: UNESCO (2008b)

Figure 4.1 India's public expenditure on education 2006–7

On the other hand, while there has been a manifest inability to meet the expenditure levels recommended by previous commissions set up by the Indian government there has been an increase in the expenditure allocations for elementary education in recent plans: the 8th plan (1992–7) allocated Rs 406,00 million, there was Rs 147,500 million in the 9th Plan (1997–2002), an allocation of Rs 287,500 million for the 10th Plan (2002–7) and Rs 275,000 million in the 11th Plan (2007–13) (Colclough and De 2010). The expenditure on education by both central and state education departments was 2.81 per cent of GDP in 2005–6, with half the amount going in elementary education (Tilak 2009). Additionally, while the revenue collected by the levy of the two per cent cess was Rs 70,360 million the budget outlay for elementary education was only over half that amount.

The outright failure of the UPA government to ensure that its own stated objective of 'at least six per cent of its GNP' being allocated to education indicates its inability to make good its political promises.[2] The contrast between the high political priority accorded to education in the CMP and the low level of additional finances made available for educational policies does beg the question of whether the UPA had given serious thought to devising a educational policy that was able to ensure universal elementary education (UEE).

To explore whether the financial shortfall was a consequence of merely inadequate resource mobilization or more serious shortcomings in policy making we turn to an evaluation of educational policy during the UPA's term in office.

Situating the education policy of the UPA

The educational objectives set out in the CMP fall far short of a new framework for achieving national or international goals. The major objective of the CMP of removing the communal aspects of educational policy while an important political platform for the UPA does not set out any new policies, limiting itself to the establishment of a review panel of experts to rectify the communalization of the school syllabus. The only clear objective outlined in the CMP, with regard to the educational sector, was achieving the objective of universal basic education, largely through the greater coverage of the MMS in schools. The greater emphasis on a political agenda rather than the setting out of a clear-cut educational policy in the CMP appears to corroborate the view that Indian policy making is increasingly becoming more about gaining political legitimacy than ensuring financial resources (Mooij 2007).

The objective of achieving UPE set out in the CMP was not a definitive policy agenda in itself but rather a furthering of the existing educational policies of previous governments to extend educational coverage, such as the District Primary Education Programme (DPEP) that was introduced in 1994 with the objective of providing universal access to school.[3] This programme was incorporated into a larger national level educational policy in 2000–1, covering all India's districts, under the aegis of the *Sarva Shiksha Abhiyan* (SSA).[4] The SSA had the ambitious objective of ensuring UPE by 2007[5] and was initially based on an 85:15 financial outlay by central and state government during the period of the 10th plan.

The mid-term review of the MDGs indicated that India was moving towards UPE with 95 per cent of children enrolled in primary school, but the retention levels upto grade five were just 79 per cent in 2005 (UNESCO 2008b).[6] While the overall objective of UPE might appear to be in sight, there were concerns expressed regarding the meeting of associated MDGs of gender parity, as the Gender Parity Index (GPI)[7] has not been attained, and the figure was 0.94 in 2005.[8] The data does cast some doubt on the ability of the SSA to deliver educational policy at the local level, through the district and muncipal authorities, respectively, in rural and urban India. The tools of the SSA for ensuring complete enrollment and retention as well as the target of gender parity, through specific programme interventions to the target groups of poor households and the education of girls, do not appear to have delivered adequately.[9]

Furthermore, there was little attempt during the UPA term in office to devise a detailed financial plan for ensuring educational delivery. In particular, the additional financial outlays at state and local level to deliver these programmes were set out within the guidelines of the existing 10th plan, where educational provision was to be based on a financial sharing of 50:50 between the centre and the states. This arrangement was based on a strict financial proviso, whereby the state governments could be denied annual plan funds if they failed to transfer their contributions to the State Implementation Committee for the previous year.[10] There was no indication in the CMP of 2004 that there would be any change in these financial arrangements to ensure that the target of UPE, that was not achieved as originally envisaged by 2007, would now be achieved during its term of office. The only additional funds to be obtained were through the imposition of an educational cess of two per cent on all central taxes to provide funds to help achieve the objective of UPE and this was to be put towards funding the MDM scheme in schools.[11]

The MDM scheme as an educational programme

The MDM scheme announced by the UPA government in 2004 as its main initiative to attain UPE was not in itself a new policy. In fact, the scheme was the consequence of a court directive in response to a writ petition filed in the Supreme Court of India in 2001 to demand India's food stocks be used to prevent hunger.[12] It was the interim order of the Court, on 28 November 2001, that directed all state governments to provide children in government and government-assisted schools a prepared mid-day meal as a measure to relieve 'classroom hunger' (Drèze and Goyal 2003).[13] Throughout the following year, there were concerted attempts by non-governmentatl organizations (NGOs) to monitor the implementation of the MDM scheme, which revealed that the initial financial outlay fell far short of the requirement to provide meals of an adequate quality. So rather than being a new focus, the MDM emerges from a set of legal and lobbying battles to ensure the 'right to food', and thereby to guarantee Article 21 of the Indian Constitution on the 'right to life', as the driver for the MDM scheme (Khera 2005). There was little indication in the CMP that the MDM was to play a part in a larger educational policy framework to achieve national and international educational objectives.

Schemes such as the MDM act by providing incentives for parents to send their children to school (Jayaram 2008). The increased attraction of schools due to the provision of a hot cooked meal is particularly relevant for the most economically disadvantaged sectors, where malnourishment of children is an endemic condition. Consequently, a MDM scheme could ensure both increased enrollment in schools as well as the improved attention of children from the most deprived sections of society. Improvement in both attendance and the increased socialization at school are also achieved by incentive schemes such as the provision of free textbooks and the awarding of scholarships for girls.[14]

The evidence regarding the effectiveness of these schemes is mixed, with some studies pointing out that the universal schemes (e.g. mid-day meals and textbooks) perform better than targeted schemes (e.g. scholarships for girls).[15] While the studies recognize that leakages do persist, they find evidence that these are considerably reduced through improved monitoring of the programme to ensure that the food does arrive at the school and is of an adequate quality (Samson *et al.* 2008). The research indicates that with increased transparency and awareness-raising measures put in place there could also be an improved attendance level in response to other school incentives such as uniforms and free textbooks (Khera *et al.* 2009).

The introduction of specific programmes that target the socially under-privileged and discriminated categories, such as gender, minority status, and disability, have been applauded by international bodies (UNESCO 2008a). It is noteworthy that in the case of India, universal programmes that cover all government and government-aided schools, such as MDM, have also been effective when administered effectively by the school authorities, though this might not reduce the gender gap, as both girls and boys appear to benefit equally from the programme (Jayaram 2008). The key seems to lie in the ability to make explicit links between educational inputs, the process of educational service delivery and the type of educational outcome that results from such a programme (Pritchett and Pande 2006).[16]

The flipside of this finding is that it cannot be presumed that funding of an educational programme within the ongoing framework of the SSA is an automatic guarantee for ensuring UPE. Achieving UPE requires an understanding of the process of educational delivery and its implication for the nature and extent of successful educational outcomes.[17] Programmes to improve educational outcomes must consequently operate within a social context that favours children from more disadvantaged and discriminated groups attending and completing school. The provision for MDM and other school-based incentives are therefore most effective where there is widespread community level support for all children being at school, i.e. full support for the principle of the 'right to education' (Khera *et al.* 2009). If school programmes are undertaken in an environment of social stratification, particularly caste distinctions, then they are unlikely to be able to ensure equal treatment of all schoolchildren and their 'right to education'.[18]

Despite contemporary evidence that institutional mechanisms should be based on every child's right to education the CMP does not indicate that the programmatic aspects, such as MDM and ICDS, are working within such constitutional requirements for the provision of education. The absence of any explicit indication of how the legislative framework would be linked to the revised educational policy indicate that interrelations between institutional reform and programme implementation were not considered at the outset of UPA's term in office.

This appears strange given the discernable shifts in public opinion on the 'right to education' following the awarding of landmark legal judgements in the 1990s (the most significant being *Unnikrishan, J.P. vs. the State of Andhra Pradesh*) with regard to the interpretation of the right to education as a constitutional right.[19] The legal judgement and the public interest that resulted led to the formation of a national coalition, the National Association for the Fundamental Right to Education (NAFRE), and a campaign for the recognition of education as a fundamental right. The demands made by civil society organizations pushing for a bill in the Lok Sabha resulted in the passing of the 86th constitutional amendment (Article 21A) in 2002 that required the state to provide free and compulsory education till the age of fourteen. Despite these major legal achievements in the preceeding years the CMP did not directly mention how it would meet the additional costs of financing such a legal obligation and nor does it refer to the 'right to education' directly.

There was also no reference, in the CMP, to the particular design of an educational programme that would directly remedy the fallings of the SSA in achieving UPE. This further suggests that the UPA had not thought deeply and hard about the specific educational outcomes that it wished to realize when it came to power in 2004. The UPA's willingness to focus solely on programmes, largely on the MDM, as a tool to accelerate UPE points to a lack of any premediated thinking on financial and administrative requirements to ensure improved educational outcomes.

The consequences of the limited remit of the UPA is also evident in its own *Report to the People* released at the third anniversary of the alliance's victory in the national polls, which identifies its major objectives and achievements in the field of education (UPA 2008). The report profiled the increase in expenditure as the pathway to success in moving towards education for all, particularly the achievement of 96 per cent of all habitations having access to a primary school and the MDM being the biggest feeding programme in the world, covering 115 million children in primary and primary-aided schools (UPA 2008). It did not make any reference to the method of financial provisioning for the final mile towards UPE. While the increased demographic coverage by educational programmes is a positive feature, this is in a context where India still accounted for 21 million of the 72 million schoolchildren in the world not in school in 2008 (UNESCO 2008a). Yet there was no underlining of the need to place the legal responsibility of the state at the centre of educational provision despite the voluble discussion in the public sphere regarding the legal obligation to uphold the constitutional right to education.

The institutional and legal processes in education

The central message emerging from the CMF was the need to remedy the saffronization of education that took place under the NDA government. It was in pursuance of this objective that the UPA government reconstituted the Central Advisory

Board for Education (CABE) on 6 July 2004. Authorizing the CABE to review and make recommendations thorough key committees put into motion a number of processes by which the legal, institutional and curricular aspects of educational policy would come into play.[20]

The first meeting of the reconstituted CABE was held in August 2004 and its members – drawn from both houses of parliament as well as experts from the worlds of academia and public life – identified key areas that needed 'detailed deliberations' and the setting up of the specific committees to deal with these areas.[21] The Minstry for Human Resource Development (MHRD) provided detailed terms of reference for each committee,[22] and reports were submitted by each committee with the key policy recommendations that were required to ensure the achievement of each objective (Ministry of Human Resource Development 2004, 2005a).

The committee reports examine the relationship of education policy with development, both in relation to economic success as well as social justice. The recommendations of the committees indicate that very careful consideration was given to both academic arguments as well as legal judgements regarding the position of education in India's development. Nor were the individual committees averse to expanding their individual remit, and the committee for girls' education recommended that:

> alongside the 86th Amendment the Government of India bring in another Act to protect the fundamental right to life of the child in the form of the right to live in a civil society with full provision by the state of both primary health needs and early educational care for children up to 6 years.
> Ministry of Human Resource Development, Government of India
> 2005b: 9

The principle that the provision of education should be based on the principle of social justice and ensure equality for all children was evident in the recommendations of the committee on girls' education and inclusion. The report repeatedly underlined the necessity for a Common School System (CSS) that was both state-funded and state-led if the education system was to ensure the inclusion of all children. It stated:

> Pursuing the common school system as the key strategy that can prevent commercialism and exploitation of education as making good quality education available to all students in all schools at affordable fees is a primary commitment of the Common School system.
> Ministry of Human Resource Development, Government of India
> 2005b: 40

The reports of the individual committees reveal they regarded their terms of reference as being part of a larger exercise of reviewing the educational system. Consequently, they indicated the benefit of working alongside the recommendations of other committees, and the synergy that might arise from conjoining policy guidelines is evident in their reports. The report argued that:

We take note of two other committees constituted by CABE whose Terms of Reference overlap the task of this Committee. One of these committees is drafting Free and Compulsory Education Bill in pursuance of the 86th Amendment to the Constitution and looking into other issues related to elementary education. The second of these committees is deliberating upon the subject of girls' education and the Common School System. The recommendations of both of these committees shall have a direct bearing upon the blueprint of Universal Secondary Education that is engaging our attention.
Ministry of Human Resource Development, Government of India
2005c: 12

The members of the committees, both in their individual and collective capacity, considered their remit in its fullest sense and engaged with the process of reviewing educational policy to ensure that education was available to all children. Each committee enunciated this core principle and reiterated that the CABE had the responsbility of advising on educational policy. It is also clear that individual committees felt it was appropriate to reflect the recommendations of previous government committees on the institutions appropriate for ensuring education, with a particular regret being expressed about the inability to implement the Common School Policy, regarded as as the 'bedrock of educational quality, social cohesion and national integration' (Ministry of Human Resource Development, Department of Secondary Higher Education, Government of India 2005d: 1).

The interpretation of these committees went considerably beyond the primary objective set out for the reconstituted CABE of overhauling the school syllabus with a view to remedying the 'saffronization' of textbooks that had taken place under the previous government. The committee recommendations, while recognizing the importance of reinstating the autonomy of the educational system, focussed on the larger question of creating an institutional process to ensure that education would be finally made available to all children and to ensure that they would all be equal citizens who could participate fully in all avenues of life.

This objective was abundantly evident in the recommendations of the committee on the regulation of textbooks, which took a wide-angle view of the role played by textbooks and recommended that their content was reviewed by an expert and independent body. Their major directive was that the educational curriculum needed to be reviewed by an institutional process that ensured independent monitoring. According to the report:

> there is an urgent need to set up an institutional facility to keep an eye on textbooks. Research on textbooks is an essential feature of a healthy education system, but in the context of the challenges we face research must take the form of inquiry into specific problems relating to the quality of textbooks and the values they convey. The institutional structure to perform this task needs to be independent of any organization, which is involved in textbook preparation.
> Ministry of Human Resource Development, Government of India
2005a: 2

Regarding education as a goal in itself and one that should not be regarded narrowly as contributory factor to national development was also emphasized by the various committees of the CABE.[23] The committees deliberating universal education, girls' education and inclusion, and secondary education were also committed to a government system of school, particularly the CSS, to ensure that UEE should not place the poor at a disadvantage. It was with the view to ensuring equality and social justice that there was an emphasis on keeping out private, and thereby commerical profit-making, schools that would require payment of fees for education by the most disadvantaged.[24]

While the CABE and its constituent committees were drawing on public consultation with experts through structures such as the Public Study Group (PSG), the UPA government also initiated the design of the National Curriculum Framework (NCF) in 2004 under the aegis of the National Council for Educational Research and Training (NCERT). The consequence of simultaneously setting into play both a review panel at the highest level (i.e. the CABE) and the review by an existing educational institution (i.e. the NCERT) led to mutually irreconcilable recommendations. The CABE committee on textbooks censored the NCERT for proceeding to review textbooks, as there was a conflict of interest in a body, such as the NCERT, that produced books undertaking such a review.

The NCF brought out by the NCERT (2005) was the subject of considerable controversy, and particularly subjected to criticism by the CABE for being an elite formulation of education that did not address the needs of the CSS adequately (Sadgopal 2005a; Kumar 2007). There were concerns raised that the new NCF, which focussed on ensuring that children from diverse regional backgrounds, located in both urban and rural environments, could participate in classroom learning did not take into account the conditions on the ground across India. The major objections raised were that the NCF was focussing its recommendations on an ideal conception of education rather than setting out an operational policy that would ensure that all children were going to school. Most vociferous were criticims that the framework was elitist, and that its focus on a wide range of resources to ensure child-centred teaching did not take into account the very limited resources in government schools across the country (Sadgopal 2005b). There were also concerns regarding a large part of the framework being based on a move from focussing on textbooks to drawing on local knowledge that would result in the teaching of 'obscurantist' ideas (Habib 2005; Ganesh 2005).

While the controversy was itself noteworthy, what is of particular importance is the reasons for such a spirited public response on the matter of educational policy. One contributory factor was the opening up of the educational field by the reconstitution of the CABE. Among the most significant features of this process was the very creation of the PSG to advise the CABE on various aspects of educational policy. The 100-member PSG was drawn widely from across India, and included academics, intellectuals, and social and political activists to respond to policy initiatives, suggest changes and ensure transparency of the process.

While the creation of a public body for consultation was laudable it was not supported by a consultative policy environment within which the PSG could operate. Consequently, there was a little sustained engagement at the various public meetings and an increasing predominance of the political agenda that tended to overwhelm the educational dimension (Sadgopal 2005a; Raina 2008). The lack of procedure in the making of policy in India appears to have stymied additional rounds of review and undermined the possibility of reaching a consensus on educational policy.

An unfortunate victim of the truncated nature of consultation that ensued over the NCF recommendations of 2005 was the important pedagogic feature of placing children at the centre of schools through child-centred learning methods, which remained inadequately debated. The lack of consensus on educational policy at this juncture bequeathed a considerable advance in public debate on the merits and demerits of adopting a rights-based approach to learning and its implications for equality of children in disadvantaged or deprived areas of the country but denied the possibility of any reconciliation of oppositional views. Such a response was particularly regrettable given new findings in Indian education that children from different economic, linguistic and gendered backgrounds acquire knowledge through their own particular social context so that any CSS must have teaching and learning methods that work within rather than disregard these social constructions (Sarangapani 2003).

The frustration of not moving forward to construct a more effective educational policy driven by clear principles based on the recommendations of seven important national committees became clearly evident in 2006. In contrast, with the earlier anticipation that the UPA government would build on the minimal formulation for the educational sector in the first parliamentary session there were now mounting concerns that the opportunity of reforming educational policy was slipping away before the very eyes of the CABE and its committees.

There also appeared to be reluctance on the part of the government to respond to the critical scrutiny of the model bill by the academic, policy and activist communities, or the serious suggestions made regarding areas of review. The biggest cause for decrying the bill was its limited conception of the role of education, particularly with the delimiting of education to the age group five to fourteen years. This exclusion was particularly iniquitous as it was the poorest socio-economic groups that were least able to meet the costs of nursery and other organized forms of pre-schooling.[25] When it became apparent that the UPA government was neither addressing the limitations of the existing model bill, nor was it redrafting the bill to do away with limiting free education to the age group five to fourteen years, there was a series of public representations undertaken by NGOs, and alliances such as NAFRE.

The backtracking by the UPA on the earlier commitment to the CSS, and the increasing evidence of a lack of serious regard for social justice was even more irksome when it came to light that the CABE committee on higher education was recommending a greater role for the private sector in education (Raina 2008).[26] Furthermore, there was evidence that the government was not intending to create financial instruments beyond the educational tax to ensure the necessary expenditure for a fully fledged CSS, which would require Rs 40,000 crores per year over and above the current expenditure for implementation (Tilak 2009).

The upshot of these events was the growing public perception that the UPA government was not serious about linking existing programmes to the recommendations of individual CABE committees to create a comprehensive education policy. A consequence of a flawed policy-making process was the generation of more heat than light on educational policy and precluded firm commitment to any framework, current or revised, that could have gone beyond political agendas (Mooij 2007).

Additionally, there was a growing view that the UPA government's reluctance to reformulate the model bill was, at least in part, due to their concern about the greater financial outlays that would be needed to make good the recommendations of the committees. While the members of the expert committees and the public study groups were focussing on the reneging of the primary principle of equality and social justice in the period 2006–8, economists were beginning to discern that the government was orchestrating a distancing process away from the committee recommendations due to its manifest inability to garner the necessary resources (Jha *et al.* 2008; Tilak 2009).[27]

By the summer of 2008, it was clear that the government was moving away from any further reformulation or adoption of the recommendations of the various committees of CABE to a position where it was indicating that the model bill should be adopted in its current form by state governments, and that the majority of the financial burden be shouldered by them as well.[28] The seeming intransigence of the UPA government indicates both weaknesses in policy making, particularly with regard to laying out procedures for negotiation and consensus building, as well as in relation to accrual of financial resources for the provision of agreed public goods. The limitations in procedure as well as in public finance resulted in considerable disenchancement with the UPA record in education and growing doubt being cast on its ability to put in place an effective education policy that will ensure the goal of UEE. Thus while the individual programmes, such as the MDM, were varyingly reviewed by critics there was unanimous agreement that there was nothing new in relation to the process by which educational policy was to be delivered during the UPA first term in office.

Achieving UEE and the agenda of inclusive development

The limitations of policy and finance that have figured prominently as reasons for the lack of a fully fledged educational policy do not only mar the educational objectives of the UPA government but also cast doubts on the ability of the government to pursue a distinctive pattern of development. This is particularly the case as the UPA has made a series of public statements regarding its intention to set out a new and more socially transformative path to development than that followed by previous governments.

The Prime Minister's Independence Day speech in 2006 emphasized the need to send all children to school and reiterated that the SSA and the MDM would be the government's initiatives to achieve this objective. He said:

> The expanded Sarva Shiksha Abhiyan will ensure that all our children go to school. Under the universal Mid-Day Meal Programme, almost 12 crore children are getting a nutritious meal at school. Through these two programmes, we will ensure that all our children complete basic schooling.[29]

The almost identical language in the CMP of 2004 and the speech of 2006, without any mention of a new directive and no allusion to changes in educational policy, beg the question of why there was no evidence of responses to the vociferous public debates in the preceding years. This absence is also surprising given the importance accorded to the empowering aspect of education in the UPA agenda.

On the third anniversary of the UPA government, 22 May 2007, the Prime Minister stated that a strategy of development that was based on 'inclusive growth' was superior to following a purely growth oriented strategy as it combined empowerment with entitlement and investment. The major contribution to be made by the provision of public goods through public investment was spelt out very clearly in this statement:

> Education empowers, improved health care empowers, employment guarantee entitles, fulfilling quota obligations entitles. Through a combination of offering entitlement, ensuring empowerment and stepping up public investment, our Government has sought to make the growth process more inclusive.[30]

There is a stark contrast between the vision conjured up by these words of an education policy that would ensure that all children are getting a quality education and an inability to realize the objective of UEE as the financing of education continues to fall short of the required level of six per cent of GDP. Furthermore, an adequate financial outlay might not be a sufficient condition for ensuring UPE, even though it is a necessary condition (Alston and Bhuta 2005). In addition, the programmes that have been successful in increasing enrollment and retention, such as MDM, do not by themselves ensure the delivery of a quality education and are successful only environments where institutional mechanisms are based on tenets of equality and social justice.[31] These shortcomings in meeting the UPA's own objective of UPE are not explicitly recognised in the 11th plan.

The 11th plan documents do trace a linkage between the UPA's development strategy of 'inclusive growth', the major plank for government planning between 2007 and 2012, and the objectives of the CMP announced by the UPA during the course of the 10th plan.[32] However, there does not appear to be any new and distinctive educational policy emerging from the objectives of the CMP. If education is to have a central role in relation to achieving 'inclusive growth' there needs to be a fundamental rethinking on the provisioning of education. In particular, there must be a commitment that the legal responsibility of the state is to be met with adequate financial resources to ensure (a) that the right to education is made available to all children as demanded by the courts and (b) that greater consideration be taken of the importance of both the content of education and the context within which education is provided, as recommended by the expert committees of the CABE.

The new development paradigm of inclusive growth cannot be met by incremental increases in individual programmes alone. If empowerment through education is to be the way forward then considerable financial resources need to be expended on the educational sector (at the very least the six per cent that has been a longstanding recommendation). These resources must also be firmly linked to an educational policy that has an established set of procedures for public consultation that will result in negotiation and consensus of the principles and processes to ensure UEE and other national educational goals.

The power of education cannot be unleashed if there is dissipation of human energies, those of expert bodies, public figures, professionals and civil society organizations, on account of a lack of institutional processes to harness the best civil society initiatives and government legislation. Educational exclusion will continue as a social mechanism unless there is the embedding of a set of institutional practices that work with social norms and community practices (Fennell 2010) to ensure that children complete education in inclusive school environments.

Conclusion

The rather limited advances made by the UPA in education indicate that while there was an intention to ensure social transformation through improving educational access, the reality is that marginal groups continue to be excluded from education. This stumbling block could become a major obstacle in achieving the desired objective of inclusive development that the UPA has adopted as its distinctive policy.

The CMP and the educational reform agenda set out under the CABE were received by the government as recommendations for remedying the earlier excesses of the NDA government rather than as a requirement to put in place both a more comprehensive policy and greater financial wherewithal to achieve the objective. The debates on the nature of educational policy, its remit, pedagogy and financing, raised by the individual committees of the CABE, were highly pertinent and showed that public consultation did create positive inputs into the policy process. It also became clear that individual programmes, such as the MDM, were important for ensuring universal elementary education. However, these improvements cannot become institutionalized without setting out procedures to design a coherent educational policy that outlines how individual programmes will work to achieve quality education for all children.

There have continued to be severe shortcomings in the creation of financial mechanisms for resource mobilization throughout the UPA's term in office. The shortfall is particularly worrying as it appears to indicate that the financial and policy promises of the CMP have yet to be realized. Consequently, political imperative appears to have been the only victor, rather than a permanent improvement in the provision of education. Educational exclusion continues to a major blot on the terrain of educational provision and with the potential to annul any advances in strategies of inclusive development, as the marginalized and excluded are drawn to adversarial and, often violent, movements in retaliation against well-intentioned but weakly institutionalized and poorly implemented policies.

Part 2
Secularism

5 UPA and secularism

Gurharpal Singh

Introduction

In contrast to the rich theoretical discussion of secularism and the Indian state (Bhargava 1998), there is a major hiatus in the literature on its political practice. This ambiguity, according to Brass (2006), arises from the fact that secularism occupies a peculiar position in the discourse in India politics because not only does it encompass state–religion relations in the conventional sense, but it is also intimately interwoven into the fabric of competing visions of nationalism; the role of religious minorities, especially Muslims, in public life; and the belief that a strong centralized state is needed to act as a buffer between India's religious communities that have a high propensity for communal conflict. These complexities, moreover, are shot through with sharp political differences between the Congress and the BJP in their contrasting conceptions of the national idea and the place of secularism within it – differences that, arguably, represent clear blue water between the UPA and the NDA. Secularism in contemporary India is therefore much more than simply an issue of the state–religion relationship; it is about highly contested political practices, 'a mentality', a 'discourse' and, above all, different constructions of Indian nationalism that have been strongly influenced by the division of the country in 1947 (Brass 2006).

This chapter, which introduces subsequent ones by Steven Wilkinson and Rochana Bajpai on related themes, has three objectives. First, using the expansive definition of secularism outlined above, it elaborates the Nehruvian normative ideal of the concept and how it has changed, particularly with reference to its political practice. Second, in response to these changes, it then discusses the UPA's CMP and the policies that were followed between 2004 and 2009. Finally, it offers some perspectives on how the record of the Congress-led UPA on the subject might be better understood.

Nehruvian state secularism and after

The starting point for any meaningful discussion of state secularism in India is the normative ideal established by the Constitution of India. Although the term secularism is absent in the text – it was inserted in 1976 as result of a constitutional amendment – the constitution does not recognize an official religion.

The individual's relationship to the state was defined as a citizen rather than as a member of a religious group, and individual and collective freedom to worship and propagate religion was guaranteed. Taken together these provisions fulfilled at least three *essential* requirements of the secular state: religious equality, religious liberty and state neutrality (Smith 1967: Chapter 4). And though no clear 'wall of separation' was established between religion and the state, Indian secularism came to be characterized by what Smith has called the 'non-preference doctrine' in which no 'special privileges were to be granted to any one religion' (Smith 1967: 381). This doctrine, or what Bhargava (1998) terms 'principled distance', summed up in the credo *sarvadarma sabha* (good will towards all religions) 'share the liberal imagination, even though the ideals cherished by liberals are realised somewhat differently in the Indian context' (Mahajan and Jodhka 2009: 6).

The Constituent Assembly rejected demands from religious minorities for political reservation, but it went a long way to conceding their cultural and linguistic claims (Mahajan 2010). The provision of Muslim personal law was conceded but with a constitutional commitment to move eventually towards a unified civil code that would embrace *all* religious communities. In addition the recognition of affirmative action for scheduled castes (SCs) and scheduled tribes (STs) and, subsequently, Other Backward Classes (OBCs) introduced an element of group rights but with a clear understanding that this was aimed at eradicating disadvantage and discrimination.

It is generally recognized that the Constitution established a form of democratic citizen-centered idea of state secularism (Bajpai 2002), and public policy thereafter was based on the precept 'of the cultural rights of faith based communities and development rights of the structurally and historically deprived groups *within every* community of faith' (Seth 2010: 55, emphasis original). However, the last 30 years have witnessed a serious erosion of this ideal because of the blurring of the distinction between cultural and religious rights of religious minorities in national and provincial social policy. Central to this development has been the demise of the Congress and its original commitment to secularism as an ideology, which 'has been battered and largely displaced with the rise of Hindu nationalism' (Brass 2010: 2). Simultaneously, the meteoric rise of the BJP and associated *Hindutva* forces, on the other hand, has been accompanied by calls for 'genuine secularism' in which religious minorities would be assimilated into Hindu *rashtra* (nation) (Singh 2000: Chapter 1). But underpinning these changes has been a seismic shift in Indian politics introduced by the implementation of the Mandal Commission Report in 1990 that has extended reservation to OBCs, thereby unleashing the mobilization of Dalit parties in northern India. This broad extension of affirmative action programs has raised basic questions about whether these programs can continue to *exclude* religious minorities (i.e. non-Hindus) and, if so, whether alternative provisions are required for them, for example Muslims, who have singularly failed to share in the development achievements of the Indian state. In sum, the loss of Congress's hegemony, the rise of the BJP and the Dalitization of Indian politics appear to have fundamentally redefined the assumptions on which Nehruvian state secularism was based.

These complex and intersecting developments pose a range of questions: how has state secularism in India fared under the Congress-led UPA since 2004? Is it, as some argue (Seth 2010), now defined essentially by a form of religious pluralism? To what extent did the policies of the UPA government (2004–9) arrest or hasten this process? The rest of this chapter aims to address these concerns, firstly, by examining the UPA's policies and how they were implemented, and secondly, by offering some perspectives on how these developments might be better understood.

UPA's CMP and secularism

The UPA's CMP gave major prominence to secularism. Of its 'six basic principles of governance', two included a commitment:

> to persevere, protect and promote social harmony and to enforce the law without fear or favour to deal with all obscurantist and fundamentalist elements who seek to disturb social amity and peace, [and] to provide full equality of opportunity, particularly in education and employment for Schedule Castes, Schedule Tribes, OBCs and religious minorities'.
> Government of India 2004: 2–3

These overarching objectives were set within specific proposals that included measures to: reverse the communalization of education under the NDA, especially in higher education; 'implement the Places of Worship (Special Provisions) Act, 1992 and seek a negotiated settlement on Ayodyha'; enact a comprehensive law to deal with communal violence; 'establish a Commission for Minority Educational Institutions that will provide direct affiliation for minority professional institutions to central universities'; achieve the social and economic empowerment of minorities through education; establish a national commission to address the welfare of socially and economically backward religious and linguistic minorities (including the possibility of reservation); adequately fund the national Minorities Development Corporation; 'provide constitutional status to the Minorities Commission and the recognition of Urdu under Article 345 and 347 of the Constitution'; 'revive the National Integration Council so that it meets at least twice a year'; and 'to take the strictest possible action, without fear or favour, against all those individuals and organizations, who spread social discord, disturb social amity, and propagate religious bigotry and communal hatred' (Government of India 2004: 5–11).

Many of the above proposals were also present in the Congress's manifesto. The Congress, it declared:

> believes *in affirmative action for all religious and linguistic minorities*. The Congress has provided for reservations for Muslims in Kerala and Karnataka in government employment and education on the grounds that they are a socially and educationally backward class. *The Congress is committed to adopting this policy for... Muslims and other religious minorities on a national scale.*
> Indian National Congress 2004: emphasis added

This proposal, moreover, was set against a background in which secularism was identified as the 'key issue' because the BJP was 'systematically undermining the very essence of Indian civilization and destroying the very idea of India'. 'The Congress', the party's manifesto warned, 'recognises that this is not a moment for a narrow pursuit of power': rather, it was '*a moment to consolidate all forces subscribing to the fundamental values of our Constitution*' (Indian National Congress 2004: emphasis added).

In short, directly or indirectly, state secularism featured prominently in the UPA's CMP and Congress's manifesto and was tied to three commitments: to 'de-communalise' some of the policy initiatives of the previous NDA; to develop policies to empower (religious) minorities; and to ensure effective and impartial governance that upheld state secularism. To what extent these objectives were realized in the policies of the UPA is the subject we turn to next.

Table 5.1 summarizes the policy initiatives taken by the UPA. We have excluded those elements of affirmative action provision for SCs, STs and OBCs in so far as they relate to secularism because these are discussed in some detail in Rochana Bajpai's chapter (see Chapter 7). The broad implications of her paper for understanding changes in the evolution of Indian state secularism, however, will be discussed in the final section of the chapter.

De-communalization

In 2002 the NDA government changed the NCERT school textbooks through a new National Curriculum Framework. Ostensibly these changes were designed to 'saffronize' public education by raising the profile of Hindu cultural norms, views and historical personalities in school textbooks by portraying other religions negatively. At the time the BJP argued that its aim was to overhaul institutions such as the NCERT and free them from the 'dynastic control' of the Congress and the Communists to present a more 'accurate' picture of Indian history and culture.

One of the first initiatives of the UPA administration was the setting up of a three-member panel by the minister for Human Resource Development to review history textbooks and replace 'objectionable portions, distortions and factual errors with historical facts' (*AsiaNews.it* 2004). For this task it chose three historians from well-known Indians universities and, in addition, drew on the Delhi Research Council of Educational Research and Training, the Ratan Tata Trust and scholars from the University of Oxford to review Hindi, English, history and mathematics books. Overall, these reviews resulted in new textbooks, but not without opposition from *Hindutva* and non-*Hindutva* groups who said that the new offerings were now equally biased, if not more full of errors.

One area in which the UPA was able to make immediate impact was in the appointment of senior academics administrators. During Murli Manohar Joshi's tenure at the Ministry of Human Resource and Development the NDA had imposed its own nominees on leading academic appointments such as the chair of the Universities Grants Commission (UGC), NCERT and the Indian Council for Social Science Research (ICSSR) and extended the framework of religious-based university education by creating deemed universities (Nanda 2004). In response

Table 5.1 UPA's policies and secularism

De-communalization	Empowering religious minorities	Governance
De-communalization of text books (2004)	National Commission for Minority Education (2004)	Aftermath of Gujarat riots (2002)
'Secular' appointments to National Council for Educational Research and Training (NCERT), Universities Grants Commission (UGC), and Indian Council for Social Science Research (ICSSR)	Ministry of Minority Affairs (2006)	Nanavati Commission Report into anti-Sikh riots (2005)
Deregulation of religious-deemed universities	Sachar Committee Report (2006)	Communal Violence (Prevention, Control and Rehabilitation of Victims) Bill (2005)
	PM's 15 Point Programme for Welfare of Minorities (2006)	Anti-Christian riots in Orissa (2008)
	Introduction of a Bill to give Minorities Commission constitutional status (2006)	Liberhan Commission Report on the demolition of Babri Masjid mosque (2009)
	Mishra Commission on Religious and Linguistic Minorities (2007)	UPA and anti-conversion legislation in the states
	Executive action to monitor and target employment of minorities in national government service (2007)	
	Menon Committee on Equal Opportunities Commission (2007)	
	Kundu Committee Report on Diversity Index (2008)	

the UPA made its own high-profile appointments such as Professor Javeed Alam as the Chair of ICSSR and Professor Sukhadeo Thorat as the chair of UGC, while also instituting an inquiry into the working of the Indian Institute of Advanced Studies at Shimla, though these initiatives were less well trailed than its efforts in schools.

Empowering religious minorities

Whereas de-communalization of education was seen as the necessary corrective step, bolder measures were taken to empower religious minorities as outlined in the CMP above. These initiatives included: enhanced educational provision for religious minorities, a new administrative framework for the management and promotion of religious minority affairs, the commission of new research to assess the socio-economic status of religious minorities as well as the case for a more robust framework for equal opportunities, and the use of executive action to monitor and target better employment recruitment to central government services.

That education was seen as the key driver of minority religious empowerment was signaled by the creation of the National Commission for Minority Educational Institutions Act (2004). The main objective of the measure was to ensure that educational provisions enshrined in Article 30(1) of the constitution, which gave minorities the right to establish and administer educational institutions of their choice, are accessible to the members of religious minority communities without unnecessary administrative encumbrance. To this effect the commission was established as an executive authority to oversee, among other things, the affiliation of minority institutions to any university of their choice as long as they fulfilled the necessary requirements. It also seeks to overcome vexatious disputes relating to the status of minority educational institutions that have all too frequently ended up in the courts, often to the detriment of minority communities themselves (Gill 2001).

The emphasis on educational empowerment was also accompanied by a new administrative framework for the management and promotion of religious minority affairs. In January 2006, the Ministry of Minority Affairs (MoMA) was created to 'ensure a focused approach to the issues related to minorities and to play a pivotal role in the overall policy, planning, coordination, evaluation and review of regulator and development programmes for the benefit of the minority communities (Muslims, Sikhs, Christians, Buddhists and Zoroastrians)' (Government of India: 2010).[1] The main purpose of the ministry is 'overall policy, planning, coordination, evaluation and review of the regulatory and developmental programmes of the minority communities' (Government of India 2010). In particular, during the UPA's tenure, MoMA has been tasked with the function to coordinate a range of programs targeted at minority religious communities (principally Muslims) in the fields of education and development by drawing on resources formerly allocated to other ministries such as the Ministry for Human Resource Development. Of particular note has been the coordination of the Prime Minister's New 15-Point Program for the Welfare of Minorities also launched in January 2006, which is focused on four areas: improving education opportunities; ensuring an equitable share for religious minorities in economic activity and employment; improving the living conditions of minorities; and preventing and control of communal riots (Government of India 2010). This initiative draws on resources allocated to other programs and, where possible, aims to ensure that 15 per cent of the total outlay is earmarked for minorities. In addition, in 2007–8 the MoMA identified 90 Minority Concentration Districts (MCDs) for socio-economic backwardness for which a multi-sector development program (MSDP) was launched in 2008–9 to address the '"development deficit" in education, skill development, employment, sanitation, housing, drinking water and electricity supply for these districts' (Government of India 2010). Although the range and number of programs managed by the MoMA is bewilderingly complex, and frequently overlaps with other initiatives by the UPA in the fields of education and development, the creation of MoMA has for the first time provided a new administrative focus to minority affairs by creating a major institutional space within central government.

MOMA's task has been further underwritten by the findings of several reports commissioned by the UPA. Foremost among these was the Sachar Committee report (Prime Minister's High Level Committee 2006), which provided the intellectual and ideological ballast for the whole raft of policies coordinated by the ministry from 2006 onwards. The Sachar Committee was set up to provide systematic information on Muslims' socio-economic status and public and private opportunities compared with other communities', and to 'to identify areas of intervention by the government to address relevant issues relating to the social, economic and educational status of the Muslim community' (Sachar Committee Report 2006: vii). Given the subject matter, it was perhaps to be expected that the report's findings and recommendations became the focus of a heated national debate. While these are discussed at some length in the subsequent chapter by Wilkinson, here I want to highlight two aspects that are likely to have a more long-term impact.

First, the report marks a decisive shift in understanding the condition of Indian Muslims from the politics of *identity* to the politics of *development*. For much of the post-1947 period the political management of religious diversity in India has been articulated in terms of creating a framework for the recognition of the religious and cultural rights of minorities while maintaining the distinction between them. Yet since the 1980s, coincidently with the rise of the BJP, some of these identities have been pathologized as anti-national, with a consequence that some minorities have struggled to articulate their demands in non-religious language. By providing systematic data on the socio-economic condition of India's Muslims, the Sachar report demonstrates that Muslims 'suffer from deprivation on every front ... and are generally extremely backward and live in the shadow of poverty' (Robinson 2007:842). This recognition has, to some extent, been accompanied by a wider public acknowledgement that public policy can no longer overlook large sections of the Indian population merely because of their religion.

Second, the report – and its subsequent policy recommendations – has conceptually introduced the language of equality of opportunity and anti-discrimination into Indian politics. To be sure, this has always been present in some measure, but these new innovations are to be found in its recommendations for an equal opportunities commission and diversity index in living, education and work spaces. These issues were subsequently examined in detail by two committees. The Menon Committee report (Ministry of Minority Affairs, Government of India 2008a) proposed an Equal Opportunities Commission Bill to prohibit discrimination against 'deprived groups' defined on grounds of sex, disability, religion, caste, and language. The Kundu Committee report (Ministry of Minority Affairs, Government of India 2008b) recommended the constitution of a Diversity Commission to oversee the encouragement of diversity in educational institutions, employment and housing societies. Taken together both these reports' recommendations represent a noticeable shift in India's approach to equality, one that moves beyond an exclusive focus on reservations to explore a combination of anti-discrimination and diversity promotion measures in pursuit of social justice. They also recognize that discrimination is not merely the outcome of social identity (e.g. caste or religion) but can take place on multiple and intersecting grounds, and that compartmentalizing it by group-specific measures may well result in the politics of resentment and competition. Finally, both these reports appear to have borrowed extensively from the new equalities legislation in the United Kingdom, Canada and South Africa, and, in introducing the concept of indirect discrimination, mark a radical departure that is likely to have significance impact if enacted into legislation (Hasan 2009).

Equally profound were the findings and recommendations of the Mishra commission on religious and linguistic minorities (Ministry of Minority Affairs, Government of India 2007). This commission was set up in 2004 with a threefold objective: to establish criteria for identifying social backward sections among religious and linguistic minorities; recommend measures for their welfare, including reservation in education and government employment; and examine the necessary constitutional and administrative changes required to implement these changes (Government of India 2007: 1). Key among its recommendations were the proposals for a 15 per cent reservation in non-minority educational institutions and central and state government jobs for all religious and linguistic minorities, of which Muslims would be given a 10 per cent reservation (commensurate with their 73 per cent share in the total minority population in India) and the remaining 5 per cent would be given to other minorities. It also called for using the same criteria for identifying backwardness among minorities, as done for members of the Hindu community, and recommended the inclusion of Muslims and Christians Dalits in the SC list for reservation – a provision which had been denied to these groups on the grounds of religion (Government of India 2007: 144–55).

Perhaps because of its potentially contentious nature the Mishra report was only tabled in Parliament in 2009. As Wilkinson and Rochana Bajpai note (see Chapters 6 and 7 in this volume), there has been a significant opposition to the proposal from the BJP and, indeed, some schedule caste groups who fear the dilution of their quotas. Most of the recommendations of the report remain to be acted upon, though despite intense pressure from Dalit and Muslim groups, the UPA continues tread wearily in translating these proposals into legislation.

Finally, as noted by Rochana Bajpai (see Chapter 7), the UPA's policy of empowering religious minorities was addressed more directly through executive action. In January 2007 to ensure a better representation of religious minorities in government service, including banks, financial institutions and the railways, monitoring and targeting were introduced by the Ministry of Personnel, Public Grievances and Pensions. To what extent these measures have had the desired effect, however, remains to be systematically evaluated.

Governance

In some ways the real litmus test of secularism for any government in India is its protection of religious minorities and the effective prosecution of those involved in acts of communal violence. Again, as this subject is discussed at length by Wilkinson (Chapter 6), here we map out the broad parameters of the UPA's record; namely, its response to the aftermath of the Gujarat riots (2002) and other episodes of communal violence, the inquires into the anti-Sikh riots of 1984, the inquiry into the destruction of the Babri mosque, and the government's record in defending freedom of religion.

Notwithstanding the UPA's tough stance against communal riots in Gujarat, its efforts to bring the perpetrators of violence to book were at best insipid. Despite the fact that there were cases pending against some of the accused, and legal precedent precluded the imposition of President's Rule, a more interventionist policy would have demonstrated clear political intent. In the event, the Congress-led UPA preferred to skirt around the Gujarat's chief minister Narendra Modi than directly confront him. And this was in no little measure due to the Congress's electoral weakness in the state where the party has to tread carefully in not appearing to appease Muslim voters at the expense of its Hindu constituents.

Similar political considerations also appear to have been in play in the coalition's management of anti-Christian violence in Orissa (2007–8). This began at the end of 2007, but new waves of attacks against Christians were triggered in August 2008 by the killing of a Hindu leader, Swami Laxanananda Saraswati, along with five other people at Tumudibandh, Kandhamal district. Reports from various sources suggested that at least 50,000 Christians in Orissa were displaced, hundreds fled their homes and took refuge in forests and many others were said to be living in relief camps. The nature of the violence and the inadequate response of the local state administration called into question the ability of the center to ensure basic law and order in the states (United States Commission on International Religious Freedom 2010: 241–54). Again, as Wilkinson (see Chapter 6) convincingly demonstrates, it was electoral and political considerations that seems to explain the center's vacillation and the ineffectiveness of the state government in dealing with the violence (the BJP was in coalition with the ruling party in the state).

Such vacillation and partisanship from the Congress-led UPA leadership was also evident in its handling of two long-running inquires: the anti-Sikh riots and the Liberhan Commission and their fallout. The inquiry into anti-Sikh riots in Delhi in 1984 was completed by the Nanavati Commission report in February 2004. Although the commission was established by the NDA, its findings clearly embarrassed the UPA led by Dr Manmohan Singh, a Sikh Prime Minister, who had to publicly apologize to the Sikh community for Operation Blue Star. The report indicted very senior Congress politicians – such as Jagdish Tytler – who had played an active role in instigating the riots. In the aftermath the government reluctantly asked the Central Bureau of Investigation (CBI) to investigate seven cases. But in March 2007 the CBI gave Tytler a clean bill of health and closed the case against him. However, this was not the end of the matter. The Congress's decision to nominate Tytler for a Delhi constituency in the general elections (2009) led to the famous shoe-throwing incident in which the party had to backtrack from Tytler's candidature and suffered some political damage in Delhi and Punjab (see Singh 2009).

The Liberhan Commission report was completed in June 2009. However, some of its findings, which implicated the BJP leadership in the demolition, were selectively leaked to the press in November 2009, forcing the UPA government to table the report before Parliament. The political furore that accompanied this act led to allegations from the BJP that the UPA was deliberately using the report to attack the party and deflect criticism from its unpopular policies (Tandon and Tuteja 2009). To date none of those identified by the report has been prosecuted.

It is in light of these political ambivalences within the Congress-led UPA that we have to view the failure of its flagship measure: the Communal Violence (Prevention, Control and Rehabilitation of Victims) Bill (2005). The bill was framed as a piece of model legislation that would prevent communal violence and, in the event of such incidents, ensure the rehabilitation of victims. Its provisions included giving more powers to the police to deal with rioters and effective measures to bring the guilty to book, including the provision of a special court. Authorities were to be empowered to declare certain areas as communally disturbed and constitute them into a single judicial zone in which the police could take preventive measures such as controlling the movement of vehicles and people in such areas. The Bill also placed heavy sanctions on police officers for neglect of duty while doubling the rates of punishment under the Indian penal code (*Times of India*, 24 August 2010).

Yet despite these provisions this proposal faced universal opposition from social activists and lawyers on the grounds that it was not the lack of legislation that prevented the control of communal conflict but the absence of political will. The Bill made no serious provisions for making the concerned authorities liable for the non-exercise of powers to prevent or control communal violence. Fifty prominent personalities, including the Chief Justice of India, rejected the 'bill in its entirety' concluding that its assumptions were so 'flawed that it cannot be remedied by amending a few components' (*The Tribune*, 17 June 2007).

Finally, we need to mention the weathervane indicator of Indian secularism: the status of religious freedom. Following the Gujarat riots, the United States Commission on International Religious Freedom placed India on its 'Countries of Particular Concern List'. In subsequent years this was demoted to the Watch List as result of the Orissa riots and the increasing erosion of freedom of religion through anti-conversion legislation passed by several states (Gujarat, Himachal Pradesh and Chhattisgarh). Much of this legislation excludes 're-conversions' to 'one's forefather's religion' while imposing heavy sanctions on proselytizing traditions for seeking new converts. This legislation, once again, raises difficult issues about the general trend to prohibit conversions. Arguably, if freedom of religion is to be taken seriously as pillar of Indian secularism then there is need for a 'shift from formal to substantive equality, and from majoritarianism to a recommitment to [a] liberal democracy with sufficient protection for minority rights' (South Asian Human Rights Documentation Centre 2008: 68).

Assessment

Given the range and extent of the UPA's policies on secularism, it is perhaps premature to offer a wholesale assessment, especially as many of the measures have yet to demonstrate the effectiveness their policy makers intended. While the latter is, no doubt, a task for further research, it is worth reflecting on some of the general perspectives on these developments, two of which are also examined in detail in subsequent chapters.

The first perspective accuses the UPA administration of wasting a historic opportunity to restore the Nehruvian ideal of Indian state secularism (Seth 2009: 15). Far from returning to the Congress of the old, it is argued, the measures taken by the Congress-led UPA administration have moved the country towards new political framework of inter-religious relations that is now characterized by 'religious pluralism' in which the political commitment to 'secularisation' has now been displaced by 'communalisation' (Seth 2010: 38). The result of the UPA's policies aimed at minorities like the Muslims, it is contended, has shifted the conventional tradition of focusing on 'backwardness' (identified with caste or socio-economic indicators) to undifferentiated total 'communities' *à la* Sachar Committee. Consequently, this has led to the reframing of Indian state secularism in a way in which the state can 'legitimately abet, even aid, the communal practices of a religious group' so that now 'membership of the state is constituted not of citizens *qua* citizens but of citizens-in-communities' (Seth 2010: 48). Paradoxically, this religious pluralism is likely to have the opposite effects from what was intended: notably, the resurgence of communal identity among the majority Hindu community that now *also* has an incentive to represent itself as a 'total' community.

For Wilkinson (see Chapter 6) the UPA's record is best understood as the product of the compulsions of practical politics, particularly, though not exclusively, the need to win elections. State secularism according to him has always had to operate within the context of popular 'soft' *Hindutva* values among the electorate. Thus although the UPA and the Congress have utilized the rhetoric of secularism to introduce the policies discussed above, a careful evaluation of *how* these policies were *selected* and *implemented* suggest that they were primarily intended for maximum political impact among the Muslim vote. Much more seriously, however, the UPA's sins of omission and commission in governance continue to betray a political ambivalence that has characterized Indian secularism since its birth. Ironically, despite the extensive measures taken by the UPA to address the Muslim 'development deficit', Wilkinson is pessimistic about the overall potential of these polices because of their narrow focus, which does not mainstream the community but further segments its concerns. Such an exclusive focus, according to him, could provide the ideal breeding ground for political radicalization, especially if these policies are perceived by its opponents as an effort to rebuild the Congress's traditional Muslim vote bank.

In contrast to Wilkinson, Rochana Bajpai (see Chapter 7) offers an alternative reading based on an extensive review of affirmative action provision during the UPA administration, including the extension of reservation to religious minorities. In her historically based account, Rochana Bajpai argues that far from symbolizing a radical departure, the UPA's record marks a continuation of a *polity-wide* policy shift first signaled by the implementation of the Mandal Commission report in 1990. The real distinction between the UPA and previous Congress administrations, it is suggested, is the recognition that religious identities can be a source of disadvantage that requires affirmative action and, as such, its use is justified on grounds of the 'egalitarian concept of social justice'. While the Congress appears to have embraced the language of reservation for non-SC and ST groups, including religious minorities, this conversion is not unrelated to building new political constituencies around identities that have been so effective in shaping Indian politics since the late 1990s (see Chapter 7).

Given the currency of the UPA's policies it is perhaps premature to offer a definitive assessment, especially as a serious evaluation of the impact of some of the more targeted measures still remains to be undertaken. The three perspectives suggested above are useful in so far as they draw our attention to the continuities and discontinuities with the Nehruvian normative ideal in UPA's record over secularism, but apart from Wilkinson's qualified approach, they tend to elide more critical readings of the nature of Indian state secularism itself that could better explain the Congress's historic ambivalence. Here the answer may lie in a more radical approach to Indian state secularism, which questions whether it applies 'only to cultural groups that remain broadly within the Hindu fold but discriminates against non-Hindu minorities' (Brass 1994: 69). For some, like Madan, state secularism in India is at best an

> ... inadequately defined 'attitude ... of good will to all religions', *sarvadarama sadbhava*; in a narrower formulation it has been a defensive policy of religious neutrality (*dharma nirpekshta*) on the part of the state. In either formulation the Indian state achieves the opposite of its stated intentions; it trivialises religious differences as well as the notion of the unity of religions. And it really fails to provide guidance for viable political action, for it is not rooted, full-bloodied, and well thought *weltanschauung*; it is only a strategy.
> (Madan 1987: 750)

This negative strategy has no particular agenda for the secularization of Indian society. It offers only asymmetrical accommodation (encapsulation) to religious minorities in terms of state neutrality and, as a result, while the state's official policy is to treat all religious communities equally, one community remains 'more equal than others – the majority Hindu community' (Upadhyaya 1992: 817). Such an outcome, I have argued elsewhere (Singh 2000), was implicit in the demographic majoritarianism built into the new state at Independence; it was also inventible in the model of Nehruvian secularism that was unable to erase M. K. Gandhi's philosophy of inter-religious pluralism as the credo of the new state (Singh 2004).

Thus while the Congress under the UPA has undoubtedly embraced the language of affirmative action for religious minorities, this conversion is not unmindful of its political potential in an era that has been defined by patronage politics where new constituencies of caste and religion can be mobilized only by promises of reservation (Chandra 2007). These considerations perhaps explain the UPA's recent decision to enumerate caste as a category in the 2011 census when for the last 60 years calls for such an enumeration have been pejoratively dismissed as a throwback to colonial engineering of 'divide and rule'. To what extent this turn in Indian public policy, which is characterized by a relentless extension of affirmative action to 'excluded group', can provide a firm underpinning for democratization and consolidation of state secularism remains to be seen, especially given the zero-sum implications of these policies from some of the groups and its potential for a wider backlash from the BJP and its *Hindutva* organizations. It is in this light that the Congress's claims to have further 'embedded' and 'consolidated' state secularism by empowering religious minorities should be assessed. Historically speaking the odds against such claims being realized are very high, and only the UPA's record in office since 2009 will determine whether it has permanently shifted the terms of trade of Indian secularism or merely reframed them under the all too familiar rhetoric of 'empowering' religious minorities.

6   The UPA and Muslims

Steve Wilkinson

The UPA and communal conflict

The UPA came to power in 2004, in the aftermath of one of the worst incidents of communal conflict in post-independence India, the 2002 Gujarat riots, in which perhaps 1,000 people died and tens of thousands were forced to flee their homes. Those riots, likely instigated by the incumbent BJP government in the state in the aftermath of a murderous attack on Hindu militants in a train at Godhra, took the form of anti-Muslim attacks by mobs of Hindu militants, abetted by the inaction of the state security forces, which were apparently under orders not to interfere. One witness in Ahmedabad told a reporter how, when a group of terrified Muslims were running towards a police inspector to ask for help, 'He burst teargas shells at us when we were running towards him for protection. When approached for help, he replied *Jao, mera to upar se order hai* (Go away, I have orders from above)' (Setalvad, 2002: 188). The few officials that were brave enough to stick their necks out and arrest those responsible found themselves quickly transferred to non-operational positions, especially if they dared to arrest those with political connections to the incumbent BJP state government.[1]

The UPA, in its manifesto and on the campaign trail, promised to do two main things to prevent communal conflict and address minority concerns. First, it promised to prevent a Gujarat-type massacre from taking place while it was at the center. Shortly after being sworn in, Manmohan Singh talked sincerely about his pain at the Gujarat massacre, and expressed his determination that minorities should feel secure in India, remarks given credence by his status as a member of the two per cent Sikh community, which had suffered heavily in the 1984 riots that followed the assassination of Indira Gandhi. Second, the UPA promised to do something about minority economic development, by appointing a committee to examine minority economic backwardness, to report within six months.

The UPA's stance on these issues reflected the very robust support the Congress and its allies got from the minority communities. In 2004, the Congress and/or its allies got 79 per cent of the Muslim vote in Bihar, 78 per cent in Tamil Nadu, 66 per cent in Assam, 60 per cent in Gujarat, 55 per cent in Karnataka, and 47 per cent in Maharashtra (where the breakaway NCP got 30 per cent). The party also did well among the regionally concentrated Christian community, winning 76 per cent of the Catholic vote in Goa and 64 per cent of Christians in Kerala (CSDS/

Lokniti 2004). This minority support was pivotal to victory in several states, so pragmatic electoral considerations on the part of the Congress and its allies, as well as the Congress party's public commitment to secularism, give it a powerful incentive to attend to minority concerns.

But the UPA also realized that it needed to tread carefully, lest it took actions that would make the BJP's claims of minority appeasement seem more credible to voters in the majority community. Most voters from the majority community want minorities to be protected and deplore rampant communalism in politics and attacks on minorities.[2] But that does not mean that majority voters necessarily like minorities, nor that they are not uneasy about government action that seems to be too pro-minority. Two thirds of Hindu voters in the 2004 CSDS/Lokniti exit poll, for instance, supported a legal ban on religious conversions, and roughly the same margin supported a ban on inter-religious marriages, an issue of special significance for the Christian community (CSDS/Lokniti 2004). Previous polls have also found solid majorities in favour of a common civil code, which would abolish separate Muslim personal law (CSDS 1996). And opinion polls in the past have found that many of the same voters who decry riots and the use of communal appeals in elections also want to build a Ram Mandir in Ayodhya.[3]

The UPA also had to bear in mind that minority concerns, though important, almost always rank lower on a list of voters' current concerns than more bread and butter issues such as employment and *bijli, sarak, pani* (electricity, roads, and water). Even during the height of the Babri Masjid agitation from 1989 to 1992, issues such as the economy, inflation and corruption almost always topped communalism in rankings of voter concerns.[4] So politicians know that while minority issues are of great salience to a small proportion of the electorate, most of the electorate has other concerns. Governments therefore have to read carefully: avoiding mass violence and communalism, whilst not being seen as too focused on minority issues at the expense of overall development and majority concerns. This delicate political balancing act accounts for the national Congress leadership's equivocal stance on the Ayodhya issue, for instance – to follow past legal judgments and let the courts work it out – and also for its occasional inaction when violence breaks out, such as Prime Minister Narasimha Rao's equivocation during the Babri Masjid movement in 1991–2.[5]

In terms of its first promise, to keep a lid on minority violence, the UPA's performance has generally been very good since 2004. As of February 2010, there have been no major Hindu–Muslim riots since 2004. Most of this success, given India's constitutional structure, has to be credited to the performance of the 28 state governments, which control law and order at the local level. As I have explored elsewhere, the highly competitive nature of state politics, and the importance of cross-cutting caste cleavages among the Hindu majority, means that Muslims are often pivotal in state politics, and they increasingly demand and get state protection in return for their electoral support (Wilkinson 2004). Even the weakest governed states, such as Bihar, seem to be capable of preventing anti-minority violence from taking place when the electoral conditions are right.

But the center nonetheless deserves credit for acting decisively on the one or two occasions when it looked as if state governments were prepared to allow events to take place that had a high risk of leading to large-scale communal violence. Most notably, in May 2006, the central government responded strongly when riots broke out in Vadodara, in Gujarat. These riots had started after the BJP mayor, Sunil Solanki, had ordered the destruction of a small Muslim shrine as part of an urban development project, an act that in the heated communal environment in the city after 2002 was perceived by many Muslims as a direct assault on their community (Bunsha 2006). In the aftermath of the destruction of the shrine riots broke out in which five people were murdered and dozens injured. But the riots ended quickly because the Congress government at the center warned the BJP government in Gujarat that it would impose central rule if the riots were not stopped quickly.[6] Because the BJP state government knew these threats were credible –the UPA had strong Muslim electoral support, and therefore had a partisan interest in displacing its rival in the state, as well as its law and order motivations – the Modi administration met the riots with a firm response (16 of the 42 people injured were hit in police firing) and quickly called in the army to quell the violence. This was in sharp contrast to the Modi government's response in 2002, when the BJP central government exerted no real pressure on the BJP state government in Gujarat, and the state allowed the riots to continue for days without strong action.[7]

The center and states also acted decisively to prevent an anti-minority backlash after the horrific terrorist attacks on Mumbai in November 2008, in which 125 were killed and 327 injured. State and central police forces were deployed in large numbers, curfews were imposed in some sensitive areas, and central officials made public comments about how the attacks should not damage the unity of the Indian people. Indian Muslim leaders also emphasized their horror at the attacks and their renunciation of the attackers, with leaders in Mumbai refusing to let the dead Pakistani attackers be buried in graveyards they controlled. And a large number of Muslims participated in demonstrations and protests against the attacks, and emphasized that these were at odds with the teachings of Islam.

The big exceptions to this generally positive evaluation of the UPA's ability to prevent violence were periodic episodes of anti-Christian violence, mainly in the eastern state of Orissa, but also in Karnataka and other states. The tribal belts of Orissa are the scene of intense competition for influence and conversion between Christian denominations and Hindu right wing organizations, such as the Rashtriya Swayamsevak Sangh (RSS) and Bajrang Dal. The largest single attack, in 2008, came after the murder of RSS activist Swami Lakshmananda Saraswati and four Vishwa Hindu Parishad (VHP) activists. This was immediately blamed on Christians, but in all probability the murders were committed by Naxalites. In the aftermath, however, there were large-scale Hindu militant attacks on Christians in Kandhamal district, in which perhaps 70 people were killed (official figures listed 43 deaths), many churches were destroyed, and several thousand homes ransacked.

Prime Minister Manmohan Singh described the attacks on Christians in Orissa as a 'shame on the nation' and spoke to the Orissa Chief Minister (CM) to urge him to 'restore normality' but evidently threatened no stronger central action.[8] Why did the center not intervene strongly to prevent these attacks in the same way it did the 2006 riots in Vadodara? A cynic would argue that Christians, with their connotations of western influence and with less than two per cent of the population, are simply less important electorally to protect than Muslims for the incumbent government, and also an attractive (and small) community for the Hindu right to polarize against. The government of Orissa, a coalition between Naveen Patnaik's Biju Janata Dal (BJD) and the BJP, was also one that the Congress was wary of destabilizing, given the possibility that it might peel off Patnaik's party from the BJP in the run up to the 2009 elections.[9] When combined with the reluctance of the BJD to destabilize the government by arresting large numbers of its coalition partner's supporters from the Sangh Parivar (especially the Bajrang Dal), this led to a period of central and state inaction over the attacks that allowed Hindu militants to kill and injure many of the minorities in the tribal areas.[10]

One final aspect of the UPA's policy on communal violence has been to encourage in some cases and not block in others various court cases and investigations into previous communal violence. There had been a few symbolic successes, such as several convictions of those involved in the 1984 anti-Sikh riots in Delhi and the continuing efforts to get first information reports (FIRs) lodged against CM Narendra Modi for his role in the 2002 Gujarat Riots (Modi is supposed to give evidence in March 2010, though whether he will is uncertain at time of writing).[11] But in general these post-event prosecutions and investigations are likely to be much less effective at preventing riots than strong central and state action when riots break out, because conviction rates are extremely low – maybe 1–2 per cent of those charged – and the legal process is very uncertain and drawn out (Wilkinson 2004). These commissions and investigations are also seen, rightly, as highly politicized. After its 2009 election victory, for instance, the UPA government finally tabled the Liberhan Commission report on the 1992 destruction of the Babri Masjid, 16 years after its appointment by Prime Minister Narasimha Rao. But this report was seen as partisan because, while it rightly condemned senior BJP leaders, such as L. K. Advani and former Uttar Pradesh CM Kalyan Singh, for their actions in withdrawing police protection from the site, it said nothing about Congress Prime Minister Narasimha Rao's own responsibility in the matter. The Congress has also come in for a lot of criticism from the Sikh community over the non-prosecution of Congress leader Jagdish Tytler (cleared in 2007) for his role in the 1984 anti-Sikh riots in Delhi, with one Sikh journalist hurling a shoe at Home Minister Chidambaram over the issue during an election campaign press conference in April 2009.

The Sachar Committee: a missed opportunity

The Sachar Committee is only the latest in a long line of initiatives and committees set up by the center to examine minority issues. Jawaharlal Nehru in the mid-1950s was deeply concerned about patterns of discrimination and exclusion against minorities. He set up a Congress sub-committee in late 1957 to examine the issue, and asked the states to provide data on minority representation, most of which was never made public.[12] And since Nehru, each new government (the BJP excepted) has wanted to establish a new commission or committee to differentiate itself from its predecessor (which is usually condemned as 'having done nothing for minorities') and appeal to minority voters. Indira Gandhi, during her first period in office, ran for election with the manifesto promise to remove the 'present discrimination against minorities in the matter of recruitment to services' (Noorani 1990). She introduced a 15-point program for minorities, with the aim of protecting their security and fully including them in the state's development policies. And in her second period of office, to differentiate her own party from the Janata Government, which had established its own national Minorities Commission in 1978, she went back on her promise while in opposition to give the Commission statutory status and instead established in 1980 her own new 'High Power Panel on Minorities', under Gopal Krishna, to examine the plight of minorities through large-scale surveys and information gathering (Noorani 1990: 2419).[13]

All these commissions have found pretty much the same thing: minorities are underrepresented in government, in primary, secondary and higher education, and in private employment. They are more likely to be unemployed, or to work in unstable self-employment, for example as artisans, mechanics and rickshaw drivers. They have lower literacy, and higher infant mortality. They also suffer from social and economic discrimination, and sometimes also from the risk of communal violence.[14] The degree of underrepresentation and threat from communal violence, however, varies from state to state and place to place, with Muslims having much better representation and levels of socio-economic development in the south than in the north. Muslim underrepresentation in government employment also varies depending on the perceived sensitivity of the position, with very few Muslims for instance in Intelligence and security roles.[15] These government findings – many of them reproduced by Syed Shahabuddin in his now defunct journal *Muslim India* – have been supplemented by many other official studies (e.g. using National Sample Survey data) and by private studies by individuals, NGOs and centers such as the Gujarat Institute of Development Research and the National Council for Applied Economic Research (NCAER).[16] They all tell a similar story.

The committees and commissions have mostly made similar recommendations. They have urged steps be taken to improve recruitment of minorities, through educational grants and by including minorities on recruitment boards. They have urged that new bodies be created to monitor employment and social discrimination. And they have largely turned their back on creating separate reservations for Muslims. Most commissions have taken the view that separate community reservations encourage divisive anti-minority political sentiments, and therefore even if they were constitutionally permissible (which is doubtful), they ought to be avoided.[17]

The chance of any of these recommendations having a real effect on Muslims' social or economic status is minimal. This is not to blame the committees, which generally contained people of high integrity and who are deeply concerned with the position of minorities. But these committees are unable to surmount two big obstacles.

First, the fact that there has been such a strong partisan element, with each government largely rejecting the efforts of the past and appointing its own committees, commissions and councils to reinvent the wheel once more, has led to a lack of continuity in minority policy as it has in many other areas. In its attempt to show it is dealing with multiple problems, the government proliferates programs: child development; coaching; scholarships; employment; medicine; university programs; minority concentration districts and many more (see, for example, Ministry of Minority Affairs, Government of India 2009). To demonstrate that the UPA is doing better than previous governments, similar programs to those in the past have been re-founded, without of course ever really becoming integrated into the way of doing things in New Delhi, the state capitals, or at the crucial district and block development levels.

Second, the fact is, as I have written elsewhere, that most issues that affect Muslims' day-to-day lives – issues such as education, security and employment – are decided much more by state governments than by the national government. The center can encourage, cajole and occasionally create pots of money to hand out to the states through centrally sponsored schemes, but it cannot do much without political will at the state level.[18] In the early 1980s, for instance, the Minorities Commission found that, despite the Uttar Pradesh government issuing directives to increase minority representation in the services in a 1972 letter, nothing had happened, and the UP's response to complaints was simply to issue the same directive again... (Ministry of Welfare, Government of India 1986: 67, 71)

The Sachar Committee followed in the vein of these earlier initiatives, though the mass of documentary evidence on Muslim backwardness it compiled, and the scale of its perambulations around the country, were larger than most of these previous efforts. Much of the value of the committee for Muslims and the Congress was performative, no doubt, the act of going round and listening to grievances and the discussion of this in the press convincing many that the Congress was with the minorities. One problem that was obvious right from the beginning was that the seven-member commission included no women, something that drew wide and justified criticism, but that it tried to address through several women-focused events held in various places. There was also storm in a teacup in the press and parliament about whether, by asking for data about Muslim representation in the army, the committee and Congress were trying to 'communalize' the army, with senior army officers particularly vocal in their protests. The irony of the army's stance, of course, and one possible reason that senior officers did not want the whole issue of recruitment opened up, is that the army still maintains class regiments, with recruits chosen on the basis of region, religion and caste, that are a holdover from the 'martial race' divide-and-rule strategy of the British. The Muslim companies from these infantry and armored regiments left for Pakistan in 1947 (except for the Madras regiments where Muslim soldiers served alongside Hindus and Christians rather than in separate units), but the Hindu and Sikh companies and regiments remained (Wilkinson 2010). The navy and air force did supply data to Sachar on Muslim recruitment, but after the political controversy over the army data this was not printed in the final report.

Most of the data that Sachar produced were not particularly new, and largely confirmed the existing picture that Muslims are worse off in terms of employment, education, access to land and access to credit, and that the community's position has if anything worsened relative to other communities over the past few decades.[19] Unfortunately, with a couple of exceptions, most of the data presented in Sachar are not terribly informative for policy purposes, because they only establish that Muslims are worse off than other communities on some dimension or the other, without establishing *why*, or controlling for other possible causes of the imbalance rather than the discrimination the committee seems to conclude is the cause. Only in a few cases did the committee try to establish the relative importance of causes of the imbalance in this way. In one study for instance it used National Sample Survey data on 20–30 year olds to find out 'if SRC [Socio-Religious Community] status affects educational attainment even after we control for economic status and other factors' (Prime Minister's High Level Committee 2006: 72–3). The committee found that, even controlling for age, gender, economic status, state of residence and rural/urban residence, being Muslim (and being SC/ST) has an important independent effect on reducing an individual's chance of graduating from college, especially for men and in towns and cities (Prime Minister's High Level Committee 2006: 73–4). In another study the committee found that Muslims have lower workforce participation rates than members of other communities, controlling for other plausible causes of workforce participation (Prime Minister's High Level Committee 2006: 107–8).

In two big areas, though, Sachar's findings were really new, though unfortunately all these findings have received much less attention in the press than they deserve. First, Sachar shattered myths about a minority that was backward because it preferred to turn inward, to Urdu and *madrasas*, rather than enter the mainstream. Sachar shows that madrasa attendance is in fact very low (only four per cent of Muslim children, compared with earlier NCAER estimates of seven per cent) and that, far from this being the first choice of parents, most Muslim parents are in fact very anxious to get their children access to the best modern sector education they can, which often means non-Urdu education (Prime Minister's High Level Committee 2006: 15f, 77).[20] Second, Sachar shows that in other important respects Muslims are also more mainstream and progressive than many Hindus think: for instance female infanticide among Muslims is lower than that among Hindus; and Muslims are eager for the most part to be educated in regular schools in the state language, rather than in minority Urdu-language schools.

The Sachar Committee's main recommendations, most importantly, were sensible and mainstream, well in line with the previous committees and commissions, though novel in some important respects, such as recommending a 'diversity index' to encourage more inclusion of Muslims. Although interviews with people close to the committee point to some differences of opinion, with some people preferring community-specific measures and others preferring better integration of Muslims within more general programs, the report as a whole came down firmly behind the latter policy.[21] One reason several committee members in favour of reservations signed on to the majority report, apparently, is because the Misra report on reservations for linguistic and religious minorities (see below) had not yet been tabled, so that members who supported reservations were not foreclosing the issue by signing on to Sachar. In general, the Sachar Committee recommended: 'inclusive development and 'mainstreaming of the Community while respecting diversity', (p. 237); better data and studies on the prevalence of discrimination (p. 239); and providing incentives to public and private sector institutions to have a diverse workforce, residential community or student body (p. 242) (Prime Minister's High Level Committee 2006).[22] Specifically, it focused on measures such as better government schools for all (which would benefit Muslims disproportionately because they are disproportionately unschooled), better technical education, better provision of credit to all, and the provision of ways for Muslim students who started education late, or started in a *madrasa*, to switch to more mainstream education (Prime Minister's High Level Committee 2006: 243ff).

Publicly, the Congress government announced it was accepting all the main Sachar Committee recommendations in May 2007, a few months after the report was received in November 2006. The Minority Commission web site states that 'The Central Government has decided to implement the recommendations of the Sachar Committee covering affirmative action, special area development, education, credit, skill development, social inclusion etc', and then goes on to list a variety of initiatives it claims are consistent with the main thrust of Sachar (Ministry of Minority Affairs, Government of India 2009). But in 'implementing' the report, the Congress has in fact put much more emphasis on communally targeted programs than on the mainstream recommendations that were central to the report. Instead of a focus on diversity and on mainstreaming Muslims into caste-, income- and poverty-based programs in the private and public sectors, the party's leaders highlighted the delivery of more funds to minority-concentration districts, special measures for Urdu, and reservations for Muslims 'on the basis of their backwardness' (a caveat to avoid the constitutional prohibition on religion-specific measures). And in fall 2009, after the election, the government finally tabled the report of the Justice Ranganath Misra Commission, appointed in late 2004 to examine the possible criteria for reservations among religious and linguistic minorities (Ministry of Minority Affairs, Government of India 2007). This report, while recognizing that it would be ideal to have uniform criteria for reservations across all religious groups, and while reiterating its commitment to a color-blind state at some point in the future, argues that given the difficulties of implementing all this in the short term it makes more sense to treat all lower and middle caste Muslims as backward and eligible for reservations. The commission recommended a total 15 per cent reservation in central services for religious and linguistic minorities with 10 per cent of that for Muslims (Ministry of Minority Affairs, Government of India 2007: 144ff).

As of February 2010, the Congress now appears to be equivocating on implementing the Misra Commission recommendations on central reservations for Muslims, due to a fierce political backlash, with Prime Minister Singh claiming that a 'national consensus is needed on the issue' (Rediff News 2006). But on the campaign trail and in policy implementation in the states, the party has been all too willing to promote Muslim-specific measures that it claimed were consistent with Sachar but had not, in fact, been recommended by the committee at all, and in some cases –notably in the case of state-level communal reservations in Andhra Pradesh and Karnataka – had been specifically rejected. The reason for Congress's political sleight of hand is not hard to see. The mainstreaming measures recommended by the committee were felt to have much less political value than promises of community-specific benefits.

One person with knowledge of the committee noted that during its visits to the states many of the state politicians were profoundly uninterested in its draft proposals to 'mainstream' Muslims within more general anti-poverty and education programs. The reason is that 'They feel community-specific programs get them more political mileage ... in states where Muslims constituted a lot of the votes.'[23] In an environment where most people, Muslims and Hindus alike, feel that the application and promotion criteria for state jobs and education are not transparent, voters and activists seem to respond more to a guaranteed payoff that, while low, is community specific, to the much more uncertain prospect of getting some share that is not guaranteed of a larger pie in the future. That explains why activists such as Syed Shahabuddin continue to press for Muslim reservations in education, government services, and legislatures, as well as the preferential allocation of bank credit, rather than greater minority inclusion within already existing categories of reservation and government allocation.[24] Shahabuddin (2007) argues that 'Personally my view is that in the final analysis, reservation is the issue, the master key to political, economic and social empowerment of a backward community' and he urges a campaign of civil disobedience and a general boycott of elections if reservations are not implemented.

To respond to such demands the Congress put much more stress in the campaign trail in 2009 on the community-specific promises than on the mainstreaming development aspects of the report.[25] The party's manifesto highlighted the award of 400,000 scholarships to minorities, special programs for 90 minority-concentration districts, and then went on to trumpet the fact that 'The Indian National Congress has pioneered reservations for minorities in Kerala, Karnataka and Andhra Pradesh in government employment and education on the basis of their social and economic backwardness. We are committed to adopt this policy at the national level.' The manifesto then went on to highlight other community specific initiatives such as a Wakf Development Corporation, a National Unani (Muslim medicine) University, and more funding for the Maulana Azad Educational Foundation (All India Congress Committee 2009).

The results of this minority-specific strategy are not hard to imagine. A large number of relatively underfunded and uncoordinated proposals will not have a large effect, on the basis of past performance, in addressing the social and economic discrimination and underdevelopment that affects the community. And among members of the majority community, doing something for minorities is ever more associated with negative connotations of 'vote banks' and 'appeasement' rather than a politically more acceptable and socially more progressive policy of mainstreaming Muslims into government on the basis of their equal rights as Indian citizens. At the time of writing (February 2010) India is once again being wracked by a debate over religious reservations, with the Congress – which under Nehru argued strenuously against them – now in the position of defending them against the BJP, which argues that they are unconstitutional and politically divisive, a view probably shared by most Indians.

A social and economic time bomb?

India has so far been fortunate to avoid alienating its 13 per cent Muslim minority from the polity, despite the fact that the Muslim community is worse off than the majority on almost every dimension. Compared to Pakistan's almost complete failure on this dimension, India's treatment of linguistic and religious minorities has been a notable success and there is much to celebrate. But there are two real danger signs for the future.

One is that social, educational and residential discrimination and disadvantage remains strongly entrenched, and does not seem to be lessening much with the expansion of the private market and general improvements in development outcomes.[26] In part because SCs have done better in recent years due to their political clout (for instance Sachar data shows that younger-age-group Muslims are now less literate than SC Hindus, for the first time), Muslims are losing relative ground to most other communities. Sumon Kumar Bhaumik and Manisha Chakrabarty, for instance, in a paper that uses NSS data, have established that the returns to education for Muslims compared with equally qualified Hindus have been declining in relative terms over the period 1987 to 1999, a period when inter-caste differences among Hindus have declined (Bhaumik and Chakrabaty 2006). And one recent study of employment practices in the modern sector (where we might think employment discrimination would be lowest) suggests that discrimination is a very big problem. This study for the first time used matched applicants with identical CVs to try to get a sense of how pervasive employment discrimination might be, a method used with considerable success by Bertrand and Mullainathan in their study of discrimination in the USA (Bertrand and Mullainathan 2003). The study sent in CVs from identically qualified upper caste Hindu, lower caste Hindu and Muslim applicants for each job advertised in a major newspaper for which these applicants were qualified over the course of a year. The object was to see which applicants received an initial call back about the job. The results were striking. An equally qualified SC 'applicant' had only two thirds as high a chance of being called back as an upper caste candidate. But the chances for Muslim candidates were even worse: a Muslim candidate had only one third as high a chance of being called back as an upper caste Hindu candidate.[27] If these results are at all typical, this suggests massive employment discrimination in the private sector.

The second danger is that, fed by this continuing discrimination and poverty at a time when many Indians' lives are visibly improving, support for extremists might begin to extend beyond the very small number of young men who have thus far joined organizations such as the now-banned Students' Islamic Movement of India (SIMI). India's Muslims are, in many states, disproportionately urban and ghettoized (e.g. 19 per cent of the urban population in Andhra Pradesh, 15 per cent in Gujarat, 21 per cent in Karnataka, 14 per cent in Madhya Pradesh, 31 per cent in Uttar Pradesh), which when combined with transnational attempts to stoke militancy, seems to provide much of the raw material necessary for both increasing minority marginality and extremism. The relationship between poverty, discrimination and militancy is not always uniform, of course, but many minority militant groups around the world seem to draw on men and women who have some education but feel that their life chances are limited and that the state, the market and the majority community are stacked against them. And it appears from data in Sachar and Basant and Shariff that this group is growing in India. One factor that surely facilitates this feeling of separateness is the increasing segregation of the Hindu and Muslim communities in cities such as Vadodara and Ahmedabad, the product of security concerns on the part of Hindus and Muslims as well as anti-Muslim housing discrimination (Wax 2009).[28]

But the chances of the government putting a very high priority on measures to improve things for India's minorities, as to some extent was done after the urban riots of the 1960s in the USA, seem very low. For the political reasons explored above, the party and its allies seem to be unwilling to substantially mainstream minority development within existing programs. And, again for political reasons, the party also seems unlikely to spend really serious money through its community-specific programs: the center lacks the money, and such proposals engender fierce criticism. A statement by Manmohan Singh to a minorities forum at the National Development Council in 2006 about the need for innovative development programs for minorities to have 'the first claim on resources' so that they could have a fair share of India's development, was met by a hail of criticism by the BJP, which argued he was trying to communalize the country.[29] BJP leader Rajnath Singh responded that 'India's resources are not to be divided on religious lines. Every Indian, irrespective of his or her religious background, has equal claim on the country's resources.' And RSS leader Ram Madhav said that: 'This is precisely the language used by Mohammad Ali Jinnah before the partition… It is unfortunate our leaders have not learnt lessons from the tragic partition. They are pursuing the same politics of religion for electoral benefits.'[30]

7 Beyond identity?

UPA rhetoric on social justice and affirmative action

Rochana Bajpai

Introduction

The ideology of the UPA has figured prominently in analyses of its policies and explanations of its electoral successes. This chapter examines the UPA's ideology on affirmative action, chiefly quotas or reservations, focusing on political rhetoric. I show that UPA rhetoric on reservations differed substantially from earlier Congress positions, both in the late 1940s, as well as in 1990. The UPA did not mark the return of the old Congress but, rather, the emergence of a new one that was much more favourable to the expansion of identity-based quotas than its predecessor. This reflected, however, a *polity-wide shift* that can be traced at the national level to the Janata Dal coalition in the 1990 Mandal debate. All governments that came thereafter – NDA as well as UPA – have extended identity-based reservations and/or favoured their expansion to new beneficiaries. Ideological differences have meant, however, that the Janata Dal, NDA and UPA coalitions differ in terms of the groups favoured as beneficiaries, as well as the mode of extension of reservations. Under the UPA, affirmative action for religious minorities has seen the greatest expansion, a process that has thus far occurred largely through executive action rather than legislation and remains overlooked by scholars.

The UPA is often distinguished from the NDA in terms of its ideology.[1] Thus, for instance, the UPA's triumph at the polls in 2004 and 2009 are widely interpreted as the electorate's rejection of communalism and identity politics more generally, in favour of old Congress values of secularism and development for all. The politics of religion, represented by the BJP, the Shiv Sena and other Hindu nationalist organizations, as well as the politics of caste, represented by Janata successor parties such as Mayawati's BSP, Mulayam Singh's SP, Laloo Prasad Yadav's RJD, Ram Vilas Paswan's LJNSP, were humbled at the polls by the Congress party, the old behemoth that promised policies based on secularism and inclusive development. In another claim for ideology, the UPA's election victories in 2004 and 2009 are believed to represent popular endorsement for its pro-poor ideology and policies. The electorate, it is claimed, rejected the NDA's pursuit of economic liberalization for the middle classes, exemplified in its 2004 'India Shining' campaign, in favour of the UPA's promise of equitable growth, welfare of the common man (*aam aadmi*) and 'weaker sections'. Also, it is argued that ideological differences have meant that the UPA's foreign policy is more focused on negotiation and compromise than the NDA's, which emphasized military instruments of power.[2]

This chapter seeks to refine our understanding of the ideological distinctiveness of the UPA, both in relation to the NDA, as well as the Congress party historically. For the most part, scholars have sought to nuance popular accounts that link electoral outcomes to the UPA's ideology. Interpretations of the 2004 or 2009 vote as national popular verdicts in favour of secularism or social justice, it has been argued, unravel on close scrutiny; at best, these explain some election results, with state-level factors and electoral alliances playing a much more important role.[3] Moving away from electoral outcomes, this chapter scrutinizes the thesis of the ideological distinctiveness of the UPA in the context of the policy process. Its focus is official rhetoric on affirmative action.

Political rhetoric is usually dismissed as little more than a smokescreen for power, offering little additional leverage for political explanation. Typically examined within the frame of self-interested behavior of politicians seeking electoral or factional power, there has been little detailed analysis of the ideas expressed in rhetoric.[4] These tend to be examined in narrow instrumental terms, and in terms of the gaps between rhetoric and reality. Drawing upon Quentin Skinner (1988, 2002), I have argued elsewhere that the principles professed by politicians, however insincerely held, provide important information for understanding policy shifts, as well as ideological and political change (Bajpai 2011). In part, this is because as Skinner has argued, professing commitment to a principle gives politicians a strong reason not to behave in ways that appear to contravene the principle – whether or not they genuinely believe in it (1988: 116–17; 2002: 156). Going beyond the actions of individual agents, however, political rhetoric yields information about collectivities, the range and distribution of ideological opinion within political parties and legislative assemblies – for instance, the different notions of social justice at play and their relative strength at a given moment. As such, political rhetoric offers an exceptional site for an empirical study of political hegemony, for mapping processes of its construction and breakdown (Bajpai 2011).

This chapter examines the UPA's rhetoric on social justice and preferential treatment in order to assess ideological continuities and shifts, both in relation to the NDA and Janata Dal coalitions, as well as the Congress's own earlier positions. Did the UPA's rhetoric and policies represent a move away from identity politics of the 1990s and a return to the old Congress focus on development? Were they distinct from previous coalitions' stance on reservations – the Janata Dal (1989–91) and the NDA (1998–2004)? Can the UPA's rhetoric help us better understand policy outcomes with respect to quotas during its tenure? Did the UPA mark a re-emergence of Congress hegemony? The focus is on political rhetoric in parliamentary debates, supplemented with information from government websites, manifestoes, interviews and press reports.

A note on terminology is necessary at the outset. In political theory debates, social justice mainly connotes distributive equality, a concern with the distribution of material resources among individuals in a society (Rawls 1971). This has been contrasted with social equality – equality of status or the absence of social hierarchy – that has been considered as independent of social justice (Miller 1999: 232).[5] In public policy debate, this roughly maps onto the distinction between the politics of identity or recognition on the one hand, and the politics of class or redistribution on the other. In my usage, social equality is not regarded as independent of social justice, but the distinction between relational and distributive equality is maintained.

The UPA, social justice and quotas: CMP and beyond

Did the UPA mark a return to older Congress conceptions of social justice that had emphasized distributive equality and sought to dissociate this from identity concerns (Bajpai 2011)? On first examination of a key rhetorical output of the UPA, the Common Minimum Programme (CMP) of May 2004, this does appear to be the case. The term 'social justice', so prominent in the political rhetoric of the 1990s as shorthand for caste-based reservations, does not find explicit mention in the CMP *at all*. Instead, the emphasis is on distributive justice. The initial statement of principles of governance, which makes no explicit mention of social justice or reservations, avows a commitment 'to enhance the welfare and well-being of farmers, farm-labour and workers'. A concern to alleviate poverty also runs through several declarations on employment, education and health. For instance, in employment, the UPA promises to 'immediately enact' a National Rural Employment Guarantee Act; in agriculture, it urges immediate steps to ease the debt burden on farmers, to 'ensure the fullest implementation of minimum wage laws for farm labour', to 'pay special attention to farmers in poor and backward states and district'. In education, the UPA government 'pledges to raise public spending in education to at least 6 per cent of GDP', to 'introduce a cess on all central taxes to finance… [universal] access to quality basic education', to introduce a centrally funded 'national cooked nutritious midday meal scheme'. In health, too, the CMP promises to raise public spending to 2–3 per cent of GDP, to introduce a 'national scheme for health insurance for poor families', and to 'keep a check on the prices of drugs', to aim for 'universal food security'. The rhetoric of the CMP thus corroborates James Manor's assessment of the UPA as social democratic rather than neo-liberal in its orientation.[6] Nevertheless, the commitment to tackling poverty is not framed in the prevailing language of social justice, an indicator, perhaps, of an identification of the social justice with quotas, and an attempt on the part of the UPA to shift its focus away from reservations.

On closer examination, however, the CMP does hint at the possibility of reservations in some areas. Reservations are implicitly indicated in two principles of governance that seek to 'fully empower women politically, educationally, economically and legally', and 'to provide for full equality of opportunity, particularly in education and employment for scheduled castes, scheduled tribes, OBCs and religious minorities'.[7] The CMP also goes on to explicitly mention reservations in the case of women. The document says that 'The UPA government will take the lead to introduce legislation for one-third reservations for women in vidhan sabhas and in the Lok Sabha.' In private sector employment, the UPA describes itself as 'very sensitive to the issue of affirmative action, including reservations', but there is caution around quotas, which are framed within broader affirmative action measures that are to be the subject of a 'national dialogue with all political parties, industry and other organizations', and mentioned only for 'scheduled caste and scheduled tribe youth'. The only other new reservation broached, tentatively, is for religious minorities, phrased vaguely as 'the welfare of socially and economically backward sections among religious and linguistic minorities'. In the section of the CMP on SCs and STs, no new legislation on reservation is mentioned; instead, the focus is on better implementation of existing reservation policies,[8] and targeted economic assistance in the form of a variety of fellowships, scholarships, and residential school schemes. OBCs are only mentioned once in the CMP, in a general list of weaker sections. Of the Mandal report recommendations for OBC quotas in higher education, which would become one of the most controversial policies prosecuted by the UPA in 2006, there is no mention.[9]

The de-emphasis on identity-based reservations characterizes other rhetorical and policy outputs of the UPA. In the July 2008 status report on the CMP, the UPA's institution of educational quotas to the OBCs is tucked away among benefits to other groups (SC, ST, religious minorities, poor), and to benefits other than reservations – new schemes for fellowships, scholarships, bank loans, residential schools for the SCs and STs are discussed at much greater length.[10] OBC quotas are described as implementation of the UPA's pro-poor agenda to 'ensure that nobody is denied professional education because he or she is poor' and to provide 'full equality of opportunity in education and employment'. Interviews with government ministers corroborate this reading of the UPA as seeking to downplay identity-based quotas. Current and former ministers for Social Justice and Empowerment among others insist that social justice is much broader in its scope than reservations. Among the UPA's achievements in social justice, those frequently cited include poverty alleviation (e.g. the NREGS), institutional innovation (e.g. setting up of ministries of Social Justice and Empowerment at the state level), and more concerted implementation of existing reservation policies (e.g. filling up vacancies).[11] Reports commissioned by the UPA have recommended more universal measures to tackle inequalities, such as a Diversity Index (Kundu Report) and an Equal Opportunities Commission (Menon Report).[12] Several policies implemented by the UPA for benefitting minorities and lower castes are development schemes that seek to improve housing, education, employment, and credit conditions for the poor. Located in districts that have a concentration of population of minorities or SCs, often these are universal benefits for the entire population of the area.[13]

In some senses, the low significance of quotas and social justice in the rhetoric of the CMP is not surprising. The recent rhetorical prominence of social justice in Indian politics and its identification with reservations is associated with the rise of lower caste-based parties (Bajpai 2006, 2010). In terms of its ideology, the Congress has historically broadly sought to reduce the salience of identity politics, and opposed quotas on religious and caste lines.[14] Before Independence, these were seen as an instrument of colonial divide and rule. During constitution-making, the Congress sought to limit the scope of reservations and only reluctantly accepted these in the case of the SCs and STs, as temporary provisions (Bajpai 2000, 2011).

Social justice in the dominant Congress view was best achieved through development not quotas; further, quotas were seen to advance development in some respects, but to detract from it in others, notably in their entrenchment of group identity (caste and religious). It may be recalled that the Mandal report, which resulted in the largest expansion of national quotas in independent India, was commissioned by the non-Congress Janata government in 1978. Largely ignored by the Congress governments of the 1980s, it was only revived at the behest of another non-Congress government – the Janata Dal – in 1990.

Did the UPA then mark a return to old Congress, in terms of an emphasis on social justice as distributive justice for all, to be achieved through universal development schemes for the poor, rather than identity-based reservations? This, I will now argue, would be an erroneous conclusion. To the picture sketched thus far, we need to add the UPA's many initiatives in support of quotas. In 2005, the UPA amended the Constitution to extend the scope of reservations to private educational institutions. The Constitution (Ninety-Third) Amendment Act 2005 inserted Article 15 (5) in to the Indian Constitution that explicitly permitted the state to 'make any special provision, by law, for the advancement of any socially or educationally backward classes of citizens or for the Scheduled Castes or Scheduled Tribes insofar as such provisions relate to their admission to educational institutions, including private educational institutions, whether aided or unaided by the state, other than minority educational institutions referred to in Clause (1) of Article 30'.[15] In 2006, legislation was passed enabling quotas in higher education for OBCs, in addition to SCs and STs who were already covered.[16] The UPA has also pressed for affirmative action in the private sector for SCs and STs.[17] Although quotas have not yet been mandated, the government has invited responses from the chambers of industry – the Confederation of Indian Industry (CII), the Federation of Indian Chambers of Commerce and Industry (FICCI), and the Associated Chambers of Commerce and Industry of India (ASSOCHAM) – on a proposal for a five per cent quota for STs and STs.[18] And despite being divided on this issue, the UPA government has moved ahead with the enumeration of caste in the 2011 census, a key demand of proponents of reservations for lower castes.[19] With regard to women's quotas as well, after some hesitation on the issue, the UPA government passed the much-delayed Women's Reservation Bill in the Rajya Sabha in March 2010, for 33 per cent reservations for women in national and state legislatures[20] although it has not yet been enacted into law.

The most significant expansion of affirmative action, however, has been with respect to minorities. While the UPA's policy towards minorities is outside the scope of this chapter,[21] a few points are relevant here. The Congress's 2004 manifesto promised educational and employment quotas for 'backward sections' among religious minorities, mentioning Muslims in particular:

> The Congress has provided for reservations for Muslims in Kerala and Karnataka in government employment and education on the grounds that they are a socially and educationally backward class. The Congress is committed to adopting this policy for socially and educationally backward sections among Muslims and other religious minorities on a national scale.[22]

The UPA government created a Ministry of Minority Affairs in 2006. Although ministers have voiced different opinions on quotas, with some favouring affirmative action more broadly defined,[23] the various commissions on minorities created by the UPA government – such as the Sachar Commission (2006), and the Misra Commission (2007) – indicate that its desired direction of movement is in favour of national quotas for minorities, particularly Muslims. The Misra report, tabled in parliament in December 2009, explicitly proposes 15 per cent reservations for religious minorities, including a 10 per cent quota for Muslims based on their proportion of the minority population.[24] While progress towards legislation remains cautious, key policy makers have spoken in favour of quotas for Muslims, including reportedly Prime Minister, Dr Manmohan Singh,[25] and the Congress party president Sonia Gandhi.[26] The extension of SC status to Dalit Muslims and Dalit Christians has been recommended by the Misra Commission as well as Satish Deshpande's study, both commissioned by the UPA government,[27] although here, as in other controversial areas, progress has been slow.

Importantly, this chapter contends that expansion of affirmative action for minorities in a sense has *already* occurred through executive action.[28] The Prime Minister's new 15-point program for minorities seeks to 'earmark' for members of minority communities 15 per cent of benefits of a wide range of existing development schemes, covering education, employment, credit, housing, training, and scholarships, essentially targeting a proportion of universal excludable benefits for the poor, to the minority poor.[29] The 15-point program also states that 'special consideration' should be given to minorities in recruitment to police forces at the central as well as state levels, and that for this purpose, 'the composition of selection committees should be representative'.[30] An Office Memorandum, dated 8 January 2007, issued by the Ministry of Personnel, Public Grievances and Pensions, Government of India states that '[A]vailable evidence indicates that the representation of Minorities in Government service and public sector employment is not satisfactory ... Government is committed to ensuring fair representation to the minorities in Government employment including public sector enterprises, public sector banks and financial institutions, and the Railways.' The heads of all departments, public sector undertakings, banks and financial institutions and quasi government organizations are instructed that it is *mandatory* to have at least one SC/ST member and one belonging to a minority community in all selection committees involving 10 or more vacancies, and desirable in the case of less than 10. They are required to submit to the Ministry of Minority Affairs half-yearly and annual reports monitoring trends in the recruitment of minorities, including in their subordinate organizations.[31] Unlike similar executive edicts from earlier eras, a rigorous, high-powered monitoring mechanism is outlined for each level of government in the new 15-point program. At the central level, each ministry or department involved is instructed to appoint an officer of at least the rank of a Joint Secretary to Government of India to review and report on the progress of the program to the Ministry of Minority Affairs. Furthermore, progress is to be monitored with reference to targets by a Committee of Secretaries (CoS), and a report submitted to the Union Cabinet.[32] Targets and performance of each department and state are published by the Ministry of Minority Affairs. Such targets do not constitute quotas in a full-fledged sense – these are not mandatory and do not have the standing of enforceable law. As in other policy areas, massive implementation shortfalls remain.[33] Nevertheless, 'earmarks' do indicate a broadening of affirmative action to include religious minorities.[34] If and when the UPA enacts legislation for minority quotas, this would entrench a process that has already begun through executive action in development policy.

In sum, the UPA represents a new Congress that is much more accommodating of identity-based quotas than the old Congress party. Through a reading of legislative debates, I will now show that, as part of the UPA, the Congress position on social justice and reservations is significantly distinct from its earlier positions both during constitution-making in the late 1940s as well as the 1990 Mandal debate. It is in the light of this normative–discursive shift in conceptions of social justice that the policies enacted by the UPA for the expansion of affirmative action can be adequately grasped. Further, I suggest that in moving to a position broadly in favour of identity-based quotas, the Congress is following a polity-wide shift that can be traced back at the national level to at least the Janata Dal in the 1990 Mandal debate. This involved the expansion of quotas under an egalitarian conception of social justice that recognized identity as a basis of disadvantage. It has been taken forward by successive administrations, both NDA and UPA: in this respect at least, there is no significant difference between Indian governments since 1990. However, in following this trend, the UPA's rhetoric and policies have reflected distinct Congress concerns. In contrast to the Janata Dal, social justice has been linked to development and national unity. In contrast to the NDA, social justice has been associated with minority rights. These rhetorical differences translate into differences in policy, in the manner in which reservations have been extended and the groups regarded as the most deserving beneficiaries. It is to a detailed elaboration of this argument that we now turn.

Contextualizing the UPA: Congress rhetoric on reservations, 1946–2007

The UPA's sanguine attitude towards the expansion of reservations stands in stark contrast to the Congress's historical wariness of quotas. During the Constituent Assembly debates, Congress representatives from both the right and the left of the party converged in opposition to legislative and other quotas for religious minorities, on the grounds that these detracted from a secular democracy and nation building (Bajpai 2000, 2011). Reservations were accepted very reluctantly, as strictly temporary provisions for uplifting 'backward' sections. When reserved seats in legislatures for religious minorities that had been included in the 1948 of the Constitution were withdrawn in 1949, Nehru commended their abolition as 'a historic turn in our destiny', confessing that he had never been convinced:

> Reluctantly we agreed to carry on with some measure of reservation ... but always there was this doubt in our minds, namely, whether we had not shown weakness in dealing with a thing that was wrong ... doing away with this

reservation business is not only a good thing in itself ... It shows that we are really sincere about this business of having a secular democracy.

Constituent Assembly debates (CAD) VIII: 329, 332[35]

Nehru spoke for many Congressmen as he said:

Frankly I would like to go further and put an end to such reservations that still remain. But ... I realise that in the present state of affairs in India that would not be a desirable thing to do ... in regard to the Scheduled Castes ... I do not look at it from the religious point of view or the caste point of view, but from the point of view that a backward group ought to be helped and I am glad that this reservation will also be limited to ten years.

CAD VIII: 331

For secular nationalists exemplified by Nehru, quotas required the recognition of religion, caste, and tribe in public policy and thereby detracted from secularism that was the desired basis of national identity (Bajpai 2011). Secularism had expansive connotations, referring to 'to the elimination (or minimization) of caste and religious groups as categories of public policy and as actors in public life' (Galanter 1984: 559). Also, religious and caste identities were considered as archaic, unbefitting for a country aspiring to be a modern industrialized nation. Above all, minority quotas were, in Congress' opinion, a creature of British divide-and-rule policy that served to legitimize colonial presence in India, had bred community consciousness and rivalry, and led ultimately to the violent partition of the country. The Congress of the late 1940s rejected the view that groups as such were entitled to representation. Quotas were rendered legitimate only as temporary affirmative action provisions for the rectification of 'backwardness', chiefly in the case of untouchables and tribals. The desired ideal was the transcendence of inter-group difference, embodied in the nationalist slogan of 'a casteless and classless society'. Congress' opposition meant that reservations were incorporated in the 1950 Constitution in a weaker form than desired by their strong proponents in the Constituent Assembly. In keeping with Congress' position, women representatives and several minority representatives renounced reservations as inconsistent with equality and national unity[36] (for details, see Bajpai 2011).

On what grounds, then were reservations for 'backward' groups admitted in the Indian constitution? Although some arguments from compensatory justice were put forward for the SCs and STs, reservations were mostly defended in Congress opinion in terms of consequentialist arguments regarding the national interest in a more socially just society. Reducing socio-economic disparities between groups was desired because it would further the 'upliftment' of sections that were dragging the nation down and inhibiting its progress, as well as the integration of 'backward sections' with the rest of the population.[37] Importantly, reservations were seen as departures from justice considerations in the present such as equality of opportunity for all individuals, albeit justifiable in terms of progress towards a more socially just order in the future. Social justice was itself ultimately valued for its contribution to national integration and development. Congress opinion, however, remained highly ambivalent on reservations. In addition to equality of opportunity, these were also seen as detracting from secularism and national unity, as casteist and divisive (for details, see Bajpai 2011).

Skepticism about the desirability and efficacy of identity-based reservations continued to characterize the Congress's position in the 1990 Mandal debate on employment quotas for the OBCs. Former Prime Minister Rajiv Gandhi was critical of the inclusion of better-off OBC families as beneficiaries:

> ... when ... you ... take some affirmative action ... you must accept that there are those people who perhaps though originally of a socially, educationally backward group, are today under no circumstances that can be described as socially and educationally backward ... once an individual has risen above a certain level ... does his family need it...?
> *Lok Sabha debates* (*LSD*) 6.9.1990 col. 490

In such criticisms, social justice was understood primarily in terms of inequalities in the distribution of material goods, and while it was accepted that these often overlapped with an inferior position in the ritual hierarchy, the implicit contention was that historical discrimination was neither a necessary nor a sufficient condition for socio-economic disadvantage. As in the Constituent Assembly debates, Congress discourse reflected concerns about reservations from standpoints of secularism and national unity. The government's policy, it was argued, was casteist, abandoning India's founding fathers' ideals of a casteless society;[38] it reinforced 'a caste and communal divide', detracted from 'a modern and scientific society' (Sourendra Bhattacharjee, *Rajya Sabha debates* (*RSD*) 9.8.1990 col. 259). In Congress criticisms of casteism in the Mandal debate, as in the Constituent Assembly debates, secular and nationalist concerns converged, with the accepted illegitimacy of caste supporting worries about the divisiveness of reservations (Bajpai 2011).

Nevertheless, as in the Constituent Assembly, the Congress reluctantly accepted employment quotas in the 1990 Mandal debate. Again, the most common considerations cited in favour of quotas in Congress discourse were those of national unity and development. For Rajiv Gandhi, 'backwardness' was a 'not just a question of ... a social wrong', but an impediment to development in an era of liberalization: 'Today we need to harness all the energies of the nation ... to compete with other countries. That can only be done if we harness all the resources of our people. That includes the most backward, the poorest ... ' (*LSD* 6.9.1990 cols 485–6).

Rajya Sabha Member of Parliament (MP) Rajmohan Gandhi gently rebuked the ruling Janata Dal for focusing exclusively on 'backward' groups:

> ... the whole House has agreed that this section is largely backward and has suffered for such a long time ... But the question is this: Are we supporting and sheltering that section only for its own sake ...? Today ... when our nation's unity is assailed from many quarters, it is all the more important that we are absolutely clear that we should strengthen and support a part because we want to preserve the unity and strength of the whole.
> *RSD* 27.8.1990 col. 343

The key legitimating terms in Congress discourse in 1990, as in the late 1940s, were national integration and development.

By contrast, when we turn to the 2005–6 debates on educational quotas for OBCs, Congress discourse appears very different. To begin with, Congress spokesmen now championed reservations primarily on grounds of social justice. The Minister for Human Resource Development, Arjun Singh, introduced the constitutional amendment enabling reservations in state-aided as well as private educational institutions thus:

> The Government is committed to the policy of reservation which ensures social justice and we will try to do everything possible to see that it happens … The entire issue that is being addressed by this Bill is the issue of 'social justice' … In the Preamble, it is said: '…. to secure to all its citizens: Justice, social, economic and political'. There can be no justice if there is no social justice …
>
> *LSD* 21.12.2005

On closer examination, social justice also appears to be construed differently in Congress discourse in 2005–6 from previous debates. Although the language used was that of opportunity, there was a shift to a focus on equalizing outcomes. Arjun Singh introduced the Central Educational Institutions (Reservation in Admission) Bill 2006 by saying: 'millions of backward classes all over the country have been looking forward to getting an opportunity for equitable access to the institutions of higher learning maintained by the State' (*LSD* 25.08.2006). The Congress party representative from Varanasi, Dr Rajesh Mishra, noted:

> Today the whole of India will agree that those who were not getting opportunity within society, they have not been able to get higher education, after this law is made when they will receive higher education then we will be capable of fulfilling the promise of social equality that we made in the Constitution … The OBC communities are not very wealthy. If you see their position at the grassroots level, they are also like Scheduled Castes and Scheduled Tribes.
>
> *LSD* 21.12.2005, author's translation from Hindi[39]

In such claims, outcome inequalities – in group shares of places in higher education and employment – were seen as evidence for inequalities in initial opportunities, a key characteristic of fair or egalitarian equality of opportunity arguments (Rawls 1971; Phillips 2004). Reservations were defended as a means of equalizing opportunities for those who suffered from educational and economic disadvantage. Social justice construed as fair equality of opportunity was much more fully articulated in the speeches of UPA's constituent lower-caste-based parties and Left allies.[40] Nevertheless, a clear shift can be discerned in Congress discourse from equality of opportunity construed mainly in terms of non-discrimination and careers open to talent in the Constituent Assembly debates, to more egalitarian notions of equality of opportunity voiced in the UPA reservation debates.

Furthermore, there was much greater acceptance by the UPA Congress of an overlap between identity and disadvantage and of the need for identity-based policies to redress disadvantage. In contrast to earlier Congress discourse, the lines of socio-economic disadvantage and caste group membership were assumed to coincide in the 2005–6 debates: no concerns were voiced about OBC quotas from distributive justice standpoints. Concerns that identity-group-based quotas detracted from equality of opportunity or fairness assessed at the level of the individual, voiced during the Constituent Assembly and 1990 Mandal debates, for instance, were absent from UPA discourse. Instead, Congressmen avowed their caste affiliation in a manner unthinkable in previous eras, and advocated identity-based policies for increasing group shares of places and resources.[41]

Was the core Congress concern of national unity then absent from UPA discourse in the 2005–6 debates? In contrast to its positions in the Constituent Assembly and the 1990 Mandal debates, no worries were voiced about identity-based quotas from standpoints of national unity. Closer inspection, however, suggests that this remained significant, but now had a positive relationship to reservations, which were no longer seen as divisive, but, rather, as the basis of nation building. This perspective is evident in the following speech by Minister Arjun Singh:

> the whole question of reservation started with the First Amendment of the Constitution which was moved by Pandit Jawaharlal Nehru which took into account all the movements which have ultimately contributed to the freedom of India ... All those social movements, whether they were in the South or in Maharashtra or anywhere else, constitute a very powerful stream in our national ethos and therefore ... [Pandit Nehru] was only taking note of what ... ultimately helped us to achieve freedom ...
>
> *LSD* 14.12.2006

As this speech indicates, reservations were legitimized through association with the Indian freedom struggle, as the basis on which unity was forged between diverse movements, and national freedom won. Given Congress's previous strong misgivings about identity-based quotas, this involved a creative reinterpretation of its history and the role of key leaders.[42] Nehru's distaste of caste-based reservations during constitution-making was papered over, as was the optimistic modernization narrative of development overcoming caste and other identities. In Congress and UPA pronouncements of this period, regional contributions to national policy were emphasized, with representatives from southern states highlighting the role of their leaders in the adoption of reservations.[43]

Development, another core Congress concern, was prominent in UPA discourse on OBC quotas but, like national unity, was now overwhelmingly construed as congruent with reservations.[44] That the benefits of India's high growth rates since the 1990s should be equitably shared among all sections of the population was a common argument in support of reservations for OBCs.[45] In some cases, where quotas were defended as distributing benefits of growth more widely, development was subordinated to the cause of social justice.[46] In other cases, the advancement of socially and educationally backward classes itself was seen as 'vital not only in the interest of achieving ... the object of an egalitarian society, but also in order that India may march forward along with other nations of the world' (Basudev Barman *LSD* 21.12.2005). A few dissenting voices were raised by independent MPs that quotas were anachronistic in a modern society and competitive market economy;[47] in the speeches of Congress and UPA representatives, however, development was largely construed as consistent with social justice.

While no legislation has yet been put forward by the UPA on minority quotas, the Prime Minister's new 15-point program for minorities and related pronouncements deploy a similar egalitarian conception of social justice discerned in the debates on OBC quotas, framed within Congress ideologies of secularism and development.[48] The Prime Minister's 15-point program focuses on redressing inter-religious inequalities in outcomes with respect to poverty, instituting targets of 15 per cent minority beneficiaries for various development schemes for the poor. As such, it draws upon the national consensus on the goals of development and poverty reduction, at the same time as directing this towards improvement of the position of minorities – of reducing their 'development deficit'. Development, as in the debates over OBC quotas, is itself put to the service of social justice, construed in terms of equalizing outcomes ('ensuring an equitable share for minorities in economic activities and employment'[49]). In his Independence Day address to the nation on 15 August 2007, Dr Manmohan Singh noted that India had made great strides in development, generating the resources needed for eradicating poverty and providing universal education and health care. The proceeds of this growth ought to be shared equitably; as such, the 15-point program sought to ensure that minorities were not left out of India's development.[50]

In sum, as part of the UPA, the Congress has substantially redefined its earlier position on reservations. It is much more accommodating of identity-based quotas, a change of position that has involved an important shift in the meaning and significance of social justice in Congress discourse, and a reorientation of its relationship to national unity and development. These discursive shifts are conducive to the expansion of identity-based reservations. As the latter are no longer seen as a threat to national unity, or involving the balancing of competing considerations to equality –detracting from equality of opportunity in the present, albeit contributing towards the creation of a more equal society in the future – the scope of reservations does not need to be restricted, as was the case in Congress discourse earlier. The expansion of affirmative action policies under the UPA – to higher educational institutions for OBCs, to the private sector, to religious minorities – has been accompanied, and facilitated, by a discursive shift conducive to these outcomes.

At the same time, the manner in which affirmative action has expanded has been informed by the Congress's core concerns of national unity, development, and secularism. The concern with national unity has been evident in the gradual pace of expansion of affirmative action, allowing time for consensus and compromise, for carrying different shades of political opinion.[51] For instance, the expansion of educational quotas for OBCs was envisaged over a three-year period without reducing the number of places for other groups, by increasing the overall number of places in higher education.[52] Similarly, the expansion of affirmative action to religious minorities remains gradual and cautious, focused on aspects on which there is a national consensus, such as tackling poverty. Congress rhetoric of secularism has meant that minorities are the priority area for reservations.

While the Congress has recast its rhetoric to support identity-based reservations, arguments for how affirmative action can contribute to the common good, benefitting all citizens, remain underdeveloped in UPA discourse, and in Indian public debate more generally. Barring general allusions to the desirability of development, and how the inclusion of minorities in mainstream institutions strengthens Indian unity,[53] there has been little elaboration in UPA discourse of the universal benefits of affirmative action. Normative debates based on the experience of the US have highlighted the educational value of integrated institutions for democratic citizenship.[54] In building a national consensus on the expansion of quotas to minorities and the private sector, the UPA would benefit from greater attention to the experience of other countries, and to policy justifications that highlight the advantages of affirmative action for all citizens.

Social justice and reservations: Janata Dal (1990), NDA (1998–2004) and UPA (2004–9) compared

I have so far argued that in terms of the rhetoric and policy on reservations, the UPA did not represent the old Congress but, rather, the emergence of a new Congress that was much more accommodating of identity-based policies. I now want to take this argument a step further, and suggest that in redefining its position, the Congress was not leading but rather following a polity-wide shift. At the national level, this can be discerned from the time of the Janata Dal government decision in 1990 to extend employment quotas to the OBCs (Bajpai 2010). All governments that came thereafter, Congress and BJP led, consolidated and extended the trend towards the expansion of identity-based quotas under an egalitarian conception of social justice.

With the 1990 Mandal debate, social justice, a long-standing rhetorical trope in Indian politics, acquired a new meaning and salience as it came to be identified with reservations (Bajpai 2010). Of course, 'social justice' was not a new semantic acquisition – the term appears in the Indian Constitution and had been employed to refer to provisions for disadvantaged groups in policy documents and debates.[55] Nevertheless, its prominence in justifications of preferential treatment, and its identification with quotas, marked a new departure. Introducing the government's decision to implement employment quotas for OBCs in 1990, Prime Minister V. P. Singh termed it as 'a momentous decision of social justice' (*RSD* 7.12.1990 col. 309). Other parties more critical of caste-based reservations, such as the Congress and the BJP, were careful to preface their objections with declarations of support for the cause of social justice (see *RSD* 27.12.1990 col. 276; *LSD* 5.9.1990 col. 418). Although professed by all parties, the connotations of social justice varied along party-type lines. In the discourse of the Janata Dal, and lower caste-based parties more broadly, social justice was elaborated as social equality, focused on inequalities of status and power. Social justice connoted that social disabilities were the primary source of the injustices that quotas sought to rectify and that social groups rather than individuals were the relevant units for its assessment. For Left representatives, social justice required tackling distributive inequalities in income, health, nutrition, and education: as such, quotas were necessary but insufficient for achieving social justice. For Congress and BJP representatives, social justice was valued ultimately, albeit in different ways, for its contribution to national unity and development: as such, some concerns that quotas could be divisive or detract from development were voiced (for details, see Bajpai 2010).

Apart from the ascendancy of social justice as a key legitimating value, the 1990 Mandal debate saw other important changes in the discourse on reservations. First, with the move to egalitarian notions of equality of opportunity, quotas were no longer seen as detracting from fairness to individuals, but as necessary for its realization in a context in which opportunities had historically been denied to certain groups on account of an unjust social system. Prime Minister V. P. Singh declaimed:

> I want to challenge first the merit of the system itself before we question whether it is on merit that we reject this individual or that ... a person or a family in this system is condemned to a social or economic order ... In that what are a child's opportunities? ... *treating unequals as equals is the greatest injustice* ... Correction of this injustice is very important ...
>
> *RSD* 9.8.1990, cols 233–4, emphasis added

Second, the empowerment of the disadvantaged became part of how the goal of equality was defined, as well as the favoured means of its realization. Quotas enabled social justice not so much by improving the socio-economic conditions of beneficiaries, but by giving them political power. Elaborating on the rationale of quotas, V. P. Singh said: '... It is not merely a question of ... alleviating the economic conditions of our people ... We consciously want to give them a position in the decision-making of the country, a share in the power structure' (*RSD* 9.8.1990 cols 232–3).

Third, social justice was extricated from the embrace of national unity that had characterized earlier Congress arguments on affirmative action: in Janata Dal discourse, national unity was not the frame within which social justice had to be defined and pursued. Among the proponents of OBC quotas, we find few concerns of the kind that had dominated Congress discourse in the Constituent Assembly: that these would consolidate caste divisions, detract from a sense of belonging to a common nation, or fuel social conflict. Instead, national unity was put to the service of social justice: advocates of OBC quotas invoked bonds of nationality to argue that better-off citizens should bear the costs of preferential treatment for the disadvantaged (for details, see Bajpai 2011).

The discursive shifts observed in the 1990 Mandal debate – the centrality of social justice, the shift to an egalitarian notion of equality of opportunity that was accommodating of identity-based quotas, and the emphasis on empowerment – all endured in the 2005–6 UPA debates on OBC reservations, and indeed expanded into a polity-wide change.[56] In the 2005–6 debates, social justice was the key legitimating value for reservations, invoked by all parties, including the Congress and the BJP. Parties competed with each other to claim social justice as part of their history. Arguments for quotas advanced by representatives from all political parties, Congress, the Left as well as regional and lower caste parties, relied largely on egalitarian notions of equality of opportunity. Unlike the Constituent Assembly debates, and in sharp contrast to the wider public debate, there was virtually no opposition to quotas as detracting from equality of opportunity or merit. Instead, representatives voiced a keen awareness of the effects of the 'environmental privileges' enjoyed by the members of advanced upper caste families,[57] the unfairness of a system of open competition in a society with massive disparities of income and education, and the small percentile differences that separated forward and 'backward' caste candidates (see, for instance, Dr K. Keshava Rao, *RSD* 8.12.2006). In the pronouncements of different political parties, the registers of social justice remained distinct. Thus democratic arguments about the participation of the disadvantaged in decision-making institutions were most prominent in the speeches of lower caste regional political parties, as were claims for reservations as a constitutional *right*.[58] Among Congress representatives, a more paternalist tone of the protection of 'weaker sections' and of the benevolence of the Nehru–Gandhi family was often in evidence.[59] An emphasis on economic deprivation was prominent in the speeches of representatives from Left parties.[60]

At the same time, in the 2005–6 UPA debates, social equality concerns were less prominent, and development and national unity were more often invoked in support of preferential treatment, relative to the 1990 Mandal debate. In part, this reflected the fact that it was the Congress party that was now leading the expansion of OBC quotas: the renewed emphasis on material inequalities, development, and national unity reflected the characteristic themes of Congress discourse. Did this then indicate the beginnings of a new Congress dominance, even hegemony, albeit under different terms? The evidence from legislative debates suggests otherwise. Not all parties shared the Congress's emphasis on national unity and development: unlike in the late 1940s, the Congress was unable to reconfigure the orientation of political discourse as a whole (for details, see Bajpai 2011). For lower caste and regional parties, social justice was the sole referent, with representatives from Southern parties claiming to be pioneers, delineating a history studded with Dravidian leaders that was distinct from, and often antagonistic to, the Congress.[61] Contending values remained entrenched in political discourse, an indicator that no party was now hegemonic.

Did the NDA governments of 1998–2004 partake of the polity-wide trend towards identity-based quotas? The NDA did enact legislation in favour of reservations. Three constitutional amendments were passed during its tenure, overruling limits on the scope of reservations for the scheduled castes and tribes.[62] The Eighty-First Amendment to the Constitution (2000) sought to allow the carry-over of unfilled quotas from one year to the next in excess of the 50 per cent limit on reservations, superseding the Supreme Court's Mandal judgment (1992) to the contrary. The Eighty-Second Amendment to the Constitution (2000) relaxed standards for promotion for the SC and ST, with the Parliament declaring, contrary to the view of the Supreme Court, that 'such relaxations would not interfere with the efficiency of the administration' (Dhavan 2008: 107). The Eighty-Fifth Amendment to the Constitution (2001) granted seniority to reservation candidates who were junior to their non-quota colleagues but had received earlier promotions through the reservation policy. In the assessment of leading Dalit politicians and activists, there is no significant policy difference between the NDA and UPA administrations on reservations for the scheduled castes and tribes.[63]

Did the policies of the NDA on reservations then diverge from its ideology, and in particular that of its leading party, the BJP? Analysts have argued that 'the compulsions of coalition politics', made the NDA government 'retain caste-based reservations to which the BJP was opposed' (Rao 2005:117). While a detailed analysis of the BJP's ideology is outside the scope of this chapter, a few points deserve mention. An examination of the debates over constitutional amendments in favour of reservations enacted by the NDA suggests endorsement of social justice and reservations, but with little elaboration by BJP leaders. The speeches of the minister in charge, Vasundhara Raje, were brief and factual, with little expansion on the meaning of social justice that had characterized the pronouncements of V. P. Singh's Janata Dal government, or the distinctive traditions of her party with regard to disadvantaged groups, as discerned in Arjun Singh's speeches for the UPA.[64] In the debates on OBC quotas during the UPA's tenure, BJP leaders did advocate economic criteria for the identification of 'backward', and voiced some worries about identity-based quotas as divisive.[65] Nevertheless, social justice had established itself as a key legitimating value, and was invoked in arguments for reservations, by the BJP as did all other parties.[66]

Social justice and identity-based reservations were also endorsed in the manifestos of the BJP and the NDA. However, the pursuit of social justice was tempered by a concern for social unity, and the focus was on different identity groups: tribes and women. The BJP manifesto of 2004 stated that it was 'a strong votary of social justice for SCs, STs, OBCs and other disadvantaged social groups' and emphasized 'two related imperatives (a) social justice is incomplete without economic justice and political empowerment; and (b) the means to secure social justice (samajik nyaya) have also to promote social harmony (samajik samarastha)'.[67] The identity groups favoured for special attention were tribal populations, described as the most neglected and deprived in terms of human development indicators,[68] and women ('every able bodied woman should have at least some source of livelihood' so as to 'enjoy economic independence within the framework of a harmonious family').[69] The NDA's 2004 manifesto was similar to that of the UPA in some respects in its rhetoric of social justice and reservations. Thus, while social justice was listed as a 'guiding principle', the schemes launched by the NDA for improving the conditions of the poor were not classed as social justice measures,[70] and reservations were not highlighted. With regard to reservation policy, the main initiatives mentioned were filling up backlogs in jobs and promotions for the SCs, STs, OBCs, and incentives to the private sector for creating more opportunities for the SCs and STs. Unlike the UPA's CMP, the NDA 2004 manifesto proposed reservations for the poor among the forward castes and promised the immediate enactment of the Bill for 33 per cent reservation for women in Parliament and State legislatures.[71] It cited the 'establishment of a separate ministry for tribal affairs' as the major achievement of the NDA with regard to social justice.[72] The BJP and the NDA thus participated in the polity-wide shift towards the emphasis on social justice and the expansion of identity-based policies. The BJP's Hindu nationalist ideology, however, meant that the aims of reservations were often assimilationalist,[73] and always opposed to special consideration for religious minorities.

Conclusion

Whereas the expansion of reservations is usually analysed in terms of the electoral interests of politicians, this essay has shown that ideology, in terms of professed rhetoric rather than the beliefs of agents, constitutes an important terrain for understanding and explaining policy shifts. The augmentation of special treatment in the Indian polity has been accompanied and facilitated by the ascendance of social justice as a legitimating value with egalitarian notions of equality of opportunity favourable to affirmative action. The new prominence of social justice and the expansion of identity-based reservations since the Mandal decision of 1990 represents a polity-wide shift, encompassing the UPA as well as the NDA, although party ideology has influenced the preferred beneficiaries and overall policy design.

Furthermore, this chapter has shown that the UPA Congress is much more hospitable, in rhetoric and policy, to identity-based quotas than the Congress party was for much of the 20th century. In particular, the UPA Congress does not regard reservations as divisive or diminishing secularism as the old Congress did: instead, several UPA initiatives have sought to establish an overlap between identity and disadvantage. The UPA era has seen the expansion of affirmative action to new areas, most notably to religious minorities, a process that has progressed substantially through executive action thus far (notably the Prime Minister's new 15-point program for minorities). In terms of policy justifications for affirmative action, the UPA has focused on the socio-economic 'backwardness' of religious minorities, building up evidence of a 'development deficit'. Development, however, is a double-edged sword for the justification of special treatment, given influential concerns that quotas are inconsistent with the growth and competitiveness in a global political economy. More inclusive arguments for affirmative action remain to be elaborated by the UPA, in terms of its benefits for all citizens and not just the direct beneficiaries. Here the UPA would benefit from greater attention to the arguments for, and experience of, affirmative action in other countries, notably the US. In general, the Congress has not yet fashioned justifications for its policies of special treatment for minorities in terms of the common good, leaving these vulnerable to criticism from the Hindu Right.

Part 3
Security

8 The UPA's foreign policy, 2004–9

Kanti Bajpai

Introduction

How did the UPA conduct foreign policy from 2004 to 2009? There was certainly an expectation that the new government would have a different agenda in domestic politics. Foreign policy is generally thought to feature much greater continuity between governments and to be above partisanship. While this is not necessarily the case, there is a view that foreign policy should not be a political football. This chapter suggests that the UPA's foreign policy was indeed significantly different, even though there were continuities with earlier policy, and that the most important explanation for the difference lies in the realm of ideology.

Since 1989, there has emerged a basic electoral choice in India between two political formations – a Congress-led or left of center coalition and the BJP-led or right of center coalition.[1] These have alternated in power for 20 years: the left of center was in power from 1989 to 1998 and then again from 2004 to 2009; the right of center from 1998 to 2004. It is argued here that the BJP-led NDA and the Congress-led UPA have conducted foreign policy in different ways. Crudely put, the NDA was more realist in its focus on relative power and the military instruments of influence whereas the UPA was more Nehruvian in its emphasis on negotiation and diplomacy. It is important to underline the relative nature of the previous statement: the NDA did not entirely ignore negotiation and diplomacy and the UPA was not altogether neglectful of power and force. Moreover, there are continuities between the two governments, if for no other reason than the fact that few governments anywhere can repudiate all the policies of their predecessors. Governments also find it in the national interest or their own narrower political interest to build on the successes of earlier governments, indeed to claim erstwhile lines of policy as their own. The UPA certainly followed some broad lines of policy that it inherited not just from the NDA but also from earlier governments going back to the Congress government led by Narasimha Rao from 1991 to 1996.[2]

The UPA inherited a foreign policy that was led by calculations of national power centered on military instruments. The centerpiece of the NDA's foreign policy was the nuclear tests of 1998 and the strategic dialogue with the US that followed.[3] With the tests behind it, the NDA sought to come to an agreement with the US on India's role in the world. A secondary objective was how to deal with Pakistan. Here too the bomb tests were crucial. By testing, the NDA hoped to smoke the Pakistanis out on nuclear weapons and, in doing so, it hoped to set the stage for discussions and negotiations.[4] In 2001–2, after the terrorist attack on the Indian parliament, the NDA government followed a similar policy based on a show of strength followed by negotiations: it mobilized the army for an attack against Pakistan and eventually came back to a negotiating stance with Islamabad. With China, the NDA once again began aggressively. In explaining India's reasons for the tests, the NDA government gestured towards the China threat (Chiriyankandath and Wyatt 2005: 203; Sridharan 2006: 82). With time, though, it reverted to a more conciliatory policy of negotiations and discussions over a wide range of issues.

The NDA government promised a more muscular foreign policy – and, in the way described here, it delivered. A quote from an aide to Prime Minister Atal BehariVajpayee captures the difference between the BJP-led NDA and its Congress predecessor under Narasimha Rao. Referring to the Rao government, he noted that after the 1998 nuclear tests 'Narasimha Rao's policy of "nothing but the economy" has been modified to read "security first and the rest will follow"' (quoted in Perkovich 2000: 442). Thus, the Vajpayee government consistently sought to follow a harder, more assertive line of policy with a softer, more accommodative line. In effect, the NDA conducted foreign policy on the back of a strong security posture, or, to put it differently, to negotiate from strength – or at least appear to do so. This posture reflected the preferences and style of the main party in the coalition, namely, the BJP.

The UPA by contrast did the opposite. It emphasized the role of negotiations and discussions and reached a series of agreements with key states, most importantly, the US. This reflected the general predilections of the Congress Party, the leader of the UPA. The Congress could have conducted nuclear tests in the 1990s when it was in power under Rao, but did not do so (Chengappa 2000: 390–407; Karnad 2002: 369–70). It could have adopted a militarized posture against Pakistan in the wake of various terrorist attacks in India after 2004 including the 26 November 2008 attack in Mumbai, but it resisted the temptation to do so. Instead, it worked diplomatically to isolate and embarrass Pakistan. It took a pragmatic view of China and continued to do business with it in spite of a hardening of Beijing's stance on the border. On the other hand, the UPA took a strong position on trade talks and climate change in the face of US concerns. It was fairly conservative with respect to summits and high-level meetings with Pakistan; indeed, its public diplomacy with Pakistan was almost taciturn even though behind-the-scenes progress was made on Kashmir. With China, too, the UPA negotiated and made some advances in terms of the broad principles governing a border solution, but, intermittently, it talked tough and augmented India's military capabilities in the border areas. The UPA also took the competition with China into other areas – Africa, Central Asia, and Latin America, above all – in relation to strategic resources and trade.

The UPA won the 2004 elections against virtually all predictions. Led by the Congress party, the coalition consisted of, in addition, various regional and national parties. It was supported, via a CMP, by the CPI and CPI (M). Manmohan

Singh of the Congress party became prime minister. Manmohan Singh had been the finance minister in the Congress government of 1991 to 1996 led by Narasimha Rao where he fashioned the economic liberalization policy that started India on its high-growth curve in the 1990s and 2000s. As prime minister, he decided to look after the foreign affairs portfolio, which he only relinquished in October 2006 when he appointed the veteran Congressman, Pranab Mukherjee, to the post of external affairs minister.

The UPA's CMP, which touches very briefly on foreign policy (it contains only five paragraphs on the subject in a document that spans 100 paragraphs), promised the following:

- It would pursue an 'independent foreign policy' keeping in mind its past traditions.
- It would 'seek to promote multi-polarity' and oppose unilateralism.
- It would work for 'closer relations and engagement with the US' but maintain India's independence on regional and global issues and deepen ties with Russia and Europe.
- It would improve ties in South Asia and strengthen regional cooperation in the areas of water, power, and ecology.
- There would be dialogue with Pakistan on a 'sustained' basis.
- It would support peace talks in Sri Lanka that 'fulfill the legitimate aspirations of the Tamils and religious minorities'.
- Issues with Bangladesh would be resolved and water talks initiated with Nepal.
- Trade and investment with China would be 'expanded further' and border talks would be 'pursued seriously'.
- Relations with East Asia would be 'intensified'.
- It would give a 'fresh thrust' to ties with West Asia (the Middle East) and continue to support the creation of a Palestinian homeland.
- In the World Trade Organization (WTO), it would protect Indian interests, in respect of farmers, industry, and intellectual property, as also the interests of the developing world (UPA 2004: 22–3).

In practice, the new government's focus, like the NDA's, was on relations with the US, Pakistan, and China. The rest of the foreign policy in the CMP did not get the kind of sustained, intense attention devoted to relations with these three powers. Following the previous government's lead, the Manmohan Singh government tried to give expression to multi-polarity by participating in two sets of triangular diplomacy – India–Brazil–South Africa and India–China–Russia.[5] It reached out to Iran, notwithstanding American warnings, although it decided eventually to abandon Teheran diplomatically in the nuclear tussle with the US.[6] On Iraq, it remained skeptical of the US-led invasion even as it resisted public criticism of Washington's policies (Schaffer, T. 2009: 165–8). With Europe, India made little headway, reflecting in part New Delhi's lack of belief in the European Union (EU) as a unified and consequential actor in external relations (Kavalski 2008: 74–7).

Close to home, while South Asia routinely occupied Indian diplomacy, there were few if any breakthroughs with India's smaller neighbours. The South Asian Association for Regional Cooperation (SAARC) remained moribund, partly because the two great issues that might vivify regional cooperation – trade and rivers – were being dealt with bilaterally.[7] As for bilateral relations with the smaller South Asian countries, the UPA, like its predecessor, paid them relatively little attention. In addition, domestic politics in the smaller states were turbulent and unstable, making engagement with them quite fraught: the unending conflicts between the various political parties and the rise of Islamic fundamentalists in Bangladesh, the quarrel between the Maoists, the king, and other political parties in Nepal, and the civil war between the government and the Liberation Tigers of Tamil Eelam (LTTE) in Sri Lanka did not encourage ambitious diplomacy on India's part. In any case, the UPA was preoccupied with the US, Pakistan, and China and wanted to project itself as a global rather than mere regional player. As for relations with West Asia/Palestine and East and Southeast Asia, these were an even lower priority.

If India was active outside its region, this was principally in two regions that were not even mentioned in the CMP and that traditionally were the graveyards of Indian foreign policy activism, namely, Africa and Latin America.[8] Here, partly as a check against Chinese ambitions, the UPA strengthened its outreach and broke with the past. India was also active globally, above all in the WTO, where it tried to act as a bridge between the developed and less developed countries, even though in the end it was New Delhi that caused a collapse of the Doha round of talks by its opposition to US, European, and Latin American stances on agriculture.[9]

India and the US: a big deal

The centerpiece of the UPA's foreign policy was the US and the nuclear deal with the Bush administration that consumed much of its energies. When the UPA came to power, there was a view that Manmohan Singh's government would be less enthusiastic about relations with the US. The NDA signed the Next Steps in Strategic Partnership (NSSP) agreement with the US in January 2004 just before it left office. The agreement outlined a common interest in combating proliferation and cooperation in four areas: civilian nuclear activities, civilian space programs, high technology trade, and missile defense (Raja Mohan 2006: 34–5). Prior to the agreement, the NDA had been involved in a series of security-related initiatives with the US – the strategic dialogue between Jaswant Singh and Strobe Talbott in 1998–9 (which focused on the nuclear issue), India's offer of bases and other facilities to the US in the immediate aftermath of the 9/11 attacks, and the possibility of sending Indian troops to Iraq in 2003 – but these had all failed to bring the two sides into any kind of agreement.[10] The NSSP, by contrast, committed the two states to cooperation in a number of areas that were not strategic in themselves but which certainly had implications for military matters. It was an open question whether or not the UPA would build on the NSSP (Raja Mohan 2006: 38–9).

In fact, the UPA very quickly built on the NSSP. On 28 June 2005, it signed a 'New Framework for the US–India Defense Relationship' during defense minister Pranab Mukherjee's visit to Washington, and on 18 July 2005, during Prime Minister Manmohan Singh's visit to the US, it initialed a Joint Statement on India–US relations, in particular on India–US civilian nuclear cooperation. The Framework contained a number of initiatives – more military exercises; multinational operations when necessary; cooperation against terrorism; enhanced defense trade including technology transfers, collaboration, co-production, and research and development in weapon systems; missile defense collaboration; exchanges of intelligence; and expanded strategic level discussions between the Indian Ministry of Defense and the US Department of Defense.[11]

The Joint Statement committed New Delhi and Washington to sign a Science and High Technology Framework Agreement; to build closer ties in space technologies and missions; and to the removal of various Indian organizations from the US' Entity List. Most importantly, the Joint Statement entailed full civilian nuclear cooperation between India and the US. India, for its part, was to put various nuclear reactors on its civilian list under voluntary controls, to continue its unilateral moratorium on testing, to work towards a fissile material ban, and to cooperate with existing non-proliferation regimes. In March 2006, India indicated which facilities it would place under an International Atomic Energy Agency (IAEA) inspection. The US, in turn, passed the Hyde Act in December 2006, which laid the basis for a formal agreement with India on peaceful uses of nuclear energy (known as the '123 Agreement') in July 2007. The UPA government survived a vote of confidence on the agreement in July 2008, the IAEA Executive Board approved a safeguards agreement subsequently, and, in September 2008, the Nuclear Suppliers' Group (NSG) made an exception to its rules for India. In October 2008, the US Congress passed the implementation legislation for the 123 agreement (Schaffer, T. 2009: 91–9).

These landmark agreements were preceded by a number of moves by India that helped pave the way. The moves were both economic and political. Thus, in December 2004, India issued an ordinance on patent laws that brought India finally into conformity with international trading norms. In January 2005, the government liberalized norms relating to Indian company veto rights over the expansion of FDI by external partners. Also in January 2005, the government signed an 'open skies' agreement with the US. In April 2005, it announced that Air India would award its contract for 50 airliners to Boeing rather than Airbus. Before the prime minister left for Washington on his historic trip, New Delhi also resolved the Dahbol/Enron issue, which had been pending since the 1990s.[12] These various policy initiatives were a boost for India–US relations and helped the US administration in constructing a new relationship as they addressed actual and potentially divisive issues that could have been exploited both in the US Congress and in the media by disgruntled and hostile forces.

The economic moves were matched by at least three key political moves. The first was India's decision to work with Australia, Japan, and the US on tsunami relief after the events of 26 December 2004 when large parts of Southeast Asia and South Asia were affected. The 'quadrilateral' worked effectively to coordinate relief efforts, and the Indian Navy played a substantial role. The US had requested India to partner the other countries, and New Delhi quickly agreed to do so (Raja Mohan 2006: 113–18).

The second political move was India's new and unexpected emphasis on the place of democracy in international order, a theme that US president George W. Bush had repeatedly endorsed since the attacks of 9/11. While India had traditionally been reluctant to use democracy in its foreign policy pronouncements, Prime Minister Manmohan Singh and some of his senior advisers, in a series of speeches in early 2005, referred to the vital role of democracy in ensuring international peace and security (Raja Mohan 2006: 89–97).[13]

Finally, a crucial political move was in respect of India's relations with Iran. After the July 2005 Joint Statement, India faced opposition to the nuclear deal in the US Congress over its perceived sympathy for Iran, which was under pressure from the Western powers on its nuclear program. The Bush administration made clear to India that there was little prospect of the nuclear deal proceeding through the US Congress if India voted against the US position in the IAEA Board of Governors' meeting on 24 September 2005. In spite of pressures within India to vote against or to abstain on the vote, the Manmohan Singh government decided to vote for the Western resolution against Iran (Raja Mohan 2006: 165–85).

These three political moves, in particular the last two, were important for passage of the legislation in the US Congress. The first suggested that India could be a military partner if the conditions were right. The second move underscored the Bush administration's argument that a non-proliferation exception be made for India on the grounds that it was a democratic power and therefore both a 'responsible' nuclear power and a long-term asset in building a US-friendly international order. The decision on Iran was even more important – without it, the 123 legislation simply could not have passed Congress, whatever India's democratic credentials, given public animosity in the US to Iran.

Why did the Manmohan Singh government put relations with the US at the center of its foreign policy and why was the nuclear deal so vital to anchoring the relationship? Broadly, there were three reasons. The first was the government's understanding that India needed to 'normalize' relations with the US given that Washington was decisive on virtually all global issues that affected India – trade, high technology, energy, climate (Raja Mohan 2006: 148). No international alliance or network could match or compensate for the US – not India–Russia, India–China–Russia, BRIC (Brazil, Russia, India, China) or IBSA (India, Brazil, South Africa), or the NAM (Non-Aligned Movement). The key hurdle to normalization was non-proliferation. Unless New Delhi could get a deal with the US that ended India's nuclear isolation, there was little chance of getting the US 'on side' on a whole range of matters. Nuclear differences colored all Indian thinking on the relationship and powerfully influenced discussions between the two states.[14] The second, more specific reason that the US was vital in the UPA's foreign policy was the rise of China and Pakistan's support of terrorism. To contain both China and Pakistan, US power was indispensable (Sridharan 2006: 85). The third reason was the nuclear program. Here the shortage of uranium fuel for India's reactors was the key, but at various times other considerations such as the modernization of nuclear technology, access to other dual-use technologies, and attracting capital for the expansion of the nuclear program were also in play. Uranium and the other resources would only become available if the US cut a deal with New Delhi that would then lead to the dismantling of controls and restrictions against India (Raja Mohan 2006: 137–46).

India and Pakistan: no deal ...but no confrontation

The NDA had used the nuclear tests to lead its foreign policy dealings with the US. It also used nuclear weapons to try to bring Pakistan to the negotiation table. Nuclearization, it hoped, would bring about military stability and would therefore usher in negotiations and cooperation over a range of issues including Kashmir (Raja Mohan 2003: 187) When Pakistan's prime minister, Nawaz Sharif, invited India's prime minister, Vajpayee, to a summit in Lahore in February 1999, the NDA's policy hopes were seemingly vindicated. The summit produced a series of agreements and the hope of negotiations over a range of issues including Kashmir and security. In July 2001, India hosted a summit at Agra, this time with the Pakistani president, Musharraf. The summit, rather hastily arranged, ended in failure, without an agreement. All through the period, there were also a series of back-channel talks on a settlement of Kashmir (Kapila 2004). In the end, though, the negotiations yielded little.

On the other hand, the tests and negotiations notwithstanding, there continued to be instabilities between the two countries. In May 1999, the two countries went to war over the intrusion of Pakistani troops into Kargil on the Indian side of Kashmir. This was followed by more instability including the hijacking of an Indian Airlines flight to Kabul; the terrorist attack on the Jammu and Kashmir legislative assembly in October 2001 and the Indian parliament in December 2001; the mobilization of Indian and Pakistani troops in the wake of the Indian parliament attack; and various highly inflammatory terrorist attacks on temples in Gujarat and Jammu in 2002 (the Akshardham and Raghunath temples) and on Hindu pilgrims in Kashmir in 2002.

The UPA inherited an approach to relations with Pakistan that emphasized military power and coercion. The Congress-led coalition, by contrast, did not resort to the use of military threats and avoided the wild swings of the NDA's policy. Even after the terrorist attack of 26 November 2008, the UPA stayed with a measured response. The attack of 26/11 was the most dramatic assault on Indian soil in the sense that it was protracted and extremely public, with television crews from all over the world broadcasting the events as they unfolded.[15] If ever there had been a case for an Indian military response against Pakistan, this should have been it. Since the mobilization crisis of 2001–2, the Indian military had increased its capabilities and worked on plans for a rapid, 'cold start', punitive strike in response to a large terrorist attack (Ladwig 2007/8). Even so, the UPA chose to exercise restraint and did not militarize its response.

From 2004 to 2009, the UPA's policy towards Pakistan consisted of several elements. First of all, the UPA stayed with negotiations and did not allow the talks to be interrupted by terrorist attacks, small and big, or any other bilateral developments. Second, the 'composite dialogue' going back to Narasimha Rao's time continued through two entire rounds, with every one of the eight groups holding meetings.[16] Third, in general, the talks were kept out of the glare of publicity. Fourth, Manmohan Singh met either Musharraf or his successors on various occasions. The Indian foreign minister, Pranab Mukherjee, also met his Pakistani counterpart. Both the prime ministerial and foreign minister meetings were kept low key and did not produce any fundamental breakthroughs. Fifth, the back-channel diplomacy adopted briefly by the NDA was resumed.

While the UPA's foreign policy towards Pakistan was one of negotiation, it did not in the end produce any very significant formal agreements. The two governments agreed to some new confidence-building measures (CBMs), the Indian consulate in Karachi and the Pakistani consulate in Mumbai were reopened, and there were agreements on resuming travel between the two countries including a bus service between the two sides of Kashmir that did not require travelers to obtain visas. In addition, in 2005, India offered to help Pakistan during the earthquake that was particularly devastating to the Pakistani-side of Kashmir.[17]

Yet, reports persisted of considerable progress informally, in the back-channel diplomacy between former Indian diplomat, Satinder Lambah, and Tariq Aziz of Pakistan (who earlier had negotiated secretly with Prime Minister Vajpayee's representative, Brajesh Mishra, the national security advisor). By 2007, they had apparently nearly produced a Kashmir settlement. Pakistani foreign minister, Khurshid Kasuri, noted of the negotiations, 'we'd come down to semicolons' (Coll 2009; Warrick 2009; Subrahmanyam 2009).

In addition to the statement by Kasuri, a number of statements by President Musharraf and Prime Minister Manmohan Singh suggest that some creative ideas on Kashmir were in flow between the two governments. Thus, in October 2004, President Musharraf stated that Pakistan would be prepared to withdraw from its insistence on a plebiscite in Kashmir. He suggested that Kashmir could be divided into seven 'self-governing' regions, that these regions could be demilitarized in phases, that the borders between the two halves of Kashmir could be softened to allow free movement of people and goods, and that religion should not be the basis for a Kashmir solution (Schaffer, H. R. 2009: 187).

The UPA's response to these ideas was unenthusiastic, probably because Musharraf had gone public before discussing them with India. Prime Minister Manmohan Singh eventually responded that there could be no redrawing of borders or a partition along religious lines. He endorsed the notion of soft borders and suggested that the reduction of troops was only possible if terrorist infiltration was reduced (Schaffer, H. R. 2009: 187). In March 2006, India followed up with one of its standard offers, a treaty of peace, security, and friendship (which Pakistan rejected on the grounds that this ignored the Kashmir issue). The Indian prime minister once again endorsed the idea of easier travel and trade across the line of control and of cooperation between the two sides of Kashmir on problems of social and economic development (Schaffer, H. R. 2009: 188).

In December 2006, Musharraf put forward another set of proposals, again on Indian television: soft borders, 'self-governance or autonomy' on both sides of the Lines of Control (LOC), a phased withdrawal of troops, and an India–Pakistan–Kashmir mechanism for joint supervision of the state. Pakistan, in addition, would withdraw the dispute from the United Nations (UN) Security

Council (Schaffer, H. R. 2009: 189). India once again reacted conservatively and noted it was studying the proposals (Schaffer, H. R. 2009: 190).

While there were no breakthroughs with Pakistan on Kashmir or on various other disputes such as Wullar, Siachen, or Sir Creek, relations did not fall to the point of military confrontation. The UPA's unwillingness to threaten the use of force, even under intense provocation (including a series of terrorist attacks in metropolitan India), helped maintain a more stable relationship. New Delhi's persistence with negotiations is worth underlining. In 2002 and 2003, the last two years of NDA rule, there were no joint statements and declarations with Pakistan. From June 2004, when the UPA took office, to March 2009, just prior to the general elections, there were 70 joint statements and declarations, relating to meetings at the highest political level as well as the various composite dialogue committees.[18] That the Congress was not easily provoked and the continuous nature of negotiations laid the basis for a potential breakthrough.

Why were there no breakthroughs with Pakistan? The biggest hurdle was domestic political developments in Pakistan, but there were also bilateral bumps in the road. By 2006, just as the back-channel and composite dialogue were gathering momentum, President Musharraf's position at home worsened dramatically in his confrontation with the judiciary and lawyers. This was compounded by the assassination of Benazir Bhutto and the accusation that the army had not provided sufficient protection, was obstructing the investigation, and may have been behind the killing. As things brightened somewhat with the return of the Pakistan People's Party (PPP) to power, the departure of Musharraf, and the retrenchment of the Pakistani military from politics, Pakistan's internal problems were compounded by growing extremism in Swat and the battle against Islamic militants. Finally, the terrorist attack in Mumbai on 26 November 2008 caused the Indian government to call off all talks with Pakistan until Islamabad cooperated with the investigation of the attack and acted to end terrorist activity. In this situation, neither Pakistan nor India was in a position to negotiate.

India and China: deepening engagement towards a deal?

The UPA's approach to China shows a similar pattern, one that put negotiations first. The NDA had used the nuclear weapons tests to signal that India would operate from a position of greater military strength and confidence. It had publicly suggested that China was one of the reasons for India's nuclear tests (Chiriyankandath and Wyatt 2005: 203). Beijing in response became increasingly critical of the tests and joined the Clinton Administration in condemning South Asia's nuclear tests. The Vajpayee government eventually mended fences. Foreign Minister Jaswant Singh visited Beijing in June 1999; India's president, K. R. Narayanan, went in June 2002; and Vajpayee made an official visit to Beijing in June 2003 (this being the first by an Indian prime minister since 1993). Chinese Premier Zhu Rongji went to Delhi in January 2002. The border talks and the security dialogue continued, without anything significant to show for it. Trade burgeoned between the two countries, from US$2 billion in 1997 to US$12 billion in 2004 (Wu and Zhou 2006). In the meantime, Chinese power continued to grow.

For India, the growing disparity in power between the two countries and the unresolved border quarrel dominates its thinking on the relationship. It is clear that China's rise is not just economic. Economic power is translating into military power and into commercial and diplomatic influence all over the world in the form of trade, investment, and resource access. Chinese forces are far better equipped than before, from indigenous production as well as purchases abroad, and the Chinese navy is slowly but surely organizing itself for entry into the Indian Ocean.[19] Chinese commercial and diplomatic influence is becoming truly global, stretching from North and South America, through Europe and Russia, Asia and the Middle East, to Central, South, Southeast, and East Asia as well as the Asia-Pacific. The unresolved border quarrel is a reminder that in spite of the rather spectacular growth in bilateral trade, relations are far from normal. The India–China border quarrel is probably the most enduring and stubborn of China's territorial problems.[20] Since 2008, the stream of news stories over Chinese troop incursions into the Indian side of the Line of Actual Control (LAC) suggests that the much-vaunted stability of the LAC is not as firm as perhaps imagined.[21] The problem for India is how to respond to Chinese influence and to settle the border quarrel, eschewing the extremes of confrontation and surrender.

The NDA had chosen to begin with confrontation. The nuclear tests and the finger pointing at China over the tests in 1998, within days of the NDA assuming power, were signs that the new government wanted to engage China in a more muscular way. In the end, as relations played out, India reverted to a combination of approaches going back to Narasimha Rao – summits and high level political meetings, regular border negotiations, confidence building, and an expanding trade relationship. With time, the Vajpayee government became more conciliatory. It added two twists to India's China policy. The first was to suggest that a special representative assume charge of the border negotiations rather than let the Joint Working Group (JWG) continue in its bureaucratic conduct of the discussions (Guruswamy and Singh 2009: 101–2). The second was to affirm that India accepted Tibet 'as part of the territory of China' whereas, going back to 1950, India had simply recognized Chinese suzerainty (i.e. control). In return, the Chinese shifted their stand on Sikkim by agreeing to border trade at Changgu on the Sikkimese side of the LAC and Renqinggang on the Tibetan side (Guruswamy and Singh 2009: 102). Chinese maps began to show Sikkim as uncontested and as falling within India (Guruswamy and Singh 2009: 102). In 2000, China also finally produced a map of its version of the middle sector of the LAC. This came after the NDA government indicated that the pace of progress on the mapping of the boundary was proceeding too slowly (*India News Online* 2000).

The UPA's policy towards China included all of the earlier four elements: summitry, round after round of border negotiations, more confidence building, and the encouragement of trade. Unlike the NDA, it did not, however, begin with confrontational statements and a show of force. There were three summits (at the level of the prime minister and president) in 2005, 2006, and 2008 (compared with four during the NDA's six years in power). The UPA, however, stepped up the rate of bilateral negotiations. Between 1980 and 1988, there had been eight rounds of border negotiations. From 1989 to 2003, there were 14 meetings. This amounted to roughly one a year for the two periods. However, from 2003 to 2007, the greater part of which saw the UPA at the helm, there were 10 meetings, a doubling of the pace (Singh 2008: 89). From 2004 to 2009, India and China issued four major joint statements –two in 2005 and one each in 2006 and 2008 – compared to one during the NDA period (2003). The confidence-building agenda moved forward, from agreements on information exchanges, troop limits in forward areas, constraints on military exercises near the borders, meetings of military commanders, and a strategic dialogue, to actual joint military exercises: the Indian and Chinese navies held a joint naval exercise in 2006 and a joint army exercise in December 2007 (Malik 2009: 172–3). Trade increased dramatically, from US$12 billion in 2003 to US$51 billion in 2008 (Wonacott 2009).

The UPA reached some important agreements with China, one of which was that the Chinese agreed to help out on bilateral river water problems. In the April 2005 joint statement, Beijing accepted that it would 'take measures for controlled release of accumulated water of the landslide dam on the river Parechu'. The two sides also agreed to exchange hydrological data on the Sutlej/Langqen Zangbo River and to move towards a similar accord on the Parlung and Lohit/Zayu Qu (Guruswamy and Singh 2009: 168). And for the first time, India and China agreed to cooperate on energy issues, in particular in the survey and exploration of petroleum and natural gas (Guruswamy and Singh 2009: 168). China also made its most supportive statement on India's bid for a permanent place on the UN Security Council, saying 'India is an important developing country' that has 'an increasingly important influence in the international arena'. China 'attaches great importance to the status of India in international affairs' and 'understands and supports India's aspirations to play an active role in the UN and international affairs'. In addition, it noted that China would consult and cooperate with India on UN reforms (Guruswamy and Singh 2009: 183).

In the November 2006 Joint Declaration, water, energy, and India's UN candidacy were featured once again. More hydrological data was to be exchanged. The 2006 Memorandum on Cooperation in the Field of Oil and Natural Gas, which provided for cooperation between government enterprises and for joint exploration and development of hydrocarbon resources in third countries, was to be implemented (Guruswamy and Singh 2009: 183). A virtually identical statement featured India's UN aspirations. The 2006 statement also endorsed each other's growing participation in various regional organizations: India in the Shanghai Cooperation Organization (SCO), Asia–Europe Meeting (ASEM), and the East Asia Summit; and China in the South Asian Association for Regional Cooperation (SAARC), as an observer (Guruswamy and Singh 2009: 190). In 2008, in the January Joint Document ('A Shared Vision for the 21st Century') many of these positions were once again affirmed (Guruswamy and Singh 2009: 193–8).

The most important document signed when the UPA was in power, though, was the agreement on 'Political Parameters and Guiding Principles for the Settlement of the India–China Boundary Question'. This document set out the broad set of criteria or understandings on the norms and protocols that would guide a solution to the border conflict. The agreement made six crucial points:

- that the two sides would seek a 'political settlement'
- that they would give 'due consideration to each other's strategic and reasonable interests'
- that in reaching a settlement they would take into account 'historical evidence, national sentiments, practical difficulties and reasonable concerns and sensitivities of both sides, and the actual state of the border'
- that the boundary should be 'along well-defined and easily identifiable natural geographical features'
- that they would 'safeguard due interests of their settled populations in the border areas'
- that finally there would have to be a 'delineation and demarcation' by civil and military officials and surveyors (Guruswamy and Singh 2009: 175–8).

This is the most explicit statement regarding the boundary, and though it does not represent a breakthrough, it is clearly a document that begins to prepare public opinion for a final agreement. The emphasis on a political and strategic settlement rather than a purely technical one (based on law or some physical principle of demarcation); the concession to national sentiments and sensitivities; the invocation of geographical features and the interests of settled populations; and the insistence that the final delineation would await work on the ground by technicians, all these showed a realistic approach to settling the issue. With these caveats, it is clear that the two governments have given themselves plenty of room for manoeuvre in relation to their publics – virtually any criticism of a future settlement can be fended off by recourse to one or more of these criteria.

Explaining the UPA's approach

This chapter has looked at the UPA's policies towards three key states – the US, Pakistan, and China – that dominate India's external relations. It has suggested that the UPA, in contrast to the NDA, stuck with an approach that emphasized patient negotiations and accommodation rather than coercion and force. Having said this, it is important to note that the UPA policies were not toothless. While diplomacy and agreements were the objectives of the UPA, while the nuclear deal certainly was a major success for the UPA (at least in terms of its own understanding), and while there was progress with Pakistan and China on Kashmir and the border quarrel, respectively, the Manmohan Singh government's foreign policy was not without teeth.

Thus, even as New Delhi negotiated the nuclear deal, it opposed US positions on climate change and the Doha round of trade negotiations. With Pakistan, while the Manmohan Singh government certainly stayed with negotiations, in spite of periodic provocations in terms of terrorist attacks, it showed that it was not in a hurry to reach an agreement. Even relatively tractable issues such as Siachen or Sir Creek, which might have been solved, remained unresolved. In 2005, while New Delhi rather reluctantly invited President Musharraf to watch an India–Pakistan cricket match, the Indian prime minister failed to respond to three invitations to visit Pakistan (Reddy 2006). In respect of China, the UPA certainly once again kept up a steady pace of negotiations and agreements and avoided name calling. However, as media reports of Chinese incursions surfaced, India's stand did toughen. The government let it be known that India was engaged in improving road and other infrastructure in Arunachal Pradesh where the incursions were most frequent, and began to move additional troops, even aircraft, into the area to strengthen defenses (Joshi 2009). More importantly, India began to compete with China diplomatically and economically in Africa, Latin America, the Gulf, and Central Asia. While the UPA's moves were relatively modest, they were noticeable, and Indian involvements are growing. This competitive strategy has been more ambitious than anything mounted by previous governments, though typically the Manmohan Singh team has moved quietly and without seeking too much publicity.

Why did the two coalitions deal with foreign policy in different ways? It might be argued that changing global and regional circumstances called forth different approaches. This is plausible except that, broadly speaking, the imperatives facing the two governments were similar – how to deal with the sole superpower, a fractious and troubling Pakistan, and a rising China.

Alternatively, one might argue that the NDA having already brandished the sword in the service of foreign policy (the nuclear tests, military mobilization), it was possible for the UPA to adopt a more normal, diplomatic, and accommodative stance. This also is a plausible argument, but what is striking is that when the UPA might have been more aggressive, such as with Pakistan in the wake of various terrorist attacks (especially after Mumbai 2008) and with China as Beijing repeatedly pricked India over Arunachal Pradesh, it chose strategic patience and the continuation of diplomacy. Even with the US, the UPA, given the extent of domestic opposition within India, particularly from the communist parties on whose support the coalition depended, could have walked away from the nuclear deal. India, after all, would have coped – as it had for the 25 years since sanctions and other restrictions were first applied to its nuclear, missile, and space programs. It is instructive that in four years of negotiations with the US, the NDA was unable to get an agreement. The UPA, by contrast, stuck doggedly to negotiations and brought them to a successful close in 2008.

A third possibility in explaining the difference in approach between the two coalitions is to attribute it to the political worldviews of the two major parties that lead the coalitions – the BJP and the Congress. The BJP is a conservative party in its ideological leanings, and the role of force and violence in its understanding of politics is that these are more or less inescapable. At best, the BJP ideologues see force and violence in tragic terms, something that humans are doomed to; at worst, they see force and violence as more or less intrinsic to politics. The Congress remains a 'left liberal' party ideologically, and the role of force and violence in politics is one that it finds repugnant. This does not mean that it abjures force and violence either in domestic or international politics. It does mean that force and violence are regarded as a last resort and as signifying a failure, rather than a functional element, of politics. If this explanation is correct, future research on Indian foreign policy should pay much greater attention to ideology – its influence but also its limits.[22]

Conclusion

Those who expected the UPA government to opt for different lines of policy in external relations were not altogether proved wrong. While global and regional imperatives forced the UPA, like the NDA before it, to focus on relations with the US, Pakistan, and China, and while there were continuities in policies towards these three crucial powers, there were significant differences as well. The realist, more coercive stance of the NDA was replaced by the more liberal, negotiatory approach of the UPA. This reflected in large part the ideological difference between the two coalitions.

With the UPA back in power after the 2009 general elections, it would be safe to predict that, if ideology is a determining factor, the Manmohan Singh government will continue with the broad approach of the previous five years. Having said this, there will be challenges ahead that will test the government's resolve including the implementation of the nuclear deal with the US, fresh terrorist outrages against India or Indian assets, and more Chinese military pressures on Arunachal Pradesh.

9 India's energy security during the UPA government

Lawrence Sáez

Introduction

Energy security can be narrowly defined as a condition whereby a country and its citizens have access to energy resources free from serious physical disruption of service (Kalicki and Goldwyn 2005: 571). However, for rapidly developing countries, such as India, energy security incorporates a broader range of overlapping dimensions. At one level, energy security has become one of the most important challenges for India's domestic economic development, namely in terms of the ability of energy supply to make economic growth sustainable as well as redistributive. As Sáez (2007a) has shown, energy security is interlinked with a country's rate of economic growth and demographic trends. At a different level, energy security acquires an internal security dimension. As Barton *et al.* (2004: 5) have argued, energy security also includes the protection from sabotage of gas supplies, nuclear power plants, hydroelectric dams, and other components of a country's energy infrastructure. Moreover, viewed from the perspective of the potential of its energy supply, energy security concerns have also shaped India's external relations. Finally, in light of the emerging concerns about environmental protection, energy security and the management of China and India's energy-related carbon dioxide ($CO2$) emissions have been central to global policy debates about climate change. In India's case, changes to the water level and the inadequate level of rural electrification could pose a severe threat to the sustainability of India's development.

This chapter examines India's energy security from the introduction of policies initiated during the first UPA government (2004–9). Following the stress given to energy security during the second term of the NDA government, the UPA government began to assert its energy security policy during the 2004 general election. By 2004, India's GDP exceeded US$691 billion, making India the eight largest economy in the world. It was during this period of growth that India's energy security came to the forefront of policy dialogues, both domestically and internationally. On the domestic front, the UPA devoted an entire section of its national CMP to the subject. On a geopolitical front, rapid growth in India's energy consumption began to be noticed internationally. According to calculations from the US Department of Energy (2009), India's net energy consumption is expected to increase by 2.5 per cent annually between 2006 and 2030. As Klare (2008: 80) notes, this rate of growth was three times larger than that of the United States and seven times that of the advanced economies of the European Union.

Measuring energy security and assessing the UPA's energy security threats

Although the concept of energy security is used extensively in policy debates, it is nonetheless a term that can bear a multiplicity of interpretative values. This author has defined energy security as a condition whereby a country and its citizens have access to energy resources without a serious physical disruption of service. In a highly influential analysis, Martin *et al.* (1996: 4) have highlighted the need to consider the subject from several angles, including limiting a country's vulnerability to disruption given rising dependence on imported energy sources, the provision of adequate supply meeting rising demand at reasonable prices, and the energy-related environmental challenges.

Some facets of energy security can measured quantitatively, typically supply-side functions such as a country's total primary energy supply (TPES) or demand-side functions such as total final consumption (TFC). According to estimates by the International Energy Agency (IEA) (2007: 444), India's total primary energy demand in 2000 was 459 metric tons of oil equivalent (Mtoe). By 2005, the figure had increased to 537 Mtoe, with an average annual volumetric increase of total primary energy demand to 15 Mtoe. This was equivalent to the entire total primary energy demand of Ireland. In May 2004, the UPA government asserted its commitment to triple power generation capacity by 2015 to over 350,000 megawatts (MW).

As a result of India's increasing presence in international energy markets, there has been a great deal of speculation on projected increases in various forms of energy consumption. In aggregate terms, India is projected to have one of the world's fastest growth rates in primary energy consumption. For instance, the US Department of Energy's *International Energy Outlook* (2009: 121) predicts that India will have an annual average percentage change of 2.5 during the 2006–30 period, second only to China's projected annual increase of 3.2 per cent (see Table 9.1).

Table 9.1 Comparison between India and the world's primary energy consumption, 1990–2030 (in Quadrillion BTUs)

	1990	2005	2006	2010	2015	2020	2025	2030	Average annual increase (%)
World	347.7	462.1	472.4	508.3	551.5	595.7	637.3	678.3	1.5
India	7.9	16.3	17.7	19.1	22.9	26.8	29.6	32.3	2.5

Source: Data calculated from US Department of Energy (2009) *International Energy Outlook*, Table A1

Abbreviation: BTU = British thermal unit.

The US Department of Energy's projections are corroborated by credible independent forecasts. In order to take into account the possible effect of policy changes, the IEA's (2006, 2007) energy use projections are based on two policy scenarios: a *reference policy scenario* and an *alternative policy scenario*. Under the IEA's reference policy scenario, there is an assumption that that no new government policy actions are taken and that energy-supply and end-use technologies become more efficient over time. In contrast, the IEA's alternative policy scenario assumes that countries adopt all of the policies that they are currently considering, leading to substantial savings in energy consumption and imports. The IEA's reference scenario (2007: 119) predicts that India's primary energy demand will increase to 770 Mtoe in 2015 and to 1,299 Mtoe by 2030. Table 9.2 shows the IEA's India energy profile and projected energy production and consumption outlook.

In general, using two separate forecasting models, it appears that Table 9.1 and Table 9.2 imply that India's projected primary energy consumption are likely to between 31.9 and 32.3 quadrillion BTUs (using the IEA and the US Department of Energy's projections respectively). As Table 9.2 shows, though, India's share of total energy production and consumption as a proportion of world total is low, roughly 3.9 per cent in 2006 and 4.5 per cent in 2030. Table 9.2 also shows that petroleum and natural gas consumption outstrips petroleum and natural gas production in 2006 and by a larger margin in 2030.

Moreover, India's rapid growth in total primary energy demand also shows some important gaps in the distribution of energy generation among different

Table 9.2 India's energy profile and projected outlook (2006 and 2030)

Category	Energy unit	2006	World total (%)	2030	World total (%)
Total energy consumption	quadrillion BTUs	17.1	3.9	31.9	4.5
Petroleum production	mbd	0.8	1.1	1.3	1.1
Petroleum consumption	mbd	2.6	3.1	4.4	3.7
Natural gas production	tcf	1.1	1.1	n.a.	n.a.
Natural gas consumption	tcf	1.4	1.4	3.9	2.4
Coal consumption	quadrillion BTUs	8.5	6.8	15.2	7.6
Nuclear energy consumption	billion kilowatt hours	15	0.1	144	4.0
Carbon dioxide emissions	million metric tons	1,111	4.1	2,156	5.0

Source: International Energy Agency, 2007.

Abbreviations: BTU = British thermal unit; mbd = million barrels a day; n.a.= not available; tcf = trillion cubic feet.

energy sources. India's indigenous production of primary energy at the time in which the first UPA government took office was heavily dominated by coal and lignite.

As Table 9.3 shows, coal and lignite accounted for 70.6 per cent of India's overall indigenous production of primary energy. As Sáez (2007a: 667) has pointed out, India's indigenous coal production is largely in the form of anthracite and bituminous coal, two coal types that have high carbon count and low calorific content. Given the polluting component of India's indigenous coal production, the first challenge facing the UPA was to even out the imbalances in India's domestic energy production with a commitment to reducing global CO_2 emissions.

India's energy security can also be discussed in terms of its strategic components. Sáez (2007a: 665) proposed that quantitative measures of energy security point to specific strategic vulnerabilities relating to a country's indigenously produced energy and to a country's domestic energy consumption needs. As such, he proposed that the ratio between a country's indigenously produced energy and the country's total final consumption be termed as *primary energy security*. On the other hand, the ratio between a country's domestically generated energy and the total primary energy supply should be referred to as *aggregate energy security*. Sáez (2007a: 666) noted that India's strategic vulnerability lies with its aggregate energy security, suggesting that 'domestically produced energy is not sufficient to meet domestic demand'.

India's strategic vulnerabilities are enhanced by the rapid growth in India's energy demand. In a thorough analysis of India and China's energy demands, the IEA has linked the growth of energy demand to rapid economic development. According to the IEA (2007: 41), 'the staggering pace of Chinese and Indian economic growth in the past few years, outstripping that of all other major countries, has pushed up sharply the energy needs, a growing share of which has to be imported'. For India, the cost of importing crude oil is quite substantial. According to the IEA (2007: 446), nearly 70 per cent of India's crude oil is imported. Likewise, India imports about 20 per cent of its natural gas.

Table 9.3 India's indigenous production of primary energy (2004)

Energy source	Energy unit	Amount	Total (%)
Coal and lignite	MT	412.95	70.6
Crude oil	MT	33.98	5.8
Natural gas	BCM	31.76	5.4
Nuclear	BkWh	17.01	2.9
Hydropower	BkWh	84.61	14.4
Wind power	BkWh	4.49	0.7

Source: Data calculated by author from TERI (2008) p. 19

Abbreviations: MT = million tonnes; BCM = billion cubic metres; BkWh = billion kilowatt hours. Although measured differently, the above energy units are considered to be equivalent.

As Table 9.2 showed, important sources of energy, such as a crude oil and natural gas, are not dominant sources of indigenously produced energy. In this sense, the dominance of coal in domestic energy production and the economic impact of large imports of crude oil and natural gas became the second most important challenge facing the UPA. As such, it is no surprise to note that the UPA's CMP proposed that it 'will immediately put in place policies to enhance the country's energy security particularly in the area of oil' (UPA 2004).

From a domestic policy perspective, energy security is essential for sustainable economic development. Given India's rapid growth in primary energy production, one of the key challenges facing the UPA was effort to link energy security with economic development. To that effect, the CMP of the UPA promised that 'an integrated energy policy with sustainable development will be put in place' (UPA 2004). Moreover, in relation to its proposed action relating to infrastructure improvements, the UPA's CMP pledged household electrification alongside an increased presence in power generation from the private sector.

The importance of linking energy security and economic development were most convincingly articulated by R. K. Pachauri, arguably India's leading energy expert and the co-winner of the 2007 Nobel Peace Prize (for his work as chair of the Intergovernmental Panel on Climate Change). In a seminal study of the relationship between energy and economic development, Pachauri (1977) championed the need for India to seek technological alternatives to energy supply from coal-based sources.

Writing in the 1970s, Pachauri correctly held the view that the consumption of non-commercial sources of energy in countries like India is concentrated largely in the rural sector. He pointed out that modernization in agriculture does 'not necessarily [bring about] a corresponding increase in overall energy consumption; to a large extent, the aggregate effect is a shift to commercial sources from non-commercial sources' (Pachauri 1977: 7). Counter-intuitively, Pachauri argued that a lack of commercial activity in the rural sector was acting as a barrier to economic development in the countryside. Pachauri believed that the consumption of energy in the household and in industrial activities is a substitute for the inputs in labor and capital. Pachauri (1977: 9) concluded that 'surpluses can be diverted either through more efficient use of energy or through the stimulation of greater energy consumption in order to free capital and labor for other production activities'.

The case of India, though, poses some problems, as the agricultural sector is one of the weakest consumers of energy. India's final energy consumption increased from 179.8 Mtoe in 2001 to 216.5 Mtoe in 2005. At present, India's sectoral energy consumption is heavily dominated by industry. As Figure 9.1 shows, industry accounts for 44 per cent of the overall energy consumption. As Figure 9.1 suggests, the third biggest challenge facing the UPA was to increase the energy consumption of the agricultural and commercial sectors at a time in which India's economic growth was fuelling energy consumption growth in industry and the residential sectors.

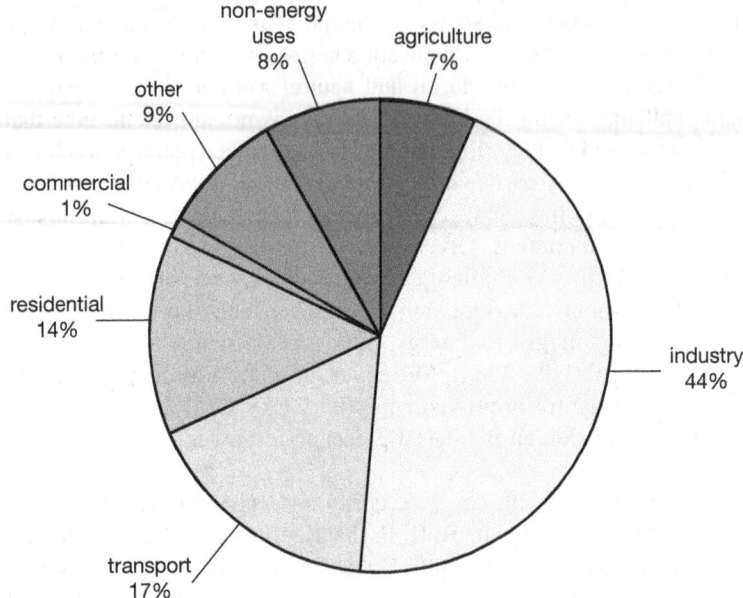

Source: Data calculated by author from TERI (2008)

Note: Non-energy uses refer to uses of energy resources for non-energy-specific purposes such as feedstock in fertilizers and petrochemical industries.

Figure 9.1 India's energy consumption by sector (2007)

Bureaucratic and institutional constraints on the UPA's energy security policy

In the previous section, we have argued that there were some important imbalances facing the UPA government, namely that domestic energy generation was dominated by coal, that crude oil and natural gas had to be imported, and that the agricultural sector was a low consumer of energy. Faced with these challenges, the UPA government gave primary importance to India's weak production of crude oil and natural gas.

In the absence of strong domestic capabilities for crude oil and natural gas production, analysts of global energy markets have highlighted the growing importance of developing nations in the global hunt for natural resources. Pant (2008) stressed the growing importance of India's energy diplomacy with its Asian neighbours, notably China. Roy (2007) also contextualized India's energy security policy options within a framework of overall energy security in Asia. However, other authors, such as Michael Klare (2008: 63), have focused their attention more precisely on what they term to be the 'Chindia challenge', whereby

China and India are rapidly displacing mature industrialized states in the acquisition of raw materials. India and China have changed the international oil market with consumption growth well above global average rates. India is the world's largest energy consumer and plans major energy infrastructure investments to keep up with increasing demand. It is the world's third largest producer of coal. Relying on statistics from the IEA, Klare (2008: 64) argues that China and India are expected 'to account for nearly half of the entire increase in global energy demand over the next quarter century, thoroughly transforming the international energy equation'.

The importance of upgrading India's energy security position was a feature of the NDA and the UPA governments. In this respect, the NDA and the UPA have coincided in identifying self-sufficiency as the key to bolster India's energy security. Nevertheless, India is in competition with other developing countries in the search for raw materials from abroad. In a speech to Indian energy officials, Prime Minister Manmohan Singh observed that 'we can no longer be complacent and must learn to think strategically, to think ahead, and to act swiftly and decisively' (Bradsher 2005).

Imaginative, swift, and decisive actions are not natural attributes of India's policy-making machinery. It is then no surprise that in an analysis of the institutional mechanisms driving India's energy security policy in particular, Bahgat (2007: 20) refers to a persistent pattern of institutional fragmentation in the discussion and implementation of a long-term energy security strategy. In addition to the Planning Commission's impact on energy security policy, India has four separate central government ministries and one independent central government department (Ministry of Coal, Ministry of Power, Ministry of Petroleum and Natural Gas, Ministry of New and Renewable Energy, and the Department of Atomic Energy) dealing with different facets of energy security policy.

The institutional fragmentation in energy security is incremented through the involvement of state-level institutions. For instance, the strengthening and enhancement of electricity transmission systems at the intrastate level is the responsibility of state transmission utilities (STUs) whilst interstate and national grid operations are the responsibility of the central transmission utility. Thus, in the absence of a fully integrated national transmission system, there are persistent problems with resource allocation, interregional power transfer capacity, and capacity addition that is commensurate with the increase in power demand.

Moreover, by virtue of India's developmental planning process, the UPA government was hampered from developing an energy security policy that differed substantially from that initiated during the NDA governments. The second NDA government oversaw a major overhaul of the energy provision statutes in India. For instance, in 2003, the federal Electricity Act was enacted consolidating all federal electricity laws and regulations. Until the enactment of the Electricity Act of 2003, the Indian power sector was governed by three principal acts, namely the Indian Electricity Act of 1910, the Electricity (Supply) Act of 1948, and the Indian Regulatory Commissions Act of 1998. Building on a conference of Chief Ministers and state power ministers on 3 March 2001, there was consensus on depoliticizing power sector reform and speeding up its implementation. In many respects, the enactment of the 2003 Electricity Act a few years later showed that there was ample bipartisan support for reforming India's anachronistic energy-related legislation.

In recent years, much of the effort to reform India's energy sector was initiated during the second NDA regime. The NDA pressed for several initiatives, including the Energy Conservation Act of 2001, which called for efficiency in energy consumption. The NDA government also introduced a number of additional energy-related initiatives and public policy programs, including the one lakh MW thermal power initiative, a 50,000 MW hydroelectric power initiative, and the accelerated generation and supply program (AG&SP).

One of the NDA's institutional successes was the launching of the accelerated power development program (APDP), later renamed the accelerated power development and reform program (APDRP). The APDRP's goal was to bring about commercial viability in the energy distribution sector. According to Rastogi (2008: 8), the original APDRP 'achieved qualified success in cutting down [aggregate technical and commercial power, AT & C] losses'. During the UPA government, the APDRP's mandate was enhanced with the establishment of automated systems for the collection of baseline data. Following the recommendations issued at the Chief Ministers' Conference on Power in May 2007, three new agencies were created to help in the implementation of new power projects. To this effect, a Standing Group of Power Ministers was created to liaise with the Ministry of Power. In addition, a subgroup of the Standing Group was formed to examine the financial feasibility of all new and existing power projects. Finally, a new body, the National Power Project Management Board, was established for the purpose of monitoring all power projects under the jurisdiction of the Ministry of Power.

One of the concerns of the NDA's electricity reform program was the financial health of state electricity boards (SEBs). In 2000–1, the Ministry of Power activated a program – called the Accelerated Development Programme – which provided financial incentives to the states for the purposes of modernizing their power administration. The NDA also supported the introduction of competition through power trading. The 2003 Electricity Act furthered this aim by introducing competition into the domestic energy production market.

Moreover, the NDA government, reflecting the multipartisan support developed during the Chief Ministers/Power Ministers conference on 3 March 2001, proposed increasing the electrification of villages. To that effect, it initiated the Rural Electricity Supply Technology (REST) mission for the purpose of providing a decentralized generation and distribution network for electrification of rural areas. In conjunction with the guidelines of the Tenth Five Year Plan for an accelerated rural electrification program (AREP), the NDA also started a program to provide electricity for one lakh villages and one crore households. In conjunction with the NDA's rural shelter initiative under the auspices of the *Pradhan Mantri Gramodaya Yojana* (PMGY) and the Minimum Needs Programme, the NDA undertook an ambitious village electricification initiative. At the time when the UPA government took power, there were an estimated 587,258 villages in India (according to extrapolations from the 1991 census), out of which 495,298 (or 84.3 per cent) were electrified. However, the panorama for rural households was more worrisome. In August 2004, there were an estimated 138.3 million rural households, out of which 60.2 million (or 43.5 per cent) were electrified.

During the NDA's first two terms of office, the other key feature of its energy policy was the enactment of important legislation relating to licensing of energy resources. The legislation, titled New Explorations in Licensing Policy (NELP), aimed to increase the speed of hydrocarbon exploration in India by enabling foreign energy-related companies the ability to bid for on-land and offshore exploration blocks. S. D. Muni and Girijesh Pant (2005) praised the NDA government's NELP. In their view (Muni and Pant, 2005: 16) 'the thrust of the new energy policy is for more and active overseas interaction and engagement with the global players both in exploration and sourcing'.

In public policy terms, India has gradually attempted to develop an integrated national energy planning framework. At the macro level, there is interaction between the energy sector and the rest of the economy, mostly in terms of resource availability, energy demand, and energy outputs. At the micro level, there is subsector planning interaction between operators who attempt to achieve reliability optimization in conjunction with a pricing policy that enables physical controls and the development of technical methods to harness energy sources.

In addition to the imprint for reform from the NDA government, the UPA was also constrained from developing a bold energy security policy as a result of India's policy planning mechanisms. In many respects, the Indian government's energy policy objectives during the UPA's first term of office were developed in the Tenth Five Year Plan (2002–7). The Planning Commission's principal programmatic initiatives on food security and poverty reduction were the *Jai Prakash Rozgar Guarantee Yojana* (JPRGY), the *Swarnjayanti Gram Swarozgar Yojana* (SGSY), and the *Sampoorna Grameen Rozgar Yojana* (SGRY).

Given these initiatives by the NDA government, it should be assumed that both the NDA and the UPA governments viewed rural electrification as a key energy policy objective. The Chief Ministers/Power Ministers conference of March 2001 stated among its resolutions the ambitious objective of completing rural electrification by the end of the Tenth Five Year Plan (i.e. in the year 2007). Likewise, in the Tenth Five Year Plan (Planning Commission, Government of India 2002, Vol. II: 914), the Planning Commission itself held the view that the rural electrification program 'is one of the most important components in rural development and as important as rural drinking water supply, health, nutrition, primary education, shelter and rural connectivity'. Although the objective of having comprehensive rural electrification was not met, the UPA government pushed forth an important piece of legislation, the Rural Electrification Policy, in 2006.

Features of the UPA's energy security policy

It would be fair to suggest that in light of the bureaucratic and institutional constraints that we have outlined, the UPA government had a difficult time establishing an energy security policy that was substantively different from the reform-minded NDA government. During the UPA's first term of office, however, specific energy security policies were pursued relating to national coordination, sustainability, and international collaboration.

National coordination

As we have discussed above, India's energy infrastructure has often suffered from weak institutional coordination between the central government and the states and among central government institutions dealing with energy. On 1 September 2004, the India Energy Forum, under the chairmanship of A. K. Sah, released a report on an integrated energy policy for India. The report proposed a set of recommendations on coordinating energy generation and supply with sustainable development. The report stressed the various factors that were essential for sustainable energy development, including making energy production and supply affordable to all classes of consumers. The recommendations of the India Energy Forum report became the blueprint for the UPA's approach to the implementation of an integrated energy policy, as stated in its campaign manifesto.

The India Energy Forum (2004: 49) report proposed new institutional arrangements to enable greater coordination among the different departments and agencies dealing with energy security. It proposed that the central government create a statutory body or apex committee entrusted with the purpose of providing guidelines for the formulation of an integrated energy policy and its associated programs. The report also proposed the creation of a taskforce within the Planning Commission for the purpose of implementing the recommendations of the programs approved by the apex committee. On July 2005, Manmohan Singh set up an Energy Coordination committee to enable a systemic approach for policy formulation in the area of energy planning and security.

The Planning Commission's goals, as outlined in the Tenth Five Year Plan, were to increase electricity capacity and to reduce import dependence on crude oil and natural gas. To this effect, the Tenth Five Year Plan (Planning Commission, Government of India 2002, Vol. I: 222) called for a mechanism for creating a strategic crude oil storage facility. The India Energy Forum (2004) report also proposed creating a strategic petroleum reserve (SPR) of a minimum of 5 million tons of crude oil, but felt that a more adequate emergency response mechanism would be the equivalent of 90 days of net imports as storage. The India Energy Forum (2004: 49) report also proposed that India follow a coordinated emergency response measure (CERM) to include stockdraw, demand restraint fuel switching options, and a potential increase in domestic output. In response, the UPA government proposed the setting up of a strategic petroleum reserve equal to 15 days of the country's consumption, over and above the holding capacity required from national oil companies. For this purpose, in 2008, the government started the process of constructing a 15 million metric ton (mmt) strategic storage facility in three sites. Initially, the state-owned Indian Oil Corporation (IOC) was to take the lead in the delivery of the reserve. However, on the advice from the Ministry of Petroleum and Natural Gas, the facilities were transferred to the Indian Strategic Petroleum Reserve Limited (ISPRL), a special purpose vehicle owned by the Oil Industry Directorate Board (OIDB).

Sustainability

A key policy contribution by the UPA government was its effort to make energy security sustainable, both in terms of its affordability and accessibility as well as on its positive environmental impact. The India Energy Forum report stated that the growing primary requirement of an integrated energy policy is to provide energy security. To achieve this aim, the report proposed 'to conserve our own resources through a balanced and judicious exploration, its efficient use through energy conservation measures, technological improvements and better man-machine interface for higher productivity and reduction in energy intensity' (India Energy Forum 2004: 34).

The issue of sustainability was also central in another influential report, the Planning Commission's India Vision 2020, which helped to guide the UPA's policy on several policy arenas. In the report, P. K. Pachauri and Pooja Mehrotra wrote an extensive analysis of the sustainability of India's natural resources. Pachauri and Mehrotra (2004: 779) opined that 'for future growth to be sustainable, it needs to be resource-efficient and environmentally accountable, requiring a long-term vision while planning for the immediate and long-term future'.

In their contribution to the Vision 2020 report, Pachauri and Mehrotra (2004: 781) identified the poor fiscal condition of SEBs, fiscal constraints leading to poor plant maintenance, insufficient generation of resources on installed capacity basis and the inadequate transmission capacity to link different regions 'as the key challenges facing India's power sector'. Although Pachauri and Mehrotra had outlined some of the institutional features that had motivated the NDA government to seek broad sectoral reforms, the key difference in their recommendations was the argument that India should fully exploit its comparative advantage in renewable energy. Thus, Pachauri and Mehrotra (2004: 804) argued that the 'development and implementation of ecologically safe, risk-free, and renewable sources of energy would help reshape the energy industry and infrastructure'.

During the UPA's first term of office, India also made important advances in securing energy security by developing its renewable energy program. One of the successes of the UPA government was the passage of a new hydroelectric policy in 2008. The policy aimed to ensure targeted capacity addition and to improve the overall reliability of the distribution system. During the consultation phase leading to the enactment of the new hydroelectric power policy, the Ministry of Power identified critical bottlenecks in the approval and operation of interstate hydropower projects. To that effect, the new hydroelectric policy had, as one of its principal objectives, offered state governments additional incentives, beyond the existing incentive of a 12 per cent allocation of free power, to collaborate in interstate hydropower projects. According to one energy analyst, the unbundling of these infrastructural bottlenecks was to be achieved by 'roping in host state governments as equity players in their projects and handing out minority equity of up to 49 per cent, over and above the 12 per cent free power entitlement for the host state' (Rastogi 2008: 11).

Another area that framed the UPA government's energy sustainability agenda was the policy proposal to initiate a distinctive energy pricing policy. In the resolutions of the Chief Ministers/Power Ministers conference of March 2001, there were recommendations for tariff determination by regulatory commissions. The resolutions also recommended that energy subsidies should be provided only to those state governments that had made specific budgetary allocations to pay central government subsidies.

Upon taking power, the UPA government initially pursued a populist policy of providing subsidies for specific energy types. Thus, in August 2004, it approved a cut in custom and excise taxes on petroleum, diesel, kerosene, and liquefied petroleum gas (LPG). However, the UPA government then refocused the direction of its policy in the energy sector by supporting a burden-sharing pricing agenda. The UPA government's proposed price band system is within 10 per cent of the range of estimated future price averages for gasoline and diesel, and the phase-out period of the subsidy on kerosene and LPG has been extended. The price band, though, included a dual pricing of kerosene sold through its public distribution system, namely by splitting consumers whose income was below the poverty line and those whose income was above the poverty line. Those consumers whose income was above the poverty line would have to purchase kerosene at market prices. In order to provide clarity to India's complex electricity subsidy policies, the UPA introduced the 2006 National Tariff Policy, which outlines the principles and approaches to tariff determination.

International collaboration

If measured in terms of public controversy, the first UPA government is likely to be remembered for its pursuance of a nuclear cooperation initiative with the United States. The pact nearly led to the withdrawal of parliamentary support from the UPA government's leftist allies, possibly prompting the collapse of the UPA coalition. As Mistry (2006: 695) argues, the Indian government's negotiation capabilities 'became smaller both because the government was weak in that Prime Minister Singh's Congress-led United Progressive Alliance (UPA) was a minority coalition government and also because the increased participation rate of domestic groups against the nuclear agreement created obstacles for negotiation'.

The full range of the impact of domestic politics and the subsequent diplomatic implications for US–India relations of the July 2005 US–India nuclear cooperation initiative will not be examined here. However, from the perspective of India's energy security, the US–India nuclear deal is interesting because it shows that by allowing IAEA inspections of commercial nuclear facilities the UPA government was keen to engage the United States in a project that would secure US expertise and the provision of fuel to safeguard reactors at Tarapur. Thus, the US–India nuclear deal could be seen to provide some enhancement to India's energy security needs.

However, in practical terms, the US–India nuclear deal was not one of the most important developments in relation to the UPA's energy security policy. The UPA's achievements in energy security policy should be depicted more broadly, specifically in reference to its distinctive outlook on international collaboration on energy. Manmohan Singh held the view that international collaboration would be a key component of India's future energy security. During his July 2005 state visit to the United States, Manmohan Singh gave a speech to a joint session of the US Congress. Singh argued that energy security 'is another area where our two countries have strong common interests'. He stressed that 'we must also tap the full potential of nuclear energy'. Nevertheless, Manmohan Singh also noted that 'we are conscious that plans to meet our energy requirements will have implications for the environment'.

The view that nuclear energy will play an important role in the provision of energy to India enjoys wide support, but tenuous empirical evidence. For instance, the US Department of Energy's 2009 *International Energy Outlook* establishes that most of the expansion in installed nuclear power capacity will take place in non-OECD (Organisation of Economic Co-operation and Development) countries, with China, India, and Russia accounting for two thirds of the projected net increase in world nuclear power capacity between 2006 and 2030. Although there are some sources of uncertainty in their projections, the US Department of Energy estimates that India will add 17 gigawatts of nuclear capacity between 2006 and 2030. Likewise, the Government of India's Department of Atomic Energy (DAE) has forecasted far more optimistic projections on the expected contribution of nuclear energy to India's overall energy mix. With the assumption of a rapid growth in additionally installed nuclear facilities in India, the DAE estimates that India will be able to generate 20 gigawatts of energy by 2020, and 44 gigawatts by 2030, twice as much as predicted by the US Department of Energy.

As Sáez (2007b) shows, though, there are sharp discrepancies between the DAE's estimates and reliable independent forecasts, such as those issued by the IEA. If we compare the DAE and the IEA's estimates for projected electricity generated by nuclear sources of energy, then we find a significant difference in their respective projections (see Figure 9.2).

As Figure 9.2 shows, the DAE's own projections about projected electricity generation from nuclear sources consistently exceeds the two projections from the IEA. The differential between the DAE and the IEA's two projections increases rapidly over time and, by 2030, DAE projections are three times higher than those estimated by the IEA. It is noteworthy that the DAE's past projections on the development of nuclear energy have been consistently off the mark. For instance, Madan (2006) and Ramana (2006) have pointed out that the DAE's past predictions for nuclear energy development have far exceeded the actual electricity generated from nuclear sources, in some instances as much as by a factor of 15 times.

Invariably, nuclear energy emerges as a source with a great potential for helping India achieve enhanced energy security. The Planning Commission itself pointed to the low contribution that nuclear energy was making to India's overall primary electricity generation. The Planning Commission's Tenth Five Year Plan (Planning Commission, Government of India 2002, Vol. II: 911) admonished: 'at present, nuclear energy accounts for only 2.4 per cent of total primary energy consumption, against a global average of 13 per cent. This is far too low.' However, as the projections about future development of nuclear energy show, nuclear energy will remain a marginal contributor to India's future energy mix.

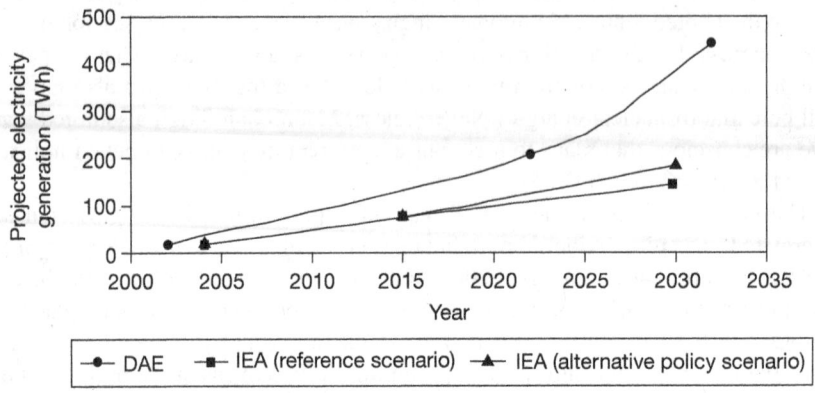

Source: Sáez (2007b); Department of Atomic Energy (2007), International Energy Agency (2006)

Figure 9.2 Projected electricity generated by nuclear sources

Clearly, the US–India nuclear deal has been rightly viewed as an important landmark in US–India relations, though not necessarily in terms of its expected contribution to India's energy security.

In contrast to the polarizing effect of the US–India nuclear deal, less visible, but equally important, were India's overtures to China, its purported international competitor for raw materials. As argued by Kumaraswamy (2007: 350), 'a cooperative approach towards China has been a prominent feature in the energy policy pursued by the Indian government since the UPA came to power in the summer of 2004'. Evidence for this change in policy includes the fact that India's Minister for Petroleum and Natural Gas, Mani Shankar Aiyar, visited China in January 2006 and signed a memorandum of understanding (MoU) for bilateral cooperation. During his visit, the often-controversial minister stressed the need for cooperation in the submission of acquisition bids in third countries and reiterated that both countries have a shared interest in seeking to lessen competition for energy supplies and in working together to discover and develop new energy supplies. During this visit, India and China signed a historic agreement in which ONGC Videsh and the China National Petroleum Corporation pledged to submit joint bids for promising energy projects in other countries.

Later that year, in November 2006, President Hu Jintao visited India and signed a 10-point resolution that included an agreement to double the volume of trade from US$10 billion to US$20 billion by 2010. The 10-point resolution reiterated the intention to 'fully implement the provisions of the memorandum of cooperation in the field of Oil and Natural Gas signed in January 2006 and encourage collaboration between their enterprises including through *joint exploration and development of hydrocarbon resources in third countries*'. The resolution also included an important agreement to cooperate in the development of civilian nuclear energy, a development that was quite similar in scope to the US–India nuclear cooperation initiative.

A second feature of the UPA government's efforts to enhance India's energy security needs was its formal commitment to the construction of the Iran–Pakistan–India (IPI) natural gas pipeline. Despite considerable pressure from the United States, India engaged in a series of bilateral and trilateral talks with its Pakistani and Iranian counterparts. As Batra (2009: 89) shows, though, the progress in the discussions was stalled on the basis of a number of critical developments. For instance, the firm entrusted with offering a feasibility assessment of the costs of constructing the 1,035 km pipeline, BHP Billiton, revised its initial project cost estimates from US$4 billion to US$7.5 billion. In addition to the unexpected costs announced by BHP Billiton, the project also floundered because Pakistan had been rumored to be interested in demanding a transit fee of US$700 million. Eventually, through intense negotiations, Pakistan agreed to a transit fee of US$200 million. Finally, the viability of the Iran–Pakistan India pipeline was jeopardized by a dispute between Iran and India on a contract relating to liquid natural gas supplies. As Batra (2009: 89) observes, 'the fact that India at the same time cast its vote against Iran in the IAEA on the nuclear issue and gas prices had gone up substantially in the international market was not mere coincidence'.

Despite these setbacks, the UPA government's cabinet approved the project in 2005. Thereafter, the construction of the IPI was expected to start in 2009 and the commencement of the supply of natural gas was due to start in 2011. India's engagement in this diplomatically tricky cross-border transnational project showed that the UPA government could pursue a very pragmatic approach to the issue of energy security. However, the UPA's pragmatism had a limit. Following the November 2008 attacks in Mumbai, the IPI project came to a standstill. As of the time of the writing, there appears to be no future engagement by India on the construction of the pipeline.

Another key feature in the UPA's energy security policy was its effort to have Indian energy giants lead a drive for international collaboration. Muni and Pant (2005) argued that one of the key obstacles hindering India's search for energy security through exploration and investment was that India was not encouraging private sector oil companies to venture abroad. Writing at a time shortly after the first UPA government had been put office, Muni and Pant (2005: 288–9) incorrectly speculated that the UPA government 'may be further reluctant in this respect as it wants to keep a tight control over strategic economic sectors, including energy'.

In order to make India more competitive in international energy markets, the UPA government promoted the gradual privatization of India's energy giants. In 1997, India's largest public sector enterprises were conferred *navaratna* (literally, crown jewel) status by the Department of Public Enterprises. Not surprisingly, India's three largest energy giants (Indian Oil Corporation (IOC), Oil and Gas Corporation (ONGC), and GAIL) account for a large proportion of public sector enterprises that have been provided with *navaratna* status. IOC is India's largest oil refinery and owns half of India's 20 existing refineries. GAIL has a 78 per cent market share of India's natural gas transmission. ONGC is India's largest exploration and production company. Since 2002, other public sector enterprises have been given *miniratna* (minor jewel) status.

During the UPA's first term of office, there were some efforts to decrease the state share of energy-related *navaratnas*. Brown et al. (2008: 238) noted that despite the gradual privatization efforts, the state still holds a prominent share of India's energy-related companies, as shown in Table 9.4.

What is distinctive about the UPA's approach to the gradual privatization of energy-related *navaratnas* and *miniratnas* is that it sought to have these firms lead a drive for international collaboration. Brown *et al.* (2008: 240) noted that one of the UPA's most noteworthy efforts to reorganize India's energy sector was to make Oil India Limited (OIL) be the fulcrum for all downstream companies preparing overseas upstream opportunities. The UPA's institutional reforms paid off. In December 2005, China National Petroleum Corporation (CNPC) and ONGC submitted a joint bid for a minority stake in Syria's Al Furat Petroleum Company. Following the success of the joint bid, Indian and China officials signed a pact of mutual cooperation establishing consultations whenever each country's energy firms were preparing to make a bid on overseas oil and gas deposits (McGregor *et al.* 2006).

The UPA's manifesto proposed that 'overseas investments in the hydrocarbon industry will be actively encouraged' (UPA 2004). As such, it is not surprising that during the first term of the UPA government, Indian oil companies were encouraged to pursue oil exploration rights in other countries. One of these companies in particular, ONGC Videsh, now has exploration activities in 17 countries (see Table 9.5). It emerged as the leading player in the international activities of Indian oil companies abroad. During the UPA's first term of office, ONGC Videsh acquired oil and gas properties in Algeria, Indonesia, Kazakhstan, Libya, Russia, Sudan, Syria, and Vietnam.

As Table 9.5 shows, ONGC Videsh has majority share in three country projects. In addition to these projects, ONGC Videsh has ongoing holdings in Nigeria, Sao Tome and Principe, Brazil, Colombia, Qatar, Egypt, and Cuba.

Table 9.4 Proportion of total assets owned by the state in India's leading energy firms

Company name	Acronym	Total assets owned by the state (%)
Indian Oil Corporation Limited	IOC	80
Oil and Gas Corporation	ONGC	57
GAIL India Limited	GAIL	74
Oil India Limited	OIL	78.4
Hindustan Petroleum Corporation	HPCL	51
Bharat Petroleum Corporation Limited	BPCL	55
National Thermal Power Corporation	NTPC	89.5

Source: Data on the proportion of the state's share of company assets has been calculated by the author from data provided by Hoover's™ Company Records (2009) Ann Arbor, Michigan: Proquest Information and Learning.

Table 9.5 ONGC international holdings

Name of the project	Owned by ONGC Videsh (%)
Sudan pipeline	90
Syria project	60
Australia project	55
Libya project	49
Vietnam project	45
Iran project	40
Block 5A project (Sudan)	24.15
Block 5B project (Sudan)	23.5
Cote d'Ivorie project	23.5
Sakhalin project (Russia)	20
Myanmar project	20

Source: Data calculated by the author from Hoover's™ Company Records (2009) Ann Arbor, Michigan: Proquest Information and Learning

The UPA's external sector developments highlighted that there are institutional mechanisms to enable growing regional energy cooperation, namely with the United States, China, and, to a lesser extent, individual European countries. However, the UPA also attempted to develop closer international energy collaboration with its neighbours. The most obvious of these regional cooperation arrangements is the SAARC. At the SAARC summit, held in Dhaka in November 2005, India proposed the creation of a South Asia energy dialogue. However, there are other existing regional networks that could facilitate cooperation in energy security arrangements. For instance, India is a founding member of the Indian Ocean Rim Association for Regional Cooperation (IOR-ARC), a full dialogue partner of the Association for South East Asian Nations (ASEAN), and a participant in the Asian Cooperation Dialogue (ACD), the ASEAN Regional Forum (ARF), the Bay of Bengal Initiative for Multisectoral Technical and Economic Cooperation (BIMSTEC), and the Mekong-Ganga Cooperation (MGC) Initiative. Under the UPA leadership, few of these regional networks were fruitfully exploited.

Conclusion

The issue of India's energy security is likely to be one of India's most crucial challenges as it emerges as a growing power in the international community. Against this backdrop, this chapter has attempted to evaluate the UPA government's policies relating to India's energy security during its first term of office (2004–9). We began by defining energy security and how it has India-specific dimensions. It is clear that the UPA government did not pursue an energy security policy that was substantially different from its predecessor, the NDA coalition government, principally because there remains ample political consensus on preventing vulnerabilities to energy security. In this chapter we have also shown that India's policy planning process limits radical departures. Nevertheless, the UPA government did establish its imprint on a limited range of energy security policy developments relating to national coordination, sustainability, and international collaboration.

Although it is encouraging to note that there appears to be some policy consensus about the need to carry out reforms that affect India's energy security, there also appears to be a great deal of inertia about tackling the actual problems affecting the provision of a reliable and sustainable supply of energy to India's citizens. Fiscally irresponsible state government subsidies of electricity and poorly functioning state electricity boards point to a breakdown of energy generation, supply, and distribution. Moreover, India's energy supply has been hampered perennially by end-user-level leakage and pilfering. In sum, the problems emanating from India's inadequate supply of energy are daunting, and without decisive action will directly undermine the gains achieved from India's economic growth in recent years. Although the UPA government's consensus-driven policies in other policy fronts have proved productive, its timidity in addressing issues relating to energy security should be a cause for great concern.

Acknowledgements

The author would like to thank Kanti Bajpai, James Manor, Subrata Kumar Mitra, and Steven Wilkinson, for useful insights and comments to earlier drafts of this book chapter.

10 Anti-terrorism and security policy

Rahul Roy-Chaudhury

Introduction

The new Congress-led UPA coalition government that took office in May 2004 had to cope with a spurt in terror and violent attacks during its five-year term. This was due to several reasons: an intensification of attacks in India's major cities (including the 'spectacular' attack on Mumbai in November 2008), the rise in home-grown Indian *jihadi* terrorism, along with terror attacks by *Hindutva* extremist groups, and, for the first time, an attack on an Indian diplomatic mission abroad. In addition, violence continued in Jammu and Kashmir and the North-east. The ultra-left wing Maoist Naxalites also expanded their influence in eastern and central India.

These attacks were carried out by diverse groups, including Pakistan-based terrorist groups with reported links to its intelligence agencies, Indian religious extremists (both Islamic and *Hindutva*), Maoists, and ethnic insurgents. Consequently, the aim of these attacks varied, including a desire to disrupt India's growing international stature and discourage foreign engagement and investment; an attempt to disrupt the peace process with India's neighbour and bitter rival, Pakistan; efforts to provoke an extreme Hindu backlash on the minority Indian Muslim population (to destabilize India by alienating and isolating its 150-million strong Muslim community); the manifestation of what might be described as an Al-Qaeda mindset or a belief in a global conspiracy against Muslims; to seek independence for Kashmir and parts of the North-east; and to overthrow the government through a 'people's war'. These attacks invariably involved the use of guns and/or explosives. The number of casualties varied, with the July 2006 Mumbai blasts resulting in the highest number of people killed in a single event in the first UPA government. Significantly, no suicide bomb attacks took place in India during this period.

The impact of these terror and violent acts also varied considerably. While the attacks in Jammu and Kashmir and the North-east did not result in any substantial policy change by the Indian government, home-grown *jihadi* terrorism had considerable psychological impact on the government although little political impact. But, the expansion of Naxalite influence through violence led to the UPA government coordinating a major anti-Naxalite operation towards the end of its five-year term. The suicide car bombing of the Indian embassy in Kabul in July

2008 also served to raise India's stakes in the stability of Afghanistan. But, it was the brazen nature of the November 2008 Mumbai attack that shocked the first UPA government and led to significant changes in India's anti-terrorism policy and the management of national security, which continue to be implemented in the second UPA government.

Early perspectives

The first UPA government had succeeded the BJP-led NDA coalition government of 1999–2004. For much of this period, the NDA government's foreign and security policy had focused on a mixture of tension and conflict with Pakistan. An attempt to build relations with Pakistan through the Lahore bus journey by prime minister Atal Behari Vajpayee in February 1999 failed, with the Kargil conflict between the two countries in May–July 1999, less than a year after their nuclear weapons tests. Pakistan's president Musharraf's subsequent visit to Agra in July 2001 resulted in a fiasco and proved a setback to relations between the two countries. The attack on the Indian parliament on 13 December 2001 by Pakistan-based terrorist groups the *Lashkar-e-Taiba* (LeT) and the *Jaish-e-Mohamed* (JeM) led to a ten-month military confrontation between the two countries, the most serious in 30 years, with over 1 million armed men facing each other across the international border and the LAC (dividing Indian and Pakistan-administered Kashmir) amidst fears of escalation of the confrontation.

The NDA's official review of the Kargil conflict, *The Kargil Review Committee Report*, highlighted grave deficiencies in the management of national security, including intelligence gathering and assessment, border management and high-level defense management. As a result, the first comprehensive review of national security management in over 50 years was undertaken in 2000–1 by a select group of ministers (GoM) headed by home minister, L. K. Advani. The subsequent declassified version of the GoM report (Government of India, 2001) recommended significant changes, including the creation of the post of chief of defense Staff (CDS), the establishment of a Defense Intelligence Agency (DIA), more effective coastal security management and greater coordination between state and central intelligence agencies. All recommendations, with the exception of the establishment of a CDS, were approved by the Cabinet Committee on Security (CCS), the highest-level decision-making body on security, and begun to be undertaken by the NDA government. The GoM report also suggested that the next such review be carried out in five years.

But it was the ensuing peace process with Pakistan that the first UPA government primarily inherited from the NDA government. This had begun with Vajpayee's 'hand of friendship' speech in April 2003 and was followed by the significant bilateral meeting between Vajpayee and Musharraf on the sidelines of the SAARC summit in Islamabad in January 2004, leading to the start of the bilateral 'composite dialogue'. Consequently, the initial focus of the UPA government did not appear to be on terrorism or domestic security, as the UPA's May 2004 national CMP made clear. Stated to be the basis for 'collective maximum performance' for the UPA's constituent political parties, the section on 'Defense,

Internal Security' was placed towards the end of this 24-page document with the focus not on terrorism, but the repeal of the controversial anti-terror legislation, the Prevention of Terrorism Act (POTA) (UPA 2004).

POTA was enacted by the NDA government in March 2002 to be tough on terrorism in the wake of the December 2001 attack on the Indian parliament. POTA included a definition of terrorist 'acts', the banning of 32 terrorist organizations (including the LeT), punishment for the financing of terrorist activities, the appointment of special courts and designated judges, and the validity of communication intercepts as evidence. POTA allowed the detention of accused personnel for up to 180 days without the filing of charges, and prevented release on bail without the consent of the public prosecutor or the judge recording that the suspect was innocent. Under its terms, confessions made before the police – whether by torture or the threat of torture – were also admissible as evidence in court, as were communication intercepts.

But, in view of concerns over the abuse of this anti-terror law primarily against political opponents, the CMP signaled a conciliatory approach. It stated that 'the UPA has been concerned with the manner in which POTA has been grossly misused in the past two years. There will be no compromise in the fight against terrorism. But given the abuse of POTA that has taken place, the UPA government will repeal it, while existing laws are enforced strictly' (UPA 2004).

The UPA government also remained 'determined to tackle terrorism, militancy and insurgency in the northeast as a matter of urgent national priority', while pursuing a 'dialogue with Pakistan on all issues ... systematically and on a sustained basis' (UPA 2004). But, in a startling omission, there was no mention in the CMP of the threat posed by the Naxalites, even though the 2003–4 annual report of the ministry of home affairs clearly stated that 'Naxal violence continues to pose a serious challenge to internal security in the country' (Ministry of Home Affairs 2004: 2–3). It added that 55 districts in nine states were afflicted with Naxalism, with Naxal outfits laying 'special emphasis on militarization of their fighting formations by acquiring new technology, particularly relating to fabrication and firing mechanism for improvised explosive devices (IEDs) and weapons' (Ministry of Home Affairs 2004: 2–3). There was also no mention of the reforms of the national security apparatus that had begun to be implemented by the NDA government.

New national security team

The UPA's new national security team of cabinet ministers and senior officials with decision-making powers appeared to be mixed in terms of effectiveness. With the cabinet led by prime minister Manmohan Singh, Shivraj Patil, a seasoned politician and former speaker of the Lok Sabha (the directly elected lower House of Parliament), was appointed as the minister for home affairs, even though he had little prior experience of such a portfolio. As home minister, Patil was directly responsible to parliament for all domestic security issues. In view of his abysmal performance, Patil was removed as home minister on 30 November 2008, days after the 2008 Mumbai terror attack, and replaced by the suave and dynamic finance minister, P. Chidambaram. Chidambaram immediately set out on an ambitious agenda to transform national security management. The first defense minister was Pranab Mukherjee, the second most powerful minister in the cabinet after the prime minister. But, with Mukherjee appointed as foreign minister in October 2006, his successor as defense minister, A. K. Antony, a former chief minister of Kerala and Congress party stalwart, was primarily focused on ending corruption in arms acquisitions, a well-known affliction of his ministry. On Chidambaram's promotion as home minister, prime minister Manmohan Singh took on the additional charge of finance minister until the end of the first UPA government.

In addition, the legendary former chief of the domestic intelligence agency (the Intelligence Bureau (IB)), M. K. Narayanan, was the powerful national security advisor (NSA) to the prime minister for virtually the entire term of the first UPA government. Initially appointed as advisor (internal security) to the prime minister, Narayanan took over as NSA in January 2005 on the sudden demise of J. N. Dixit, a former diplomat and foreign secretary. As NSA, Narayanan played a key role in exercising control over the two powerful intelligence agencies, the domestic IB and the external Research and Analysis Wing (R&AW) of the cabinet secretariat. Although the chiefs of these two agencies traditionally reported to the home minister and prime minister, respectively, they would now often report directly to Narayanan. The most prominent IB chief during the first UPA government was Ajit Doval, an Indian Police Service (IPS) officer, even though he had a short tenure as chief, and that of R&AW was P. K. Hormis Tharakan, also an IPS officer, who served as chief in 2005–7.

Spurt in terror and violent attacks

Although the CMP had not highlighted terrorism, the UPA's new national security team quickly began to focus on this issue with the spurt in terror and violent attacks taking place. These attacks emanated from six main sources. The most significant were carried out predominantly by Pakistani nationals belonging to major Pakistan-based terrorist organizations, including the LeT and the JeM. These groups were widely believed to have links with Pakistan's security establishment, especially its military intelligence agency, the Inter-Services Intelligence (ISI) Directorate of the Pakistan army. Such attacks were exceedingly complicated in terms of response as they required countermeasures such as diplomatic pressure to be applied beyond India's borders. This was also the case for the sporadic attacks on Indian workers in development and civil reconstruction projects in Afghanistan, and the attack on the Indian embassy in Kabul on 7 July 2008, which killed 54 people, including two senior Indian diplomats and two Indian security personnel. India blamed 'elements' in Pakistan, essentially the ISI, for planning the July 2008 suicide attack on the Indian embassy, in association with the Pakistan-based Afghan Haqqani terror network.

In contrast, response to attacks by home-grown Indian *jihadi* groups, such as the Indian Mujahideen, could be carried out within the country, even though its links with the LeT were widely reported. While terror attacks in Kashmir were largely carried out by Pakistani or other foreign nationals belonging to the LeT or the *Harkat-ul-Mujahidin* (HUM), involvement of indigenous Kashmiri militants belonging to the *Hizbul Mujahideen* (HM) were rare. Attacks in the North-east emanated from a mix of Indian tribal and ethnic groups, while those in the largely rural and heavily forested parts of central and eastern India emanated from the Naxalites. While no cross-border support to the Naxalites was reported, some North-east groups established training camps across the border in Bhutan, Myanmar and Bangladesh, with reports of covert links with some intelligence officials in Bangladesh.

Although the first major terror attack took place in Kashmir the day after Manmohan Singh was sworn in as prime minister, it was the terror attack in the middle-class heart of the nation's capital on 29 October 2005 that jolted the government (see Table 10.1).

Table 10.1 Selected major terror attacks during the first UPA government (22 May 2004 – 21 May 2009)

Date	Location	Target	Group	No. of blasts	Killed	Injured
23/05/2004	Pir Panjal, Jammu and Kashmir	Military families bus	Hizbul Mujahideen (HM)	1	28	7
15/08/2004	Dhemaji town, Assam	Independence day parade	United Liberation Front of Asom (ULFA)	1	22	40
02–03/10/2004	Dimapur, Nagaland; Assam	Railway station; markets; electricity and gas infrastructure	National Democratic Front of Bodoland and ULFA	9	44	100
29/10/2005	New Delhi	Markets and bus	LeT	3	66	210
07/03/2006	Varanasi, Uttar Pradesh	Hindu temple; railway station	Indian Mujahideen	3	21	62
11/07/2006	Mumbai, Maharashtra	Trains	Students Islamic Movement of India (SIMI) or Indian Mujahideen & LeT	7	186	714
08/09/2006	Malegaon, Maharashtra	Mosque	Hindutva extremist group (suspected)	3	38	125
18/02/2007	Panipat, Haryana	Samjhauta Express train from Delhi to Lahore (Pakistan)	Hindutva extremist group (suspected)	2	68	50

continued overleaf

Date	Location	Target	Group	No. of blasts	Killed	Injured
18/05/2007	Hyderabad, Andhra Pradesh	Mecca mosque	Hindutva extremist group (suspected)	1	9	70
25/08/2007	Hyderabad, Andhra Pradesh	Outdoor amphitheatre; restaurant	Indian Mujahideen	2	43	80
11/10/2007	Ajmer	Sufi shrine	Hindutva extremist group (suspected)	1	3	30
23/11/2007	Lucknow, Faizabad Varanasi, Uttar Pradesh	Courthouses	Indian Mujahideen	6	13	59
13/05/2008	Jaipur, Rajasthan	Markets	Indian Mujahideen	9	65	200
07/07/2008	Kabul, Afghanistan	Indian embassy	Haqqani faction of Afghan Taliban	1	41	141
25/07/2008	Bangalore, Karnataka	Bus stand; near a hospital; army school; shopping centre; checkpoint	Indian Mujahideen	8	2	15
26/07/2008	Ahmedabad, Gujarat	Markets; hospital	Indian Mujahideen	17	53	110
13/09/2008	New Delhi	Markets; underground station; park	Indian Mujahideen	5	30	100
29/09/2008	Malegaon, Maharashtra	Near hotel	Hindu extremist groups Rashtriya Jagran Manch (RJM) and Abhinav Bharat	2	7	80
29/09/2008	Modasa, Gujarat	Mosque	Rashtriya Jagran Manch (RJM) and Abhinav Bharat	1	71	nk
30/10/2008	Guwahati; Kokrajhar; Barpeta Road; Bongaigaon, Assam	Markets; official buildings; oil refinery	ULFA	9	83	300
26–29/11/2008	Mumbai, Maharashtra	Railway station; cafe; Jewish centre; luxury hotels	LeT	na	164	300

Source: IISS Armed Conflict Database at http://www.iiss.org

Abbreviations: na = not applicable; nk = not known.

Three bomb blasts took place in two crowded markets and a bus, killing 66 people and injuring over 200, believed to be the handiwork of the LeT. Within a few months, bomb blasts at a Hindu temple and the main railway station in Varanasi killed 21 people and injured over 60; this was the first major attack carried out by the Indian Mujahideen. On 11 July 2006, seven bomb blasts took place within minutes of each other on suburban trains in Mumbai killing 186 people and injuring 714, while paralyzing the transportation and communication networks of India's financial and commercial capital. Subsequent police and intelligence investigations focused on a tie-up between an Indian Islamic militant group, the Students' Islamic Movement of India (SIMI) and the LeT; investigations also later focused on the Indian Mujahideen with LeT support.

Within a period of 14 months – from August 2007 to October 2008 – the Indian Mujahideen carried out bomb blasts in the major cities of Hyderabad, Lucknow, Varanasi, Jaipur, Bangalore, Ahmedabad and New Delhi, killing over 200 people and injuring nearly 600. This indicated the radicalization of a small section of India's Muslim community, with perhaps, a pan-islamic Salafi jihadist mindset of the sort attributed to members of Al Qaeda elsewhere. At the same time, *Hindutva* extremist groups were responsible for bomb blasts on 29 September 2008 at Malegaon in Maharastra and Modasa in Gujarat, which killed 8 people and injured over 80. The leader of the *Hindutva* extremist group, the *Rashtriya Jagran Manch* (RJM), Sadhvi Pragya Singh Thakur, was arrested for these blasts, along with members of the *Abhinav Bharat* (AB), including, for the first time, a serving officer in the Indian army, Lt. Col. Srikant Prasad Purohit. Investigations later also focused on suspected *Hindutva* extremist groups being responsible for an earlier terror attack in Malegaon (8 September 2006), along with the bombing of the Samjhauta Express train on 18 February 2007 (which killed nearly 70 people, mainly Pakistani nationals), and bomb blasts on the Mecca Masjid in Hyderabad (18 May 2007), and a prominent sufi shrine in Ajmer (11 October 2007), all of which had earlier been blamed on local Islamic extremist groups or the LeT with suspects held in prison. Meanwhile, major Naxal attacks included the killing of 55 security personnel in Chhattisgarh on 15 March 2007 and 38 police and commando personnel who drowned after their boat capsized from gunfire at the Balimela reservoir in Orissa on 29 June 2008 (see Table 10.2).

But, the most prominent terror attack during the first UPA government took place in Mumbai on 26–28 November 2008, when 10 terrorists armed with guns and explosives attacked several targets, including two luxury hotels and a Jewish centre, killing 164 people and injuring 300 people in a siege that lasted 60 hours. The sheer aggression and audacity of the attack shocked India and the world, which received live television broadcasts of the siege. For the first time, foreign nationals were specifically targeted and 26 killed. Nine out of the ten terrorists were killed; the tenth, Ajmal Amir Kasab, was captured by Indian security forces to face trial in Mumbai. All ten terrorists were Pakistani nationals belonging to the LeT.

Although the LeT has been active in Kashmir, which it aims to liberate from India, it is not a Kashmiri group. Its headquarters are located in Muridke, near Lahore in Pakistan's Punjab province. The overwhelming majority of its personnel

Table 10.2 Selected major attacks by Naxalites during the first UPA government (22 May 2004 – 21 May 2009)

Date	Location	Target	Killed	Injured
20/11/2004	Chakia, Uttar Pradesh	Police truck	18	5
24/06/2005	East Champaran, Bihar	Police station; banks	21	0
03/09/2005	Bijapur, Chhattisgarh	Security personnel	24	nk
28/02/2006	Dantewada, Chhattisgarh	Government-supported anti-Naxal group truck	25	40
17/07/2006	Errabore, Chhattisgarh	State-government-run civilian relief camp	31	100
04/03/2007	East Singhbhum, Chhattisgarh	Lok Sabha MP (JMM, Sunil Kumar Mahato)	4	–
15/03/2007	Rani Bodli, Chhattisgarh	Police- and government-supported anti-Naxal group camp	55	11
27/10/2007	Chikhadia, Jharkhand	Cultural event	18	8
15/02/2008	Nayagarh, Orissa	District armories; police stations	15	5
29/06/2008	Balimela reservoir, Orissa	Police and commandos light patrol boat	38	8
16/07/2008	Malkangiri, Orissa	Policemen	21	nk
01/02/2009	Gadchiroli, Maharashtra	Police patrol	15	–
09/02/2009	Nawada, Bihar	Police and civilians at a cultural show	11	3
21/05/2009	Gadchiroli, Maharashtra	Police patrol	16	–

Source: IISS Armed Conflict Database at http://www.iiss.org

Abbreviation: nk = not known.

are non-Kashmiris – largely Pakistani Punjabis and Pushtuns. Its aims and objectives are not limited to Kashmir; they are far grander. In addition to dealing with Kashmir and India, the LeT aims to wage jihad against non-Islamic governments in Southern and Central Asia, as well as against the West. The LeT is widely reported to have links with the Al Qaeda terrorist organization.

India's response

India's response to these terror attacks varied considerably. The terror attacks in Jammu and Kashmir and the North-east did not result in any significant change in government policy. The army and paramilitary forces continued their long-standing counter-terrorism and counter-insurgency operations in Kashmir even though the level of violence has reduced considerably since 2004, amidst signs of heightened militant activity and infiltration across the LAC. In 2008, the number of violent incidents in Jammu and Kashmir in comparison to 2004 had decreased by over 70 per cent to 708; the number of civilians killed had reduced by nearly 90 per cent to 91; and the number of security forces killed decreased by nearly 75 per cent to 75 (Ministry of Home Affairs 2009: 6). Subsequently, there was an increase in the role and involvement of the state police, with greater actionable intelligence being obtained from the local population. The system of unified headquarters, chaired by the chief minister, with senior representatives of the state government, army, central paramilitary forces and other security agencies continued to function in the state (Ministry of Home Affairs 2009: 6). The reduction of army troops from urban areas also took place, to be partially replaced by paramilitary and state police forces. The high voter turnout of 60 per cent at state elections at the end of 2008 was a boost to the local administration, as was the smooth conduct of the Lok Sabha elections in May 2009. However, defense minister Antony ruled out the repeal of the Armed Forces (Special Powers) Act, which provided the armed forces with immunity and extraordinary powers of arrest and detention in Kashmir as well as parts of the North-east, despite pressure from the local administration in Kashmir.

Meanwhile, the North-east continued to suffer from myriad local insurgencies, tribal and ethnic clashes, irredentist claims and problems associated with illegal immigration from neighbouring Bangladesh – all fuelled by narcotics trafficking, the proliferation of small arms and light weapons, and kidnappings and extortion. Surrounded by China, Bhutan, Myanmar and Bangladesh, this landlocked region is linked to central India only by the 22 kilometer-wide Siliguri corridor, known as the 'chicken neck'. Delhi, whose neglect of the region has certainly exacerbated its problems, is currently focusing on a 'carrot and stick' approach to the insurgencies, whose transnational dimensions make this a matter of foreign as well as domestic policy (International Institute for Strategic Studies 2004).

Army and paramilitary counter-insurgency operations continued in the major insurgency-affected provinces of Assam, Nagaland, and Manipur. Amidst pressure from the central government, Bhutan had taken military action in December 2003 against insurgent camps deep inside the dense jungles of southern Bhutan, alongside the Indo–Bhutan border; this had been followed by Myanmar in January 2004 (International Institute for Strategic Studies 2004). Until the election of the new Sheikh Hasina government in January 2009, Bangladesh had denied the presence of United Liberation Front of Asom (ULFA) militants in the country.

Meanwhile, the principal leaders of home-grown *jihadi* terrorism, primarily those of the Indian Mujahideen, were widely believed to have been arrested or killed by the end of the first UPA government. These included Indian Mujahideen (IM) co-founder Abdul Subhan Usman Qureshi and Mohammed Sadiq Israr Ahmed Sheikh, although recruitment reportedly continues to take place (International Institute for Strategic Studies 2009). Leaders of Hindu extremist groups, such as the RJM and the AB were also arrested.

But, it was the brazen nature of the November 2008 Mumbai attack that shocked the UPA government and led to diplomatic pressure – with a hint of military action – against Pakistan as well as to the enactment of a new anti-terrorism law and significant changes in the management of national and coastal security, which continue to be implemented in the second UPA government. The first UPA government's new counter-Naxal policy also included central government coordination of a major anti-Naxal operation.

Diplomatic pressure

Both the major terror attacks in Mumbai in July 2006 and November 2008 sharply raised tensions with Pakistan and disrupted their peace process. Although the government was initially cautious about blaming any particular terror group for the July 2006 attack, it soon began to implicate Pakistan in the blasts. On a visit to the blast sites in Mumbai on 14 July 2006, prime minister Manmohan Singh told reporters that the terror modules were 'instigated, inspired and supported by elements across the border without which they cannot act with such devastating effects' (Daily News and Analysis 2006). In a hardening stance, two days later, he noted Pakistan's commitment in January 2004 that its territory would not be used to promote terrorist acts, and that these commitments needed to be 'backed by action on the ground' (International Institute for Strategic Studies 2006a).

Islamabad, which had been one of the first capitals to condemn the bombings, refuted Singh's insinuation that the Mumbai bombers had received support from Pakistan as 'unsubstantiated allegations' (International Institute for Strategic Studies 2006a). It also emphatically stated that it did not allow its territory to be used against any other country, and strongly urged that the peace process continue. Nonetheless, the foreign secretary-level talks with Pakistan were subsequently postponed and talks with Pakistan were suspended till March 2007 when the first meeting of the joint anti-terrorism mechanism took place.

Even as the November 2008 terror attacks were underway, prime minister Manmohan Singh stated in a deeply emotional voice that it was 'evident that the group which carried out the attacks is based outside the country' and added that 'we will tell our neighbours that their territory being used to carry out attacks in India will not be tolerated' (International Institute for Security Studies 2008). Soon afterwards, foreign minister Pranab Mukherjee blamed 'elements in Pakistan' for the attack (External Affairs Minister Mr. Pranab Mukherjee's Suo Motu statement in Parliament 2009). In January 2009, Singh raised the ante by asserting the involvement of 'official agencies' in Pakistan, which Islamabad denied. Calling Pakistan the 'epicenter of terrorism', India demanded that it act against those responsible for the attacks (Indo-Asian News Service 2009).

With both countries putting their armed forces on alert, there was considerable media speculation that India would mount a 'surgical' strike or carry out a 'limited' military operation against LeT camps and infrastructure in Pakistan. But, this did not take place nor was there any military mobilization on either side. Instead, India focused on mounting international pressure on Pakistan through the US and the UK to take action against LeT personnel and dismantle its infrastructure.

Although Pakistan belatedly admitted that Kasab was a Pakistani national and the attacks were partly planned in Pakistan, it denied all accusations of official Pakistani involvement in the Mumbai attack. The trial in Pakistan of seven suspected conspirators of the Mumbai terror attack, including LeT commander Zakiur Rehman Lakhvi, remains slow-paced. While India blamed 'elements' in

Pakistan for continuing to nurture and fund the LeT, it upped the ante in 2010 following the confessions of LeT operative David Coleman Headley aka Daoud Sayed Gilani, and now holds serving officers of the ISI or 'retired' military officers employed on contract by the ISI (although not its leadership) responsible for planning and coordinating the 2008 Mumbai terror attacks. These accusations have been strongly denied by Pakistan. Yet, with the alleged 'mastermind' of the Mumbai attacks, LeT chief Hafiz Muhammad Saeed's release from house arrest, India continues to face the threat of another major LeT terror attack.

New anti-terror legislation

In order to enhance security after the Mumbai attacks and respond to incessant opposition BJP criticism that the government was 'soft' on terror, the UPA government toughened its anti-terror legislation. This served to bolster already existing anti-terror legislation, primarily the ordinary Code of Criminal Procedures, the Unlawful Activities (Prevention) Act (UAPA) of 1967 and the National Security Act of 1980 (although the latter is notably a preventive, not a punitive, law). Although India's first specific anti-terror law, the Terrorist and Disruptive Activities (Prevention) Act (TADA), had been enacted in 1987, it was allowed to lapse in 1995 in view of its misuse against political opponents. Subsequently, the tough anti-terror POTA enacted by the BJP-led NDA in 2002 was repealed by the UPA government in 2004, in accordance with the CMP. In its place, the UAPA was amended in 2004 to make provisions for dealing with terrorist offences and terrorist organizations.

As a result of the 2008 Mumbai terror attack the UPA government further amended UAPA though the Unlawful Activities (Prevention) Amendment Act 2008 (of 16 December 2008) by strengthening the provisions for dealing with terrorism. This new legislation provides extensive and wide-ranging powers to the police in the event of suspicion or the involvement of a suspect in a terrorist act; a new clause empowers an officer to search any premises or arrest any person about whom he or she has 'reason to believe or knows' has a 'design' to commit an offence under the Act. Failure of organizations and individuals to furnish information under the Act required by an investigative officer is also punishable with imprisonment for up to three years. Police custody of suspects has been doubled to 30 days.

Most controversially, the period for which terror suspects can be held without charge has been doubled from the existing 90 days to 180 days, the longest for any democratic state, although the court can limit detention to 90 days. Although this is similar to the repealed POTA, confessions to the police remain inadmissible as evidence in the court of law as do interception of messages or telephonic communication.

Creation of a new federal investigative agency

After failures in the past to create a federal investigative agency, due to opposition from a number of state chief ministers that law and order was a state subject, and not on the concurrent or central lists, the Indian government finally pushed through legislation establishing a new National Investigative Agency (NIA) in December 2008. The NIA Act sets up the NIA at a national level to investigate terrorist offences under eight major laws, including the Atomic Energy Act and the Anti-Hijacking Act.

Operating under the jurisdiction of the central government, NIA officials have the unique mandate to investigate and prosecute on a country-wide basis terrorist cases with inter-state and international ramifications. All other cases lie with state governments. In addition, special courts for speedier trials are also being set up. Special judges are to be appointed within seven days of any scheduled offence. Appeal provisions will lie with the division bench of the High Court, who are expected to deal with an appeal within three months. The first chief of the NIA, Radha Vinod Raju, was a highly experienced police officer with considerable experience in high-profile criminal investigations.

Strengthening the intelligence establishment

In a comprehensive review of intelligence collection, analysis, assessment and coordination, the GoM report on national security (February 2001) reportedly recommended measures such as the formation of a Multi-Agency Centre (MAC) for intelligence coordination, the boosting of the Joint Intelligence Committee (JIC), which was tasked to assess intelligence, and the creation of the DIA. But, implementation of these measures lagged in the UPA government. While the MAC had been created in the IB in the home ministry, it was not empowered; JIC expansion did not take place; and the DIA chief invariably found himself locked in an administrative battle with the chief of military intelligence rather than being responsible for the coordination of military intelligence from all three service headquarters.

But, in a welcome step the NSA, M. K. Narayanan, revived the JIC by appointing a stand-alone chairman and separating it from the National Security Council Secretariat (NSCS) (Varadarajan 2010). This was the correct decision as it was quite impractical for the NSCS staff to perform the tasks of long-term strategic policy planning as well as intelligence coordination and assessment. These tasks are fundamentally different and require quite different expertise. While the former requires a fundamental understanding of key medium and long-term global strategic trends along with access to largely non-classified material, the latter requires short-term tactical perspectives based, to a large extent, on classified information provided by the intelligence collection agencies. If anything, a separate but related group, possibly within the JIC, was also needed to perform strategic tasking functions as it was difficult to ensure objectivity in tasking from those involved in tactical assessment functions. But, this move was not accompanied by a commensurate increase in the total staff strength of the NSCS and JIC (Varadarajan 2010).

Following the 2008 Mumbai terror attack and the absence of action-orientated intelligence from R&AW, several steps were also undertaken to strengthen the intelligence establishment. On 31 December 2008 the MAC was bolstered with a broader and compulsory membership and empowered to function as an inter-agency counter-terrorism centre aimed at analyzing intelligence flowing from varied sources, especially state intelligence bureaus, as well as coordinating follow-up action. Twenty-nine subsidiary MACs (SMACs) have been established in several state capitals. The home minister also now chairs a daily security and intelligence meeting, which includes the NSA, home secretary and IB and R&AW chiefs (Chidambaram 2009). The IB and the State Intelligence Bureaus (SIBs) are also being expanded. In addition, the establishment of a National Intelligence Grid (NATGRID) has been planned to evolve online real-time intelligence flows between the centre and the states, as is also the establishment of a controversial National Counter Terrorism Centre (NCTC) (into which MAC is to be incorporated) by the end of 2010.

Security restructuring

Due largely to the Mumbai terror attack, the 2009–10 interim defense budget passed on 16 February 2009 with general elections a few weeks away, steeply increased defense spending by a third to Rs 141,703 crores (US$32 billion), in contrast to an increase of a tenth the previous year. The recruitment of security personnel was a key requirement, with India possessing less than half the international average of available police per 100,000 people. Accordingly, home minister Chidambaram plans to expand police forces by 400,000 in the next three years (*Rediff News* 2009). India is spending additional funds on the modernization and expansion of its seven paramilitary forces, including the setting up of 38 new battalions (about 39,000 security personnel) in the Central Reserve Police Force (CRPF), and the acquisition of arms and equipment for its police forces, while fast-tracking arms and equipment for its commandos and special forces. The National Security Guards (NSGs) are to be strengthened and provided regional hubs. The Special Branch of state police forces is also being restructured. A new unique identity card (UIC) scheme for each citizen is to be implemented in the next three years.

Overhaul of coastal security

At the same time, a major overhaul of India's coastal and maritime security, whose inadequacy enabled the terrorists to reach Mumbai's shore, is being carried out. But, deficiencies in India's coastal security were fairly well known. The February 2001 GoM Report had warned:

> *India's long coastline and coastal areas have remained largely unprotected and unguarded.* The presence of the Coast Guard is minimal. For a country of our size, the Coast Guard must be a strong and vibrant organization. There is also need for a greater clarity in the role of the State Governments vis-à-vis the Coast Guard in so far as shallow water surveillance of the coasts is concerned.
>
> International Institute for Strategic Studies 2008, author's emphasis

Even though these recommendations had been approved by the CCS, they were yet to be implemented at the time of the 2008 Mumbai terror attacks.

In jurisdictional terms, the marine police of individual coastal states and island territories were responsible for patrolling and surveillance from the shoreline to the 12 nautical mile limit of the territorial waters, with the coast guard responsible for the 12–200 nautical mile maritime zone comprising the contiguous zone and the exclusive economic zone (EEZ). The navy's responsibilities were largely focused on the high seas. However, in practice things were quite different. Most coastal states did not have marine police forces or police stations focusing on the coastal or offshore environment; nor did they have sufficient funds, infrastructure or manpower to carry out these tasks. As a result, there were overlapping tasks and jurisdictions among the coastal states, the coast guard and the navy, with little responsibility or accountability.

Following the establishment of a marine police force in the Andaman and Nicobar Islands, the 2001 GoM report recommended the establishment of specialized marine police in all coastal states and island territories. As a result, a coastal security scheme was formulated and approved by the CCS in January 2005, which aimed to establish 73 coastal police stations, 97 check posts, 58 outposts and 30 operational barracks by 2010. Yet, this was badly delayed, with minimal implementation by late 2008.

Facing considerable criticism for the lack of coastal security, Indian naval chief Admiral Sureesh Mehta acknowledged a 'systemic failure' but maintained that neither the navy nor coast guard had received any actionable intelligence from the country's intelligence services. Subsequently, on 28 February 2009 defense minister Antony announced five key steps to bolster coastal security (Government of India, Ministry of Defence, 2009).

- *First.* The navy was designated as the nodal authority responsible for overall maritime security, both coastal and offshore. The navy would be assisted in these tasks by the coast guard, the state marine police and state agencies.
- *Second.* The coast guard was to be additionally responsible for security in the areas patrolled by the marine police, from the shoreline to 12 nautical miles. The director general coast guard was to be designated as commander coastal command and would be responsible for overall coordination between central and state agencies in all matters relating to coastal security. A new coast guard regional headquarters in Gujarat, under the newly created post of commander coast guard, north-west, was to be established to look after surveillance of the coastal state. In addition, nine coast guard stations were to be set up at Karwar, Ratnagiri, Vadinar, Gopalpur, Minicoy, Androth, Karaikal, Hutbay and Nizamapatnam, to be integrated with coastal police stations and police check posts.
- *Third.* To better coordinate navy–coast guard functions, Joint Operation Centres (JOCs) were set up at Mumbai, Vishakapatnam, Cochin and Port Blair under the charge of existing naval commanders-in-chief, to be designated as commanders-in-chief of coastal defense. These centres were to be jointly manned and operated by the navy and coast guard with inputs from

central and state intelligence and other agencies, with the navy controlling all
navy–coast guard joint operations.
- *Fourth.* The coast guard and marine police were to be strengthened and
expanded. A new air squadron with Dornier maritime surveillance aircraft
was to be activated in Porbandar in Gujarat. The navy was to be provided a
new specialized force, the *Sagar Prahari Bal* (Maritime Protection Force),
comprising a thousand personnel and 80 fast interception craft for protecting
naval assets and bases. The coast guard was to acquire additional ships,
aircraft and helicopters, as its current fleet of 74 ships, 45 aircraft and 8,000
personnel was inadequate for its tasks, representing a third of required capability. The intelligence set-up of the coast guard was also to be improved.
- *Fifth.* A national command, control, communication and intelligence network
for real-time maritime domain awareness between the operations rooms of
the navy and the coast guard was to be established. A chain of radar stations
was to be set up on the coast and island territories to include sensors for
identification of vessels near the coast. A vessel and air traffic management
system for all offshore development areas was to be carried out.

In addition, on 18 June 2009 the government set up a high-level committee under
the chairmanship of the cabinet secretary to review measures taken for coastal security at regular intervals. The other members of the committee include the chief of
naval staff, secretaries of all the ministries concerned with coastal security including
defense, home and petroleum, and the chief secretaries of all coastal states.

In essence, these steps are to enhance maritime and coastal security, notwithstanding confusion between the navy and coast guard over the relationship
between existing naval commanders-in-chief designated as commanders-in-chief
of coastal defense and the director general coast guard designated as commander
coastal command. While the former are to head JOCs on coastal defense with the
navy controlling all navy–coast guard joint operations, the latter, in a contradictory manner, is to be responsible for overall coordination between central and
state agencies in all matters relating to coastal security. Also, it remains to be
seen how effective coordination between the navy and coast guard, along with
other ministries/departments/agencies will actually be. Nonetheless, joint navy–
coast guard exercises to counter terrorism have been held, with the involvement
of local fishermen. India's new maritime doctrine (August 2009) also incorporates
new constabulary missions for the navy, including counter-terrorism and antipiracy operations. For the first time it states that India's maritime forces could be
deployed on specific counter-terror missions 'both independently and as cooperative endeavours with friendly foreign naval and coast guard forces' (International
Institute for Strategic Studies 2010: 336).

International cooperation

India has also attempted to bolster international cooperation to counter terrorism
through the UN and the SAARC, with mixed results. India's Draft Comprehensive
Convention against International Terrorism, submitted to the UN, awaits further

action. India has also established bilateral JWGs on terrorism, to coordinate and share intelligence on terrorists and related infrastructure (for instance, administrative, financial and logistical) with other countries including the US, Israel and the EU.

India's most important foreign intelligence relationship is with the US, notwithstanding the latter's well-publicized penetration of India's intelligence community in the past. US electronic communication intercepts of the Haqqani terrorist network enabled the Indian embassy in Kabul to improve security at its mission hours before the July 2008 suicide car bomb blast. Subsequently, the *New York Times* reported unnamed US government officials as stating that evidence existed to support claims of ISI complicity in the attack (Swami 2008). US intelligence also reportedly warned Indian security officials of a potential maritime attack against Mumbai at least a month before the November 2008 attack (CNN 2008).

But, even though the SAARC Regional Convention on the Suppression of Terrorism was adopted over 20 years ago, followed by an additional protocol in 2004, little has been actually achieved. At the 15th SAARC summit in Colombo in August 2008, the leaders of the eight SAARC member countries (including India, Pakistan, Bangladesh and Afghanistan) drew attention to the growing linkages between terrorism, narco-trafficking, and the illegal trafficking of fire arms and people. This underscored the need to address these problems in a comprehensive manner. Accordingly, they reiterated their commitment to strengthen the legal regime against terrorism and signed the 'SAARC Convention on Mutual Legal Assistance'. This expects member countries to grant to each other the 'widest possible' measure of mutual legal assistance in criminal matters. In compliance with the convention, once a SAARC member nation encounters a terrorist attack, it would provide the member nation with a broad framework for SAARC member states to mutually cooperate and assist in tracking down criminals and freezing their capital, as well as in the investigation and prosecution of crimes. However, implementation is lacking. The Colombo declaration also stated that member nations resolved to implement all international conventions relating to combating terrorism and recognized the salience of the wide-ranging anti-terrorism United Nations Security Council Resolution 1373 (2001), which called for the suppression of terrorist financing and improved international cooperation.

Countering Maoists/Naxalites

With nearly 300 people killed in Naxalite violence in the first four months of 2006, the level of violence exceeded that in Kashmir for the first time. With this intensification of violence, prime minister Manmohan Singh in April 2006 described the Naxalites as India's 'single biggest internal security challenge' (International Institute for Strategic Studies 2006b). Yet, their influence continued to expand during the first UPA government. Naxal violence in 55 districts in 9 states in early 2004 had spread to 87 districts in 13 states five years later (Ministry of Home Affairs 2009). The worst affected states included Chhattisgarh, Andhra Pradesh,

Jharkhand, Bihar, Orissa, West Bengal and Maharashtra. In 2008, 1,591 incidents of Naxalite violence resulted in 721 killings; in the first eight months of 2009, 1,405 incidents of Naxal violence resulted in 580 killings. Whereas 231 security force personnel were killed in Naxal violence in 2008, 250 were killed in the first eight months of 2009 (Ministry of Home Affairs 2009).

The most significant Naxalite attacks shifted from the eastern province of Andhra Pradesh to the central province of Chhattisgarh. On 3 September 2005, the Naxalites killed 24 security personnel in Dantewada. On 28 February 2006, 25 people were killed and 40 injured in a landmine blast near Eklagoda village in Dantewada. On 17 July 2006 approximately 400 Naxalites attacked a controversial civil militia *Salwa Judum* (peace campaign) camp at Errabore, killing 31 villagers. In one of the most prominent attacks so far, 55 police/security personnel were killed by Naxalites at Rani Bodli on 15 March 2007.

Although the Naxalites were formed nearly 40 years ago during the peasant uprising in Naxalbari village in West Bengal – from where they derive their name – the key difference today is that their organization, the Communist Party of India – Maoists (CPI (Maoists)), are far better organized and coordinated, and ideologically motivated, with greater reach. Their extreme left-wing ideological basis remains the establishment of a Maoist 'people's government' through a revolutionary armed struggle or 'people's war'. The Naxalites are spurred on in large parts of rural India by stark poverty, severe unemployment, tribal and caste inequalities, the absence of land reforms and bad governance.

The focus of Naxalite attacks continues to be in rural areas; in some parts they run a parallel administration collecting 'taxes' and meting out rough justice. But, the Naxalites have not yet carried out a major attack in an urban area, nor has any high-value political target been killed by the Naxalites. Their most high-profile attack on 1 October 2003 against Andhra Pradesh chief minister, Chandrababu Naidu, failed. But, in March 2007, they shot dead a member of parliament, Sunil Kumar Mahato, in Jharkhand. In October 2007 they also killed the younger son of former Jharkhand chief minister Babulal Marandi in Jharkhand.

Attempts by the central and state governments to tackle this low-intensity guerrilla war lack coherence and focus, with potentially grave economic and political consequences. While the central government advocates a 'carrot and stick' approach through a nuanced political and developmental strategy, provincial governments responsible for law and order by the federal constitution continue to see it largely as a 'policing' problem. Also, inter-provincial security coordination in intelligence and joint operations remains weak, compounded by a lack of intelligence on the ground.

Nonetheless, the central government has raised 11 battalions of the paramilitary CRPF for counter-Naxal operations, deployed additional security forces when requested by the states, released additional funds to bolster state and local police and intelligence forces, and provided key mine detection equipment, satellite imagery and armored vehicles to provinces. Central government-funded employment-generation and social security schemes, such as the national rural employment guarantee program, also incorporate the tribal belt of central and eastern India.

In October 2004, a task force – under the chairmanship of the special secretary (internal security) in the home ministry – was established; in September 2005, a standing committee of Naxal-affected chief ministers, chaired by the central home minister, was set up to coordinate measures to deal with the Naxalites. The latter proposed the creation of an inter-provincial task force to coordinate police action. In addition, an empowered group of ministers (EGoM) under the chairmanship of the home minister was set up to review and monitor all aspects of a coordinated approach to Naxalite violence, as was a coordination centre chaired by the home secretary and an Inter-Ministerial Group (IMG) headed by the newly appointed additional secretary for Naxal management in the home ministry.

Even though home minister P. Chidambaram announced that the government was ready to hold a dialogue with the Naxalites provided they give up arms – a precondition that they rejected – the ban on the CPI (Maoists) as a terror organization was formally renewed on 22 June 2009. This brought into sharp focus differences over the use of air power against the Naxalites. While the air force wanted to use force against the Naxalites in self-defense during surveillance and search and rescue operations, the government refused permission to do so. A new anti-Naxalite force, the Commando Battalion for Resolute Action (CoBRA), was also being set up under the command and control of the CRPF. Subsequently, the central government prepared to coordinate a new anti-Naxalite plan that included the deployment of over 40,000 central police personnel in states worst affected by the Naxalites. In addition, development aid has been promised for the worst Naxalite-affected areas. Yet, Naxalite leaders including general secretary of the CPI (Maoists), Muppala Lakshman Rao (alias *Ganapati*), chief of the Central Military Commission, Nambala Keasava Rap (alias *Basavaraju*), and chief of the military wing, Mallojula Koteshwar Rao (alias *Kishenji*) continue to evade arrest.

Conclusion

The new Congress-led UPA coalition government that took office in May 2004 quite suddenly had to cope with a spurt in terror and violent attacks during its five-year term. The most prominent was the November 2008 Mumbai attack that shocked the government and led to significant changes in India's anti-terrorism and security policy. These included new and harsh anti-terror legislation, the creation of a new federal investigative agency, the strengthening of the intelligence establishment, security restructuring, overhaul of coastal security, international counter-terror cooperation, and countering Maoists/Naxalites. Several of these changes are ambitious and continue to be implemented in the second UPA government. Nonetheless, these changes represent a major reform of India's national security and management and anti-terror policies, although their outcome remains to be seen.

11 Conclusion

Gurharpal Singh and Lawrence Sáez

If the performances of governments in India were measured in relation to their public pronouncements or legislation passed, then India would probably rank among first world states. Fortunately, as most hardened observers of Indian politics know only too well, there is a vast chasm between official public policy pronouncements and their effectiveness (Weiner 1990; Echeverri-Gent 1993; Jenkins 1999). Seminal analyses of comparative public policy formulation (e.g. Smith 1973) suggest that governments in developing countries have a tendency to formulate broad, sweeping policies. However, governmental bureaucracies in these countries often lack the capacity for the implementation of such idealized policies. Examined from this perspective, interest groups, opposition parties, and affected individuals and groups often attempt to influence the implementation of policy rather than the formulation of policy. In a large, diverse federal country such as India – in which the main agent of executive action is often the state government – it is not always policies or legislation that makes the difference between governments, but their *implementation*. This gap, between policy and implementation, between passing legislation nationally and seeing it executed at the local level, is a little understood black box in Indian public policy.

Sometimes this disjunction arises because governments deliberately – and intentionally – frame policies in ways that make their execution difficult (Nayar 1992). Sometimes it is the result of insufficient resources being allocated to policies or the introduction of vague pieces of legislation that make their implementation meaningless (Sáez 2009). At other times this ineffectiveness is the product of states appropriating the center's initiatives for their own ends (Jenkins 1999, 2003; Sáez 1999, 2002; Sinha 2005). Yet, more often than not, for most governments in New Delhi, whether they are coalitions or not, there is a considerable mismatch between policy intent, its actual design and the eventual outcome – an all too obvious dissonance that in no little measure is related to contemporary governance, underpinned as it is by the exigencies of coalition politics.

As the second UPA government (2009–?), with only a year and half into its new term of office, appears to be unraveling before a series of corruption scandals, there is the all too familiar feeling of *déjà vu* with its whiff of scams and rampant cronyism de-railing the administration.[1] In public discourses at least, the analogies between Dr Manmohan Singh's Congress-led UPA and Nehru's Congress now seem widely off the mark and may well remain as the fanciful imaginings of party courtiers. Indeed, as the ghost of Bofors[2] once more rears its head, all the claims of the first – and probably the second – UPA government are in a danger of being washed away in a tidal wave of graft (Ramakrishnan 2011).

However, even the harshest critics of the UPA would recognize that it is probably unfair to view the record of its first administration in light of its current difficulties. The selection of chapters presented in this volume provide detailed insights into what we identified at the outset as areas of policy representing clear blue water between the NDA and the UPA: issues of governance, secularism and security. But translating these differences into policy has proved difficult. Most of the chapters draw our attention to some common challenges that were encountered in delivering on these fronts. For example, as Fennell has demonstrated, in education the UPA missed a great opportunity to establish a coherent educational reform: far too often there were contradictory and overlapping initiatives. Such duplication was also in evidence in the approach towards minorities. The chapters by Singh, Wilkinson and Rochana Bajpai all highlight the overlapping initiatives that sometimes worked to negate the original intent of the CMP. In some areas, for instance federalism and energy security, there was a marked reluctance to take long-term decisions, though the nuclear fuel processing deal with the US was a notable exception. As result, Sáez has concluded, the implications for energy security in the medium term remain quite serious and it is questionable whether even a significant expansion in nuclear power can adequately fulfill India's energy needs. Yet, perhaps most important of all, political considerations played a major part in tempering UPA's delivery on the key issues. In dealing with the fallout from the 2002 Gujarat riots, or the proposal from the inquiries and commissions on minorities, the Congress-led UPA proved itself more adept at exploiting their rhetorical advantage rather than delivering firm outcomes. In fact, in some cases – Liberhan Commission, the anti-Sikh riots and the pogroms against Christians in Orissa – one could argue that it was deliberately duplicitous. And though, arguably, this is perhaps to be expected in the rough trade that is politics, especially in India, the feigning of intent was also accompanied by under-resourcing some flagship schemes. Thus, in education, Fennell observes, the UPA's under-funding of key programs has reinforced the trends towards exclusion and marginalization.

Nowhere has the contrast between the UPA's rhetoric and its actions been starker than in dealing with the minorities, especially Muslims, whose votes were crucial to the coalition's electoral victory in some important states in the 2009 general election.[3] The Mishra Commission report, which, through affirmative action, offers a mechanism for translating many of these proposals into policy, was only tabled before Parliament in November 2009 without an 'action-taken report' – which would make clear whether its recommendations had been accepted by the UPA government or not. Less than half of the funds that were allocated to minority schemes in the Eleven Year Plan (2007–12) in its first three years (2007–10) have actually been spent. In the much publicized MSDP for minorities focusing on 90 districts of Muslim concentration, only half of the promised funding had been outlaid. Overall, among the Muslim groups campaigning for the full realization of the UPA's promises there is a pervasive feeling of inaction, delay and systemic under-funding (Rajlakshmi 2011).

Such shortfalls in policy implementation, it could reasonably be argued, are the natural hazards of any government. However, in the case of the first UPA administration, this defense would appear to be threadbare, as some of its policy commitments on governance, secularism and security, as we have seen in the chapters presented in the volume, formed the core of the Congress party's manifesto and the UPA's CMP. In the event, the first UPA administration performed poorly in these fields and frittered away a historic opportunity to undertake long-term structural reforms in the economy, governance and social policy that could have firmly signaled a radical reforming agenda and would have been a worthy successor to the Congress administration in 1991 that had ushered in economic liberalization.

If the first UPA administration failed to live up to its own CMP, then what are the distinctive legacies of the government? What, if any, is likely to be its historical imprint on contemporary Indian politics? Drawing on the chapters presented in this volume, we would like to draw attention to four aspects.

First, the UPA experience suggests that *ideology matters*. This not to argue that ideological differences can explain *all* the substantive policy variations between the Congress-led UPA and the BJP-led NDA coalitions. The rise of caste and regional parties has accelerated the non-ideological pursuit of political interest. Similarly, India's centralized Five Year plans have a tendency to pre-empt large deviations in policy across different governments. Rather, it is to note, as Manor, Bhattacharyya, Fennell, Rochana Bajpai, Kanti Bajpai, and Sáez have done, that it is important for framing polices, for the political rhetoric that is used to construct and deliver them, and for identifying the targeted social recipients of government action – OBCs, minorities, and women. In all these areas the Congress-led UPA made great play of its idea of an India that is religiously tolerant and secular, accommodates pluralism and diversity, and in which social justice and equality go in tandem with the economic growth of today's 'shining India'. This emphasis may well have been accentuated by the bitter experience of Hindu nationalism in government with its exclusive conception of India, or the need to rebuild Congress's historic relationship with India's minorities. Nonetheless, it provided a governing framework that has proved to be not without significant levels of political support. That the Congress-led UPA was unable restore this framework to its pristine Nehruvian ideals is, of course, an entirely different matter.

Second, *style matters* as much as policy substance. As shown in Adeney and Sáez (2005), the BJP-led NDA government had marked a sharp break with previous administrations in crucial policy areas. Its external and domestic policies were characterized by such excesses as 'coercive diplomacy', hegemonic assertion of *Hindutva* values (particularly in education policy), and unrivalled political belligerence. In contrast, the Manmohan Singh–Sonia Gandhi leadership of the UPA signaled a distinctly different style, one that has privileged quiet diplomacy, a negotiatory approach and the traditional emphasis on consensus. These differences were not insignificant. According to Kanti Bajpai, they were central to UPA's measured response to the 2008 terrorist attacks in Mumbai, in dealing with China on the thorny issue of the boarder and trade and, above all, in the strained negotiations with the US and Pakistan. They were also a valuable resource in dealing with domestic policy issues such as education and federalism and troublesome coalition supporters (e.g. the Left parties). This style, perhaps best epitomized in the steely, but quiet determination of the Prime Minister himself, Dr Manmohan Singh, became the new brand name of a 'responsible' rather than 'resurgent' India.

Third, the first UPA administration signals the Congress party's conversion to reservation-based identity politics. Since the implementation of the Mandal Commission, the political landscape in India has changed irreversibly with the rise of Dalit parties and Hindu nationalism. Yet, despite the loss of its hegemony – in the 1990s and early 2000s – for almost a decade the Congress eschewed coalition politics and struggled to overcome its innate opposition to the extension of reservation to non-SCs and STs. Nationally the first UPA government, as Rochana Bajpai has explained at length, signaled something of a sea change on the party's outlook. Today an egalitarian conception of social justice buttresses the political case for the extension of identity-based reservations. In this respect the Congress was a late convert to a *polity-wide shift* initiated by the Mandal debate. In announcing its embrace of the new realities of Indian politics, it has also sought to exploit their political potential. Hence, the reservations for the Muslim OBCs have been proposed on grounds of their 'development deficit', a manoeuvre that is, ironically, intended to eviscerate the element of 'identity' in the discussion of the Muslim question in India. Hence the decision to enumerate caste in the 2011 census despite a long-standing opposition to such an enumeration since Independence. And hence the new architecture of equal opportunities – the proposals for an equal opportunities commission, the diversity index – and the commitment in principle to consider reservations in the private sector. As a recent convert to reservations, beyond the traditional categories accepted by the Constitution (1950), the Congress party now exudes the zeal of a neophyte. In so doing the Congress and its allies – especially in light of the post-2011 census results' implications for reservations – may well succeed in out-manoeuvring their opponents in the next Lok Sabha elections.

Finally, the UPA experience has ushered in what Manor in his chapter has termed *post-clientelistic politics*. Manor's account of the UPA's anti-poverty programs has shown that most were formulated against the background of a weak Congress party organization that was largely moribund or dominated by flatterers and fawners. Thus, in the absence of a party organization that can deliver or build effective networks of patrons and clients, the Congress-led UPA has opted for mass programs as a better way to deliver and – presumably – secure governance. This strategy, of course, has been underwritten by a growth in government revenues and a desire to position the Congress party, at least in the public imagination, as a progressive pro-poor social democratic party. But it is a high risk strategy. Not only does it encourage outbidding by its opponents (e.g. BJP) but it also has the echoes of political populism *à la* Indira Gandhi and her slogan '*garibi hatao*' (eradicate poverty). As the dismal records of many a state populist leader in India attest, for a weak leader-centered party such policies are destined to end in grave disappointment, however they are framed or 'better' targeted at the poor. True, thus far, the UPA has been fortunate in avoiding a balance of payments crisis or a severe fiscal crunch. But in a less benign economic climate, on the other hand, post-clientelistic politics are a recipe for a demand overload that has conventionally been associated with social democratic parties (King 1975).

Clearly the Congress-led UPA government came to power at a critical juncture in India politics when many of the accepted conventions of post-1947 politics were turned on their head by the experience of the BJP-led NDA coalition government. As such it not only had the opportunity to restore the *status quo ante,* but also to undertake a radical transformation that would have created substantial hurdles in the path of any future BJP-led NDA administration committed to reversing its achievements. Although it is probably too premature to write the final epitaph of this administration, it would certainly not be too uncharitable to say that the first UPA government (2004–9) was not so much a big bang as a damp squib. With corruption, issues of national security and the specter of communal violence now engulfing the second UPA administration in power, suddenly it has the look of a tired and exhausted Congress administration of old.

Notes

Chapter 2

1. I am grateful to the Nuffield Foundation for a research grant that enabled me to travel to India to study the 2009 general election. This chapter was written before the publication of a special number of the *Economic and Political Weekly* containing detailed studies of the 2009 election by members of the National Election Study. For further details, see *Economic and Political Weekly* 44, no. 39 (26 September– 2 October 2009), 33–203.
2. See, for example, Fareed Zakaria in *Newsweek*, 23 May 2009. His article used more moderate language than euphoric references in the Indian press to the 'Gandhi Whirlwind' (*Economic Times*, 4 June 2009) and to 'Rahul The Man. The Magic. The Politics' (*Outlook* cover, 1 June 2009). But *Newsweek*, which Zakaria edits, followed up his report with another by Sudip Mazumdar entitled 'A revolution is underway in India' on 8 June 2009.

    Two other commentators whose judgements are usually very sound echoed this view in more measured terms: Chris Morris of the British Broadcasting Company (BBC) (who spoke of Rahul Gandhi's decision to 'rebuild the party from the grassroots' as if significant progress had been made on this task) and Vir Sanghvi, both speaking on television on 16 May 2009. (To his credit, Sanghvi corrected himself in an NDTV interview on 23 May.) For further examples, see Ashok Malik in the *Hindustan Times*, 17 May 2009; and the *Times of India*'s description of the National Rural Employment Guarantee Scheme as a 'game changer' on 21 May 2009.

    For a more careful assessment of the degree to which poverty initiatives helped Congress and its allies, see *Frontline*, 5 June 2009, pages 5 and 9.
3. The differences between voting patterns by different age groups were small, but Congress and its allies fared better as the ages of voters increased. Here are the figures:

Breakdown of votes for parties by age group, Lok Sabha Election 2009 – All-India

Age (years)	Congress (per cent)	Congress allies (per cent)	BJP (per cent)	BJP allies (per cent)	Left (per cent)	BSP (per cent)	Others (per cent)
Up to 25	28.6	7.0	20.4	5.5	7.6	6.5	24.4
26–35	28.8	8.3	19.8	6.6	5.9	6.2	24.4
36–45	28.7	8.3 %	19.1	7.5	7.0	6.4	22.1
46–55	30.5	7.8	19.1	5.3	8.1	6.0	23.1
Over 56	32.8	7.9	17.8	6.0	7.3	6.2	22.1
Total	29.7	8.2	19.3	6.3	7.0	6.3	23.3

Source: CSDS Post-poll data. (I am grateful to K.C. Suri of the National Election Study for providing this information.)

4 Average ages in various Lok Sabhas

1952	46.5	1984	51.4
1957	46.7	1989	51.3
1962	49.4	1991	51.4
1967	48.7	1996	52.8
1971	49.2	1998	46.4
1977	52.1	1999	55.5
1980	51.4	2004	55.5
		2009	52.6

Source: *Deccan Herald*, 21 May 2009

5 Interviews with Congress strategists from Uttar Pradesh, Madhya Pradesh, Andhra Pradesh and Karnataka in New Delhi, Hyderabad and Bangalore between 19 May and 3 June 2009. Rahul Gandhi was not interviewed, but he made it clear he had decided not to accept a ministerial post and to focus instead on regenerating the party because he knew that that task remained to be completed.
6 Not all of these initiatives were *explicitly* described anti-poverty programs, but all appear to have eased the plight of the poor – at least to a limited extent.
7 Interviews in New Delhi in late 2004 and early 2005.
8 Interview, New Delhi, 11 February 1992. He did not say these things publicly. He preferred to say little, in order to avoid public controversy – and even clarity – since he (rightly) believed that they would undermine his efforts to promote change.
9 Interview with N.C. Saxena, former Member-Secretary of the Planning Commission, New Delhi, 4 June 2009. But for a sobering perspective on this, see his article in *Outlook*, 10 March 2008.
10 One of the few commentators to have grasped this is S. Varadarajan, writing in *The Hindu*, 19 May 2009.
11 I am grateful to Renana Jhabvala for stressing this point, and to Santhosh Mathew for further information about this initiative. The program began on 1 April 2008. It operates call centres round the clock to ensure that families facing emergencies obtain swift assistance. Poor families receive a smart card that enables them to obtain services without resorting to middlemen. The central government pays 75 per cent of the costs and state governments pay 25 per cent (Ministry of Labour and Employment, Government of India 2010a).
12 That was made clear in the *Times of India* review of the programs, 3 June 2009, and it is apparent from this writer's field research on the implementation of the NREGS in rural Madhya Pradesh in November–December 2008. But a good deal less money has been siphoned off from that scheme than the more gloomy reports have claimed.
13 He is completing a doctoral thesis at the Institute of Development Studies, University of Sussex.
14 Its full title is the Scheduled Tribes and Other Traditional Forest-Dwellers (Recognition of Forest Rights) Act.
15 I am grateful to Pratap Banu Mehta for stressing this point.
16 The same is true of most state governments that are controlled by other parties with weak organizations, as Dilip Padgaonkar noted in television discussions on 16 May 2009. After the state elections of May 2011, *all* Indian states were governed by parties (or alliances of parties) whose organizations were weak.
17 These comments are based on interviews in New Delhi in July 2007.
18 This is based on interviews with members of the National Advisory Council that worked with Sonia Gandhi to devise these initiatives, New Delhi, 2 and 3 June 2009. I have discussed this in more detail in Manor 2010.
19 Interview, New Delhi, 2 June 2009.

20 See for example, *Times of India* (New Delhi), 13 May 2009; *Hindustan Times*, 15 May 2009; and *Times of India* (Hyderabad) 17 and 19 May 2009. This is also based on interviews with reporters who had worked extensively in rural areas at four newspapers in Hyderabad (18–19 May 2009) and Bangalore (21–22 May 2009).

21 This comment refers only to the *present* Karnataka government. That state has, for the most part, *not* suffered poor leadership over the years (Raghavan and Manor 2009).

For further evidence of the current government's failure to seize crucial opportunities, consider its non-response to the new national health insurance scheme for poor people (the *Rashtriya Swasthya Bima Yojna*), which has proved to be immensely valuable to vulnerable families. Six Karnataka districts were selected for the initial phase of the scheme. But while over one hundred thousand families were enrolled in it in each of ten other states (and over one million families in Kerala), Karnataka (and Orissa) has at the time of writing in mid-2009 registered *not one* family (Ministry of Labour and Employment, Government of India 2010b).

22 Interview with one of those architects, New Delhi, 29 January 2009.

23 I am grateful to the CSDS team for this information.

24 They add that 'The balance was tilted in favour of the central government in the Hindi-speaking states that have historically lacked a regional identity. As expected, the regional tilt was more pronounced in the case of the states in the south and the Northeast' (Yadav and Palshikar 2009a: 405–7).

25 I am grateful to K.C. Suri of the National Election Study for providing this information.

26 This may change as the international financial crisis reduces India's economic growth rates and thus government revenues, and as belt-tightening occurs to reduce the fiscal deficit that has lately increased. But at the 2009 national election, the pattern is clear.

Chapter 3

1 Bhagwan Dua (1979) in his classic study of President's Rule in India argued that Article 356 had been misused most often by both the Congress since the 1950s, and the Janata Party led Union Government (1977–80) on partisan grounds. The Janata coalition, he argued, followed only in the footsteps of the Congress party, and even surpassed it, by dissolving none Congress-ruled state assemblies in 1977 by a single Presidential order, which was unprecedented (p. 612). He said that 'Mrs. Indira Gandhi used the instrument for partisan reasons but also for personal reasons with a view to liquidating dissent against her autocratic rule' (p. 612). In another classic article, Dua (1985) pointed out rampant patrimonialism of Indira Gandhi during her last term in power (1980–4) in the making and unmaking of all Congress chief ministers of states purely on very narrow partisan, and personal grounds. Dua (1985: 803) writes that 'In the process, the state legislatures were becoming increasingly irrelevant, if not redundant, in the making and unmaking of chief ministers.' Dua (1985: 804) commented: 'Over the years, therefore, her own conception of good management of state politics was reduced to one principle: keep all state leaders on perennial probation.' However, since 1994, after the Supreme Court verdict in the famous *S. R. Bommai vs. the Union of India*, the use of Article 356 has been subject to many limitations. This is one reason why the Union Government has since been cautious in using this Article.

2 The figures were 47.3 per cent in 1986 and 54.8 per cent in 1994 for India. For further details, see Watts (1999: 47). The figures went up during the 1990s due to a more centralizing turn under the Congress-led government at the centre during 1991–6.

3 The pre-poll allies of the UPA were: RJD, DMK, NCP, PMK, TRS, JMM, MDMK, All India Majlis-e-Ittehadul Muslimeen (AIMIM), People's Democratic Party (PDR), Indian Union Muslim League (IUML), RPI (A), RPI (Gavai) and Kerala Congress (Issac) (KC (I)).

4 The TRS, an ally (with five Members of Parliament) of the UPA (2004–9), left the coalition on 23 September 2006, and all its members including its leader Mr K. Chandra Sekha Rao, Union Labour Minister, resigned from Lok Sabha, and the

Ministry, respectively, on the grounds of the UPA's failure to implement its promise in the Common Minimum Programme, namely, the formation of a separate State of Telengana carving up Andhra Pradesh. The party leader Mr Rao alleged: 'In fact, both Mrs Gandhi [Sonia Gandhi] and Mr Reddy [Congress party Chief Minister of Andhra Pradesh] donned Telengana colours with our map for the separate State when they went on the election tour in the region.' (For further details, see http://www.thehindu.com/2006/09/24/stories/2006092421550100.htm, accessed 15 November 2009.) The TRS joined the NDA on 10 March 2009, as the BJP had stated that it stood for small States! It is also not true that the UPA has sat idle on the issue because the UPA government had constituted a Committee with Pranab Mukherjee, now Finance Minister, as its chairman to look into the matter. On 8 January 2008, the UPA government formed the Second States Reorganization Commission to reorganize India further and to consider the creation of new states.

5 It is stated forcefully in the document: 'We are definitely for strong states, but on no account do we want a weak Centre. The concept of strong states is not necessarily in contradiction to that of a strong Centre, once their respective spheres of authority are clearly marked out' (Kurian and Varughese, quoted in Bhattacharyya 2009: 111).

6 Two things must be stated here for clarity. First, in the past, it was during the Congress-run government at the Centre that Jammu and Kashmir suffered, and the provisions of Article 370 were compromised. Second, the NDA was, and is still, ideologically committed to deletion of the very article that assures Jammu and Kashmir's special status within the Indian federation.

7 It is reported that some 20 States have availed themselves of the benefit of the debt waiver.

8 The latest criteria with weightage of tax devolution is as follows: population (16 per cent); income (62.5 per cent); areas (7.5 per cent); index of infrastructure (7.5 per cent); tax efforts (5 per cent); and fiscal discipline (7.5 per cent). See Rao and Singh (2005: 201).

9 For further details on its application for medical help to the people in Assam, see http://sentinelassam.com/state2/story.php, accessed 20 December 2009.

10 This may not be entirely true because attempts since the 1990s have been made to revive such institutions, and the National Commission to Review the Working of the Constitution (Government of India 2002) report also strongly recommended in favour of the same. For instance, the Inter State Council (ISC) held its first meeting on 10 October 1990, and held ten meetings until December 1996. It is reported that the ISC had adopted all the 247 recommendations of the Sarkaria Commission relating to Centre–State relations, and 179 recommendations have been implemented. (For further details, see http://interstatecouncil.nic.in/agenda_isc.htm, accessed on 8 November 2009.)

11 Article 355 of the Indian Constitution states: 'Duty of the Union to protect States against external aggression and internal disturbances ... It shall be the duty of the Union to protect every State against external aggression and internal disturbance and to ensure that the Government of every state is carried on in accordance with the provisions of this Constitution.'

12 Even the Punchhi Commission in its 'Introductory' passage pointed out many of the limitations of the local government bodies. Note the following concern of the Commission: 'The Constitution was amended to rectify the situation by giving these institutions Constitutional status with the hope that they would function as a third tier of governance. However, empowering them adequately remained a challenge' (p. 10). For further details, see Punchi (2008, 2010).

13 See, for instance, Bhattacharyya (1998, 2002), Jha and Mathur (1999), Mitra (2001), Jain (2005), and Baviskar and Matthew (2009).

14 See, Thomas Issac and Chakraborty (2008, especially 91–2) and Bandopadhyay (2008).

15 Press Information Bureau for the Ministry of Rural Development. (For further details, see http://pibmumbai.gov.in/scripts/details.asp?releaseId=E2009FR37, accessed November 9, 2009.)

16 The Jana Sangh, the BJP's immediate political predecessor, had organizational units along administrative lines, as depicted above, which was at variance with the INC's linguistically federal organizational structure, particularly since 1917, which was to become the standard approach widely accepted throughout India.
17 The Telengana Statehood demand has not been conceded by the UPA Government-appointed Srikrishan Commission, which submitted its report on 6 January 2011 (*The Statesman*, Kolkata, 7 January 2011). As a result, since 6 January 2011, Andhra Pradesh has again been witnessing outbreaks of violence.

Chapter 4

1 The consistency of policy objectives as an established criteria for assessment has been in place since the celebrated work of Jan Tinbergen in the 1960s (Tinbergen 1967).
2 Stewart (2009) points out that a state unable to ensure service delivery should be deemed to have failed. In this sense, the Indian state has consistently being unable to ensure educational outlays of the order of 6 per cent of the GDP, and should be regarded as failing in some sense.
3 Duflo (2004) points out that the methodological approach to selection and implementation within the DPEP make its difficult, if not impossible, to undertake a comprehensive evaluation of the programme.
4 Both the DPEP and SSA have been introduced within the larger political framework of decentralization, whereby service delivery has been shifted from the central administration to the individual districts who receive funds through the relevant state governments. The 73rd and 74th amendments to the Indian constitution, which granted the district, block and village institutions constitutional recognition and to urban municipalities and its constituent wards, respectively, have been particularly important in placing the district at the centre of development policy, through their emphasis on Panchayati Raj institutions.
5 The SSA initially set itself a near impossible goal of achieving UPE by 2003, which was subsequently moved to 2007.
6 The figures for 2002–3 were around 77 per cent and 60 per cent respectively (Fennell 2006).
7 Gender Parity is taken to be achieved when the gross enrolment rate for girls and boys is between .97 and 1.03.
8 The GPI in 2002–3 was just under 0.90 for India (Fennell 2006).
9 These targeted programmes, such as MDM in schools and the provision of special girls' schools, the Kasturba Gandhi Balika Vidyalayas, of this flagship programme of the Ministry of Human Resource Development (MHRD) have not yet yielded success in terms of retention or improvements in educational quality.
10 MHRD website.
11 The CMP does not make any reference to other forms of financial resource mobilization nor does it declare any new financial outlays.
12 This petition also heralded the start of a national Right to Food Campaign during 2002–3 across India by a coalition of non-governmental organizations.
13 'Classroom hunger' is a term that is used to explain why children from very poor families are unable to concentrate on lessons because they have come to school without eating anything. The implications of school meals is therefore not only to ensure increased enrollment in schools but also improve the quality of children's educational learning experience.
14 The *Report to the People* (UPA 2008), released on the third anniversary of the UPA, also emphasizes the importance of targeted funds for improving the educational attainments of minority and deprived groups.
15 The recent Public Report on Basic Education in India (PROBE) study conducted in 2006 does show that mid-day meals were an important feature in increasing access and attendance (Samson *et al.* 2008). This finding is contradictory to the international

financial institutions (IFIs) view that targeted programmes are more effective as they focus on the most disadvantaged rather than providing a generalized subsidy (King *et al.* 1997).

16 The incentives are effective when they work with poor and marginalized groups to overcome obstacles to accessing education. See Fennell (2006) for an analysis of conditions within which gender-based educational programmes were effective in South Asia.

17 The DFID-funded Research Consortium on Educational Outcomes and Poverty (RECOUP) conducted research in four countries, Ghana, India, Kenya and Pakistan, between 2005 and 2010 to understand the educational experiences of individuals in poor communities, and its implications for personal identity, decision making, skills and employment. The research design and methodology used across six different projects has highlighted the need to link the process by which education is accessed, and how and in what manner teaching and learning occurs, within the social, political, economic and cultural context of the community, and is critical in defining and evaluating educational outcomes. This is an area that has only recently become a subject of independent study in the field of education and development.

18 Ramachandran (2004) points out that schools often replicate the hierarchies in society at large.

19 *Unnikrishan, J.P. vs. the State of Andhra Pradesh*, A.I.R. 1993 S.C. 2178.

20 The CABE was established in 1920 as the highest advisory body to the government on educational policy with the power to engage in public consultation. It was dissolved in 1923 on account of governmental financial difficulties. The institution was revived in 1938 and continued to be active till 1994, when its membership was not renewed at the end of its term of office.

21 The following seven committees were set up subsequent to the meeting in August: (i) Free and Compulsory Education Bill and other issues related to Elementary Education, (ii) Girls Education and the Common School System, (iii) Universalisation of Secondary Education, (iv) Autonomy of Higher Education Institution, (v) Integration of Culture Education in the School Curriculum, (vi) Regulatory Mechanism for the Text Books and Parallel Textbooks Taught in Schools Outside the Government System, and (vii) Financing of Higher and Technical Education. (See http://www.edu.nic.in/cabe/cabe-order7.htm.)

22 The committee on free and compulsory education was required to 'suggest a draft of legislation envisaged in Article 21-A of the constitution' and to examine matters relating 'to achieving free and compulsory education'.

23 The committee on girls' education recorded its strong disapproval regarding girls' education as a merely a contributory factor to a narrow growth perspective. Its first recommendation was that an 'Instrumentalist approach i.e. girls' education for fertility control, better health care, decreased expenses on health care and decreased infant mortality rate etc. needs to be vehemently opposed' (Ministry of Human Resource Development, Government of India 2005b).

24 The longstanding opposition to the entry of commercial organizations into education that was evident within these expert bodies was in relation to the imposition of fees rather than in relation to their ability or inability to provide quality education. There is considerable evidence that there are already a substantial number of non-state providers in education in India who are changing the terrain of Indian education (Fennell 2007).

25 The exclusion of this group was also inexplicable given the commitment to early years indicated through the highlighting of the ICDS programme in the CMP.

26 The introduction of private providers, taken to mean the corporate sector, in India has been a contentious matter. Educationalists are opposed to it on the grounds that this would emphasize the profit motive, which goes against the principle of providing education to the poorest and the most disadvantaged. The government's consideration of the private sector appears to be driven by its own financial limitations and

consequent inability to provide an adequate number of educational institutions to meet demand in the tertiary sector.
27 DiJohn (2007) has shown that governments that consistently under-resource education display a sign of failure of accountability. The importance of being able to meet policy objectives by an adequate amount of public expenditure is, on the other hand, an example of a fully functional state institution.
28 The shift from 50:50 to a 15:85 share of expenditure envisaged in the 11th plan was proceeded with, notwithstanding the new policy requirements. This is very similar to the ongoing use made of allocations made under the 10th plan. There appears to be little appetite in the government to make distinctive changes in expenditure outlays, and the educational cess went a very small way to provide additional funds, with most of it being absorbed by the MDM scheme during the 10th plan.
29 Independence Day Speech 2006.
30 Downloaded from India Newsline at http://www.news.indiamart.com/news.../-inclusive-growth-ke-15755.html, 6 May 2010.
31 In the RECOUP research on the provision of schools in poor communities a common finding that has emerged across all research sites is that the poorest and most marginalized families are unable to get adequate education from the state system and 'dropping out' is the most common way of registering their discontent.
32 The 11th plan document is entitled 'Towards Faster and More Inclusive Growth' and sets out a new paradigm that ensures that growth is broad-based by bringing expenditure on education, health and infrastructure to the foreground. The outcomes that the plan envisages from such investment is through empowering the disadvantaged, i.e. those who have been excluded on the basis of caste, religion, gender and disability.

Chapter 5

1 The UPA also introduced a bill to give constitutional status to the Minorities Commission. This bill was introduced as an amendment in 2004 and reached the committee stage in 2006, but does not appear to have passed. As late as June 2009 the minister for Minority Affairs was promising to reconsider the matter to give constitutional status to the Minorities Commission.

Chapter 6

1 'Modi ties hands of cops who put their foot down'. *Indian Express*, 26 March 2002, p. 1.
2 See, for example, the CSDS poll for *India Today*, 31 August 1996, in which 63 per cent agreed that 'Government must protect interest of minorities', and the CSDS exit poll in 2004 in which 83 per cent agreed with the same proposition.
3 *India Today*, National Opinion Poll, 15 August 1993.
4 The exception was in December 1992 itself, just after the demolition, when 44 per cent of voters said that Ayodhya was the most important issue, the only time the issue got more than 15 per cent from May 1991 to May 1992. *India Today*, National Opinion Poll, 15 August 1993, p. 49. See also 'The Issues that Matter', *India Today*, 30 April 1992, p. 16; and Hindu–CPPS Opinion Poll, 25 January 1993 (CSDS 1996).
5 For Sonia Gandhi's stance on the issue, see *Outlook India*, 23 June 2003, pp. 25–8.
6 'Army Deployed in Vadodara', *The Statesman Weekly*, 6 May 2006.
7 Under the Indian constitution, central paramilitary and military forces may only intervene with the permission of the state governments, unless the center imposes President's Rule on a state. The latter action is rarely taken over communal violence (only five times from 1950 to 1996, for example, though many huge riots took place in this period), and has never been taken by the center against its own party in a state over this issue.

8. 'A Shame on Nation: Manmohan', *The Hindu*, 29 August 2008.
9. Patnaik's party ultimately broke with the BJP just before the elections and went on to triumph in both the Lok Sabha and Vidhan Sabha elections in the state.
10. Patnaik subsequently claimed that the riots had been an issue in the coalition breakup: 'We all know the way the BJP's sister organization were indulging in violence in Kandhamal. My government did the best to arrest these people' (Karan 2009). But at the time of the riots his government was much more equivocal in its stance.
11. '1984 Anti-Sikh riots: High court upholds life sentences for three', *Indian Express*, 7 December 2009.
12. See, for example, Uttar Pradesh State Archives (Lucknow), Box 957, GAD File 49H/1958, 'Inquiry made by the Government of India about the employment of members of the minority communities.' For background on the 1957 committee see Humayun Kabir (1968) *Minorities in a Democracy*, Calcutta: KL Mukhopadhyay, pp. 40–6.
13. For debates over the Gopal Krishna report, which was presented to the Congress government in June 1983, but was not released to parliament until after the Janata Government took office in 1989, see *Lok Sabha Debates*, 9 May 1984.
14. For instance in 1984 the Krishna panel found that Muslims were 11 per cent of the population but had less than 2 per cent of government jobs. *Lok Sabha Debates*, 9 May 1984, p.11. Some of the National Sample Survey data was released in Abusaleh Shariff (1995) 'Socio-economic and demographic differentials between Hindus and Muslims in India', *Economic and Political Weekly* 30, no. 46 (18 November), 2947–53.
15. Vijay Karan, the ex-head of the Central Bureau of Investigation (CBI), was quoted in the mid-1990s as saying that 'It is a sort of unwritten code. Everybody knows about it and it is accepted as a fact' (Sanghvi 1994).
16. These studies are comprehensively summarized in Mushirul Hasan (1997) *Legacy of a Divided Nation: India's Muslims since Independence*, New Delhi: Oxford University Press.
17. This was the view, for instance, of the 1957–9 committee (Kabir, p. 47)
18. As a member of parliament pointed out during a debate on the Ahmadabad riots in 1970: 'The Central Government may say that they have appointed the National Integration Council, that they are appointing a Committee through the National Integration Council ... Conferences are held, Resolutions are passed, but what is the use? These Conferences and these Resolutions do not stop the communal orgy' (Imam 1970).
19. For much more on the specifics of the data and recommendations in Sachar, see Wilkinson, S. 'A comment on the analysis in the Sachar report', pp. 832–6, and the other papers in the *Economic and Political Weekly*'s special edition on Sachar, *Economic and Political Weekly* 42, no. 10 (10 March 2007).
20. Asim Khwaja has found the same pattern explains *madrasa* attendance in Pakistan (Khwaja *et al.* 2006).
21. Personal interviews by the author, 10 September 2009 and 11 December 2009.
22. The author of this chapter presented his findings on communal issues to the committee in New Delhi in March 2006, and got some flavor of the differences of approach within the seven-member committee and among the supporting staff and advisors.
23. Personal interview by the author, 10 September 2009.
24. *Muslim India*, 1 March 2007.
25. The Equal Opportunity Commission was the only measure to get significant attention in the main manifesto.
26. The best source on this, much of which reanalyses the data presented in Sachar with better methods, is Rakesh Basant and Abusaleh Shariff (eds) (2010) *Oxford Handbook of Muslims: Empirical and Policy Perspectives* (New Delhi: Oxford University Press), especially the chapters by Anil Deolalikar on 'The performance of Muslims on social indicators', Sonia Bhalotra and Bernarda Zamora on 'Social divisions in education in India', Vani K. Borooah 'On the risks of belonging to disadvantaged groups: a

Bayesian analysis of labour market outcomes', Sumon Kumar Bhaumik and Manisha Chakrabarty on 'Earnings inequality' and Jeemol Unni on 'Informality and gender in the labour market for Muslims'.
27 These studies and others are presented in Sukhdeo Thorat and Katherine S. Newman. (eds) (2010) *Blocked by Caste: Economic Discrimination in Modern India*, New Delhi: Oxford University Press.
28 See also Mona G. Mehta's 2010 University of Chicago PhD. thesis, 'Corrosive Consensus: Democracy and Everyday Ethnic Conflict in India', which explores increasing social segregation and ghettoization in Gujarat.
29 'Minorities must have first claim on resources: Manmohan Singh', *The Hindu,* 19 December 2006. Singh's full statement was: 'We will have to devise innovative plans to ensure that minorities, particularly the Muslim minority, are empowered to share equitably the fruits of development. These must have the first claim on resources.'
30 'BJP, RSS, flay PM's remarks on minorities', *Times of India*, 9 December 2006, http://timesofindia.indiatimes.com/articleshow/754456.cms (accessed 13 September 2009).

Chapter 7

1 For an analysis of the NDA's policies, see Adeney and Sáez (2005). Ideological difference from the NDA and BJP is prominent in the self-descriptions of the UPA and the Congress party. The Congress's 2004 election manifesto began with the claim that the election was not just 'between one party and another. It is a clash of sharply competing values, of diametrically opposite ideologies.' Available at http://www.qbtpl.net/congress/congress_menifesto.htm.
2 See the contribution by Kanti Bajpai in this volume.
3 See contributions by James Manor and Steve Wilkinson in this volume.
4 For instance, the rhetoric of social justice in the 1990 Mandal debate is often dismissed as a little more than a cloak for the factional and electoral interests of Prime Minister V. P. Singh. Similarly, the 2006 Mandal decision is seen as an attempt by Arjun Singh, Minister for Human Resources, to assert his authority and counter his growing marginalization within the Congress Party.
5 A recent strand of egalitarian scholarship emphasizes continuities between distributive and social equality, although egalitarian theorists differ on how the two are related (Phillips 1995; Young 1995; Wolff 1998; Anderson 1999; Fraser and Honneth 2003).
6 See the contribution by James Manor in this volume.
7 The key slogan of the Congress's 2004 manifesto is 'economic growth with social harmony'. Social justice appears further down in its priorities of governance, in the form of a commitment to equality of opportunity 'in every way for dalits, adivasis, OBCs and religious and linguistic minorities'. It is referred to as *saman avsar* rather than the more common term for social justice, *samajik nyaya* (http://www.qbtpl.net/congress/congress_menifesto.htm).
8 The CMP states: 'All reservation quotas, including those relating to promotion, would be fulfilled in a time-bound manner.'
9 By contrast, the 1989 election manifesto of the Janata Dal-led National Front coalition had promised that the 'recommendations of the Mandal Commission [i.e. OBC quotas] will be implemented expeditiously' (cited in Jaffrelot 2003: 238).
10 The extension of higher education quotas to the OBCs was considered by the minister responsible, Arjun Singh, to be the highlight of his tenure (see *Indian Express* 2009) but has not been prominent in official lists of the UPA's achievements.
11 Personal interviews by the author, 7 and 8 January 2010. The 2008 report on the implementation of the CMP claims that 'in an unprecedented special drive to clear the backlog of vacancies for reserved posts', over 53,000 vacancies have been filled. The government has also relaxed 'the 50% reservation ceiling on a one-time basis to fill up OBC vacancies as a separate category'.

12 Kundu Report (*Report of the Expert Group on Diversity Index*, Government of India, 2008, available at http://minorityaffairs.gov.in/newsite/reports/di_expgrp/di_expgrp.pdf); Menon Report (*Equal Opportunity Commission: What, Why and How? Report by the Expert Group to Examine and Determine the Structure and Functions of an Equal Opportunity Commission*, Government of India February 2008, available at http://minorityaffairs.gov.in/newsite/reports/eoc_wwh/eoc_wwh.pdf). The Equal Opportunities Commission is meant to supplement existing commissions, whereas the Diversity Index is intended as an alternative to reservations. Their recommendations are not yet policy.

13 Thus, for instance, as per the Prime Minister's 15-point program for minorities, key development schemes for schools, crèches, employment, and training are to be located in minority concentration districts (MCDs), defined as those where at least 25 per cent of the population belongs to minority communities (http://minorityaffairs.gov.in/newsite/pm15points/pm15points.asp). In the 2009–10 budget speech, a new scheme (*Pradhan Mantri Adarsh Gram Yojana*) was announced, covering in the pilot stage 1,000 villages with a high concentration of SCs. Several objectives of this scheme are universal (e.g. reduction of the incidence of poverty by at least 50 per cent within three years, universal adult literacy, compulsory primary education, reduction of infant and maternal mortality rates). For further details, see http://socialjustice.nic.in/pmagy.php.

14 Of course, in practice, the Congress has often focused upon particular identity groups, both in its electoral strategies as well as its social composition, but in its official rhetoric, has largely sought to transcend identity divisions.

15 The full text of the constitutional amendment is available at http://indiacode.nic.in/coiweb/amend/amend93.htm. The Amendment overruled Supreme Court decisions, which had excluded unaided private institutions from the purview of reservations. It also clarified that education institutions at all levels and in all areas were subject to reservations, and affirmed the autonomy of minority educational institutions, which were excluded from purview of the Bill (Dhavan 2008: 118–19).

16 The Central Educational Institutions (Reservations in Admission) Act, 2006. This also brought the elite Indian Institute of Technology, Indian Institute of Management and All India Institute of Medical Sciences within the scope of the reservations policy (Dhavan 2008: 147). The Congress's 2004 manifesto mentions that it is the only party that has 'provided for reservations in its organization for the scheduled castes, scheduled tribes, OBCs, minorities and women' (http://www.qbtpl.net/congress/congress_menifesto.htm).

17 The party's 2004 manifesto says: 'The Congress will create a national consensus on the issue of dalits and adivasis getting a reasonable share of jobs in the private sector' (http://www.qbtpl.net/congress/congress_menifesto.htm). Former minister for Social Justice and Empowerment and current Lok Sabha speaker, Meira Kumar, is a key advocate. Prime Minister, Dr Manmohan Singh, has also spoken in favour of affirmative action in the private sector (see *Indian Express* 24 May 2010).

18 Although key government ministers have voiced skepticism, favouring affirmative action more broadly defined over quotas (see *Indian Express* 4 July 2009), the UPA government has also at times put pressure on the private sector for instituting some form of quotas.

19 Lower caste-based parties, such as the Samajwadi Party, the RJD and the Janata Dal (United) (JD (U)), have long demanded the enumeration of caste in the census. The UPA cabinet was divided on the issue, with the skeptics including Human Resources Development Minister Kapil Sibal, Defense Minister A. K. Antony, Sports Minister M. K. Gill and, possibly, Home Minister Palaniappan Chidambaram. Advocates included the Law Minister Veerappa Moily, Social Justice and Empowerment Minister Mukul Wasnik, and Textiles Minister Dayanidhi Maran (views on ministerial positions compiled by the author on reports in the *Indian Express* from 26 May 2010, 27 May 2010, and 2 July 2010).

20 UPA II passed this legislation with the help of the BJP and the Left, in the face of staunch opposition from UPA I allies such as the Samajwadi Party and the RJD. OBC leaders, such Mulayam Singh Yadav, Laloo Prasad Yadav, and Sharad Yadav, who had stalled its passage for 14 years, remained bitterly opposed. Sonia Gandhi reportedly pushed for the legislation over equivocation within the government, a pattern repeated across political parties of the right and the left, with Sushma Swaraj (BJP) and Brinda Karat (CPI (M)) leading opinion in their parties in support of the Bill (personal interviews by author, 20 December 2009 and 9 January 2010).

21 See contributions by Wilkinson and Singh in this volume.

22 For further details, see the Congress party's 2004 manifesto (http://www.qbtpl.net/congress/congress_menifesto.htm).

23 Personal interviews by author, 25 December 2009; see also *Indian Express* 31 March 2010 and *Indian Express* 1 April 2010.

24 *Report of the National Commission for Religious and Linguistic Minorities*, Ministry of Minority Affairs, Government of India, 2007. Full text available at http://minorityaffairs.gov.in/newsite/ncrlm/ncrlm.asp.

25 *Indian Express* 9 July 2010.

26 *India Today* 23 May 2010.

27 As per the Indian Constitution and the Scheduled Caste order of 1950, only Hindu and Sikh Dalits were eligible for SC benefits. In 1990, the Janata Dal government extended these to Buddhists (following Dr Ambedkar, a substantial portion of Dalits had converted to Buddhism). Dalit Christians and Dalit Muslim communities are included in lists of Backward Classes in several states, but are not yet eligible for Scheduled Caste status, which brings a higher level of benefits. The Scheduled Tribes' category, by contrast, does include Christian and Muslim tribal communities. The Misra report recommends the deletion of Para 3 of the Constitution (Scheduled Castes) Order 1950 'so as to completely de-link the Scheduled Caste status from religion and make the Scheduled Castes net fully religion-neutral like that of the Scheduled Tribes' (para 16.3.5, http://minorityaffairs.gov.in/newsite/ncrlm/ncrlm. asp). Satish Deshpande's influential study found substantial evidence of social segregation, occupational segregation and economic exploitation among Christian and Muslim Dalits, concluding that their conditions were 'not so distinct' from Dalits of Hindu and other faiths, and that 'there is no compelling evidence to justify denying SC status to DMs and DCs' (*Dalits in the Muslim and Christian Communities: A Status Report on Current Social Scientific Knowledge* prepared for the National Commission for Minorities, Government of India, by Satish Deshpande with the assistance of Geetika Bapna, available at http://ncm.nic.in/pdf/report%20dalit%20%20reservation.pdf).

28 The fact that minority benefits have expanded through executive action, rather than legislation, likely explains their relatively uncontroversial passage thus far. This parallels the career of economic reforms in the 1990s; see Jenkins 1999, Varshney 1999.

29 These include employment schemes (e.g. *Swarnjayanti Gram Swarozgar Yojana*), housing schemes (e.g. the *Indira Awas Yojana*), and bank credit under priority sector lending, as well as various scholarship and training schemes. The Prime Minister's 15-point program clearly states that in addition to 'the location of a certain proportion of development projects in minority concentration areas … *wherever possible, 15% of targets and outlays under various schemes should be earmarked for minorities*… Ministries/Departments concerned will earmark 15 per cent of the physical targets and financial outlays for minorities' (emphasis added by author). The new 15-point program was announced by Prime Minister, Dr Manmohan Singh, at his 2005 Independence Day address as having 'definite goals which are to be achieved in a specific time frame' (http://minorityaffairs.gov.in/newsite/pm15points/pm15points_eguide.pdf). The new 15-point program follows previous declarations of similar nomenclature made by Indira Gandhi in 1983 and Rajiv Gandhi in 1985, but strengthens and expands these substantially, in terms of numerical targets, range of development schemes included, as well the monitoring mechanisms envisaged.

30 See http://minorityaffairs.gov.in/newsite/pm15points/pm15points_eguide.pdf.
31 For further details see http://minorityaffairs.gov.in/newsite/pm15points/DoPT_guidlines.pdf. Included here is a memorandum, dated 16 August 1990, enunciating a similar policy, presumably issued by the Janata Dal Government, but without the crucial requirement of monitoring reports.
32 The 15-point program outlines a detailed monitoring mechanism for the state/Union Territory and district levels. The state level committee is to be 'headed by the Chief Secretary', to include members from departments 'implementing the schemes under the 15 Point Programme, representatives from the Panchayati Raj Institutions/ Autonomous District Councils, three representatives from reputed non-governmental institutions dealing with minorities ...' A similarly constituted committee is envisaged at the district level, 'headed by the Collector/Deputy Commissioner of the district'. See http://minorityaffairs.gov.in/newsite/pm15points/pm15points_eguide.pdf. Setting group targets in the various development schemes for the poor appear to be a model that is being emulated in the case of the SCs – see http://socialjustice.nic.in/pdf/pmagy-guidelines.pdf.
33 See, for instance, http://timesofindia.indiatimes.com/india/Only-5-of-Plan-funds-spent-on-minorities/articleshow/5594621.cms#ixzz0x4KeYIbz, http://www.ummid.com/news/December/20.12.2009/upa_schemes_for_minority_welfare.htm. However, minority numbers in employment in public sector banks and financial institutions, railways and paramilitary forces also show strong increases in the wake of the Prime Minister's new 15-point program. See 'Minority share in govt jobs up', at http://economictimes.indiatimes.com/articleshow/6073773.cms.
34 Here affirmative action in India is becoming more similar to Malaysia in that expansion is occurring in the policy area of development, in tandem with tackling poverty, and is being done through the executive branch, bypassing substantive legislative debate. I am grateful to Dr Graham Brown for discussion of this point.
35 See also Patel's letter accompanying the advisory committee report of 11 May 1949. *CAD* VIII: 311.
36 For instance, Hansa Mehta noted: '[We have] ... never asked for reserved seats, for quotas or for separate electorates. What we have asked for is social justice, economic justice and political justice. We have asked for equality' (*CAD* I: 134). In the later stages of constitution-making, the abolition of legislative quotas for religious minorities was pressed among others by the Minorities Committee Chairman and Christian leader Dr H. C. Mookerjee. For more details, see Bajpai 2011.
37 For example, in a typical speech, Pandit G. B. Pant held: '... we must do all we can to bring them up to the general level, and it is a real necessity as much in our interests as in theirs that the gap should be bridged. The strength of the chain is measured by the weakest link of it and so until every link is fully revitalized, we will not have a healthy body' (*CAD* II: 312).
38 Vasant Sathe castigated the government for dividing the country on caste lines: '... the people who participated in the freedom struggle ... had said that our dream is to create a casteless society in this country ... Manu in ancient times deformed our society by dividing the people on the basis of their birth ...You are now trying to bring Manu through Mandal ...' (*LSD* 5.9.1990 col. 458–60). Rajiv Gandhi noted: '... Unfortunately, the step that we are taking today, the manner in which it has been put, is a casteist formula. While accepting that caste is a reality, we must dilute that formula ...' (cited in Dhavan 2008: 144).
39 Interestingly, equality is denoted by different terms in the Hindi speeches – *samanta, samarupta* – some of which appear consistent with differential treatment.
40 Basudev Barman (CPI (M)) noted: 'in a society where equality of status and opportunity is not there and where glaring disparities in incomes exist and persist, there is no room for equality in any sense ... treating unequals as equals is the greatest injustice and correction or elimination of this injustice is very important ...' (*LSD* 21.12.2005).

41 See, for instance, speeches by Janardhan Poojary, *RSD* 22.12.2005, and K. Keshava Rao, *RSD* 18.12.2006.
42 Chinta Mohan noted: '... the entire credit goes to the Congress Party and its leadership who removed untouchability from this country. They brought social justice to this country. They brought a powerful Constitution for this country...' (*LSD* 21.12.2005). In passing, the speech commends Dr Ambedkar for giving India a 'beautiful Constitution', but is mainly homage to the Nehru–Gandhi family.
43 For instance, Congress OBC representative K. V. Thangkabalu noted: '... the first Constitutional amendment ... was introduced and passed at the insistence of our great leader the late Kamaraj, the then Chief Minister of Tamil Nadu. The then Prime Minister of India, Pandit Jawaharlal Nehru accepted his proposal ... for the welfare of the weaker sections of the society in this country. That is how the concept of reservation came into the political system' (*LSD* 14.12.2006).
44 Congress themes linking social justice to development and national unity are clearly evident in the INC manifesto 2004, available at http://www.qbtpl.net/congress/congress_menifesto.htm.
45 Former Congress Minister Janardhan Poojary, for instance, argued in favour of reservations as 'Even ... a construction worker, a factory worker, a farmer in the field ... all the persons in the society contributed for this growth rate of eight or nine per cent' (*RSD* 18.12.2006).
46 See, for instance, Professor Ramdass, *LSD* 14.12.2006.
47 Industrialist Rahul Bajaj (Independent) opposed the Bill. He argued: 'in a globalized world of today, there are no entitlements. Everybody has to earn his place in the society. And if we have 50 per cent ... entitlements and reservations ... we are creating a society which does not learn to compete hard, and, does not want to compete with the rest of the world' (*RSD* 18.12.2006). Tathagatha Satpathy (Biju Janata Dal) lamented: '... Today, we are in a backward race, and we want to become more and more backward so that we get the benefits of this nation ... If you say, on the one hand that there is no merit ... on the other hand, you are saying globalization ... we want to be competitive internationally ... this is a very reactionary mindset, and I hope [we] will ... think of the nation ... of India's future; and not become caste ridden, religion ridden, petty or small, but grow beyond all that ... rise above personal greed and party interests' (*LSD* 14.12.2006).
48 Secularism in Congress discourse today has distinct connotations from those in the 1940s, connoting solicitousness of minorities. For further details, see Bajpai 2002.
49 http://minorityaffairs.gov.in/newsite/pm15points/pm15points_eguide.pdf.
50 http://timesofindia.indiatimes.com/India/PM-addresses-the-nation-on-60th-Independence-Day/articleshow/2282424.cms#ixzz0x4NH9EJu.
51 This is described in the 2004 Congress party manifesto thus: 'The Congress way is the way of dialogue, not discord. The Congress way is the way of accommodation, not acrimony ... The Congress unites the Indian nation through consensus...' (http://www.qbtpl.net/congress/congress_menifesto.htm).
52 'First signal after the decision: not all 27% at one go', *Indian Express* 24 May 2006.
53 Speaking in support of the 93rd Constitutional Amendment's exclusion of minority educational institutions from reservations, Professor Saifuddin Soz noted: 'if the downtrodden people, the Scheduled Castes and the Scheduled Tribes, the OBCs and the minorities do not join the political mainstream, how can we strengthen the edifice of the Indian unity? ... all development, all peace, all relief is there because of the Constitution of India, because of the thinking of the Founding Fathers of the Constitution. [Thomas Friedman noted] ... Muslims have not taken to extremism. Why? It is because over a long period of time, they became partners in India's democratic polity, in secularism' (*RSD* 22.12.2005). Responding to concerns about the divisiveness of reservations, Dr K. Keshava Rao noted: '... if you look into South Africa or any report in America, you will find that they vouchsafe for the fact that inclusiveness and trying to take the minority along will strengthen the quality of life, quality of education, and quality of the polity' (*RSD* 18.12.2006).

54 Elisabeth Anderson has argued that integrated institutions (schools, universities) teach individuals 'of different walks of life to *learn* to live together on terms of equality', which in turn '... is the indispensable social condition of democracy ...' (2002: 1223). For arguments on similar lines comparing the US experience with the Indian case, see Weisskopf 2004 and Nussbaum 2008.
55 The Kaka Kalelkar report, for instance, contains numerous references to social justice, used to denote special treatment for 'weaker sections', including the OBCs (*Report of the Backward Classes Commission*, 1956: vol. I.). When the report was discussed in Parliament in 1965, however, the government spokesman opposed the use of caste criteria as 'contrary to the first principle of social justice' in their unfairness to the other poor (cited in Galanter 1984: 178).
56 Prior to this, in 1995, the then Congress administration had amended the Constitution to allow quotas in promotions for the SC and ST – for details of the debate, see Dhavan 2008, Chapter 2.
57 See, for instance, Professor Basudev Barman (CPI (M)): 'in a society where equality of status and opportunity is not there and where glaring disparities in incomes exist and persist, there is no room for equality in any sense ... treating unequals as equals is the greatest injustice and correction or elimination of this injustice is very important ...' (*LSD* 21.12.2005).
58 The emphasis on reservations as a constitutional right, as Andre Beteille (2005) points out, blurs the distinction between enabling provisions (employment and educational quotas) and mandatory provisions (legislative reservations) of the Constitution.
59 Janardhan Poojary, for instance, noted that Arjun Singh who belonged to the royal family was looking after the backward classes, and that the Nehru family had always protected the weaker sections of society (*RSD* 18.12.2006).
60 Prasanta Chatterjee (CPI (M)), for instance, welcomed 'the step towards ensuring equality of access to higher education to a larger number of economically deprived students ... Wider policy to change and alter the socio-economic system is ... necessary' (*RSD* 18.12.2006).
61 References to leaders of Dravidian movements were prominent in this debate. L. Ganesan (MDMK) noted: 'Reservation is not an end in itself; rather, it is only a means to an end. Social justice is the end. For this principle ... our Thantai Periyar ... suffered ... When many of you people never heard about social justice, our own Thanthai Periyar started the movement for social justice ...' (*LSD* 14.12.2006). See also A. Krishnaswamy (DMK), *LSD* 21.12.2005; *LSD* 14.12.2006.
62 For details of the Supreme Court judgments and the tussle of the Court with Parliament post-1990, see Dhavan 2008.
63 Personal interviews by author, 19 December 2009, 7 and 8 January 2010. According to the current minister for Social Justice and Empowerment, Mukul Wasnik, the main difference is in the monitoring and implementation of policy – e.g. many more unfilled vacancies have been filled under the UPA (personal interview 7 January 2010).
64 Vasundhara Raje stated: 'The Government has proven its *bonafides* time and time again not just by mere platitudes but by action. We have brought in two Constitution Amendments and intend to shortly issue orders to restart the special recruitment drive ...' (*LSD* 28.11.2001). 'The Government has been fully alive to the need to protect the interests of the depressed classes and to further the agenda of social change through positive discrimination that is basically the corner stone of the Constitution of India ...' (*LSD* 23.2.2001).
65 See for instance S. S. Ahluwalia, *RSD* 21.12.2005.
66 For instance, opposing the exemption of minority educational institutions from the 93rd constitutional amendment, Ananth Kumar held that 'universal reservations' were needed, and that the UPA government was creating 'a new conflict between social justice versus minorityism' (*LSD* 21.12.2005).
67 http://www.indian-elections.com/partymanifestoes/party-manifestoes04/bjp.html. The 1998 National Agenda for Governance of the NDA had promised a national

charter for social justice 'based on the principle of social harmony', which was not put forward – see P. S. Krishnan, 'Imperfect sympathy', *Frontline* 26(7), 28 March – 10 April 2009.
68 The BJP 2004 manifesto mentions the NDA's initiatives to create a separate ministry and financial institution for STs and promises to extend the land rights of tribal groups to forest lands, which 'in addition to providing them livelihood security, will also help in preservation of our forests ... as the original inhabitants ... tribals are the best protectors of our depleting forest and wildlife resources' (http://www.indian-elections. com/partymanifestoes/party-manifestoes04/bjp.html).
69 Ibid.
70 These include the *Sampoorna Grameen Rozgar Yojana*, termed 'the biggest food-for-work program since Independence', the *Antyodaya Anna Yojana* and the *Sarva Shiksha Abhiyan* (http://www.indian-elections.com/partymanifestoes/nda.html).
71 It also mentions a 2 per cent 'national integration quota' for 'students from Jammu & Kashmir, North-East, Andaman & Nicobar Islands and Lakshwadeep Islands in educational institutions across the country' (http://www.indian-elections.com/partymanifestoes/nda.html).
72 http://www.indian-elections.com/partymanifestoes/nda.html.
73 The idioms of cultural nationalism, in the form of Sanskritised Hindi words, for instance, are prominent in the NDA manifesto.

Chapter 8

1 I include the governments of Deve Gowda and I. K. Gujral in the Congress/left of center side of the ledger. Their politics were also inspired by the old Congress of Nehru and Indira Gandhi.
2 On the NDA's external policies, see Chiriyankandath and Wyatt (2005); Kundu (2005); and Sridharan (2006).
3 For further details on the dialogues, see Talbott (2006); and Raja Mohan (2006): 17–21.
4 This argument is made by Narang (2009): 140.
5 On the India–China–Russia triangle, see Nadkarni (2010); and on India–Brazil–South Africa, or IBSA, see Shrivastava (2008: 136–7).
6 On India–Iran relations, see Pant (2009).
7 On bilateral cooperation in the region, see Burgess (2009).
8 On India's growing interest in Africa and Latin America, see Emmott (2008: 153–4); *The Economist* (2008); and Avendano and Santiso (2008: 222–30).
9 On the role of India at Doha, see Mortished (2008).
10 The possibility of India sending troops to Iraq is discussed in Raja Mohan (2006: 29–30) and Schaffer, T. (2009: 166–7). India–US military cooperation made some progress in the period 2001–2 including high-level contacts between the forces, military exercises, and arms sales (see Raja Mohan 2006: 101–2). At the operational level, Indian ships escorted US naval assets on their way to the Gulf through the Strait of Malacca (see Raja Mohan 200): 103–5).
11 On the Framework, see Raja Mohan (2006: 118–30).
12 See Raja Mohan (2006: 87–9) for this account.
13 On India's view of the role of democracy in its foreign policy, see Raja Mohan (2008); Cartwright (2009); and Muni (2009).
14 See Raja Mohan (2003: 87–94) on the role of nuclear weapons.
15 See Sanghvi (2009) on a series of articles that appeared in the *Hindustan Times* newspaper during the Mumbai attacks and for a month afterwards.
16 The composite dialogue between India and Pakistan includes: Kashmir; 'peace and security'; Sir Creek; Siachen; Wullar/Tulbul Navigation Project; terrorism; economic and commercial cooperation; and promotion of friendly exchanges.
17 See *BBC News* (2005).

18 These figures are compiled from the website of the Ministry of External Affairs, Government of India, New Delhi (www.mea.gov.in).
19 On the Chinese navy, see Li (2009).
20 See Fravel (2008) on China's various territorial conflicts and its approach to dealing with them.
21 Incursions by Chinese forces rose from 140 in 2007 to 280 in 2008 (see Arnoldy 2009).
22 Narang (2009) makes a similar argument about the importance of party politics and ideology in his fine, recent study of India's strategic missile tests. At the heart of his analysis is the different view of nationalism held by the BJP and Congress. See also Bajpai (2009: 36–8) for BJP–Congress ideological differences.

Chapter 11

1 As of the time of the writing of this book, several corruption scandals have emerged. One of the more prominent ones, popularly referred to as the 2G spectrum scam, involved alleged irregularities in the auctioning of 2G spectrum auctions. To date, India's telecommunications minister, A. Raja, has been forced to resign from the cabinet. Preliminary estimates on the alleged misappropriation of resources, roughly 1.74 lakh rupees, could make the 2G spectrum scam the single largest corruption scandal involving public officials in India.
2 The so-called Bofors scandal was one of the most important corruption scandals in India in the 1980s. Allegations of bribery by a Swedish arms manufacturer (i.e. Bofors AB) to Indian middlemen implicated India's prime minister, Rajiv Gandhi, and contributed to the inability of the Congress party to form a government after the 1989 general election.
3 Chhibber (2009: 60) argues that central government policies strongly influenced voter choice among Muslim respondents and that 'Muslims were more likely to say that the central government mattered when they cast their vote'. Yadav and Palshikar (2009b: 41), though, warn against overstressing the importance of the Muslim vote in returning the UPA coalition to power and they show that overall the 'UPA as a whole lost about 4 percentage points among the Muslims largely as a result of disassociating from the RJD'. Similarly, Alam (2009: 94) shows that Muslim support for the Congress party during the 2009 general election appeared to be strongest in states where there was a bipolar state-level INC–BJP electoral contest (namely Delhi, Gujarat, Karnataka, Madhya Pradesh, Maharashtra, and Rajasthan), but not necessarily in other settings.

Bibliography

Adams, J. and Somer-Topcu, Z. (2009) 'Moderate now and win votes later: the electoral consequences of parties' policy shifts in twenty-five post war democracies', *Journal of Politics*, 71: 238–48.
Adams, J., Clark, M., Ezrow, L. and Glasgow, G. (2004) 'Understanding change and stability in party ideologies: do parties respond to public opinion or to past election results?', *British Journal of Political Science*, 34: 589–610.
Adeney, K. (2005) 'Hindu nationalists and federal structures in an era of regionalism', in K. Adeney and L. Sáez (eds) *Coalition Politics and Hindu Nationalism*, London: Routledge.
Adeney, K. and Sáez, L. (eds) (2005) *Coalition Politics and Hindu Nationalism*, London: Routledge.
Aggarwal, R. and Bhan, M. (2009) 'Disarming violence: development, democracy and security on the borders of India', *Journal of Asian Studies*, 68: 519–42.
Alam, S. (2009) 'Whither Muslim politics in India', *Economic and Political Weekly*, 40: 92–5.
All India Congress Committee. (2009) *Lok Sabha elections 2009 – manifesto of the Indian National Congress*, New Delhi: All India Congress Committee, http://aicc.org.in/new/home-layout-manifesto.php (accessed 14 September 2009).
Alston, P. and Bhuta, N. (2005) 'Human rights and public goods: education as a fundamental right in India', Center for Human Rights and Global Justice Working Paper, *Economic, Social and Cultural Rights Series*, 5, New York: NYU School of Law, http://www.chrgj.org/publications/docs/wp/Alston&Bhuta%20Human%20Rights%20and%20Public%20Goods%20-%20%20Education%20as%20a%20Fundamental%20Right%20in%20India.pdf (accessed 1 July 2010).
Anderson, E. (2002) 'Integration, affirmative action and strict scrutiny', *New York University Law Review*, 77: 1195–271.
Appleby, P. (1953) *Public Administration in India: Report of a Survey*, New Delhi: Government of India.
Arnoldy, B. (2009) 'Growing number of China incursions into India lead to a strategy change', *Christian Science Monitor* (29 September), http://www.csmonitor.com/World/Asia-South Central/20090929/p06s06-wosc.html (accessed 27 February 2010).
Arora, B. (2004) 'Political parties and the party systems: the emergence of new coalitions', in Z. Hasan (ed.), *Parties and Party Politics in India*, Delhi: Oxford University Press.
Arora, B. and Verney, D. (eds.) (1995) *Multiple Identities in a Single State: Indian Federalism in Comparative Perspective*, New Delhi: Konark Publishers.
Asian Development Bank. (2007) *Energy Efficiency and Conservation in India*, Manila: Asian Development Bank.

AsiaNews.it. (2004) 'The Singh government wants to cleanse school textbooks of Hindu nationalism', 7 January, http://www.asianews.it/news-en/The-Singh-Government-Wants-to-Cleanse-School-Textbooks-of-Hindu-Nationalism-1069.html (accessed 13 July 2010).

Austin, G. (1999) *Working a Democratic Constitution: The Indian Experience,* Delhi: Oxford University Press.

Avendano, R. and Santiso, J. (2008) 'The impact of China and India on Latin America', in C. Jaffrelot (ed.) *The Emerging States: The Wellspring of a New World Order,* London: Hurst and CERI.

Bagchi, A. (2003) 'Rethinking Indian federalism: changing power relations between the centre and the state', *Publius: The Journal of Federalism,* 33: 21–42.

Bahgat, G. (2007) 'India's steers new course toward energy reform', *Oil and Gas Journal,* 105: 20–4.

Bajpai, K. (2009) 'The BJP and the bomb', in S. Sagan (ed.) *Inside Nuclear South Asia,* Stanford, CA: Stanford University Press.

Bajpai, R. (2000) 'Constituent assembly debates and minority rights', *Economic and Political Weekly,* 35 (21–2) 1837–45.

Bajpai, R. (2002) 'The conceptual vocabularies of secularism and minority rights in India', *Journal of Political Ideologies,* 7: 179–97.

Bajpai, R. (2006) 'Redefining equality: social justice in the Mandal debate, 1990', in Mehta, V. R. and Pantham, T. (eds) *Political Ideas in Modern India: Thematic Explorations,* Sage Publications, 326–39.

Bajpai, R. (2010) 'Rhetoric as argument: social justice and affirmative action in India, 1990', *Modern Asian Studies,* 44 (4) 675–708.

Bajpai, R. (2011) *Debating Difference: Group Rights and Liberal Democracy in India,* New Delhi: Oxford University Press.

Bandopadhyay, D. (2008) 'Guiding role of central finance commission regarding states counterparts', *Economic and Political Weekly* 43: 27.

Barton, B., Redgwell, C., Rønne, A. and Zillman, D. (2004) *Energy Security: Managing Risk in a Dynamic Legal and Regulatory Environment,* Oxford: Oxford University Press.

Batra, R. K. (2009) 'Natural gas pipelines: geopolitics, affordability, security dimensions', in L. Noronha and A. Sundarshan (eds) *India's Energy Security,* London: Routledge.

Baviskar, B. and Matthew, G. (eds) (2009) *Inclusion and Exclusion in Local Governance: Field Studies from Rural India,* New Delhi: Sage Publications.

BBC News. (2005) 'India offers Pakistan $25 million in aid', *BBC News,* 27 October, http://news.bbc.co.uk/1/hi/world/south_asia/4381982.stm (accessed 28 February 2010).

Bertrand, M. and Mullainathan, S. (2003) *Are Emily and Greg more employable than Likisha and Jamal? A field experiment in labor market discrimination,* NBER Working Paper No. 9873, http://nber.org/papers/w9873 (accessed 14 September 2010).

Beteille, A. (2005) 'Matters of right and of policy', *Seminar,* 549.

Bhambhri, C. P. (2006) *Sonia in Power: UPA Government 2004–2006,* New Delhi: Shipra Publications.

Bhambhri, C. P. (2007) *The Indian State and Political Process,* New Delhi: Shipra.

Bhargava, R. (ed.) (1998) *Secularism and Its Critics,* New Delhi: Oxford University Press.

Bhattacharyya, H. (1998) *Micro-Foundations of Bengal Communism,* Delhi: Ajanta.

Bhattacharyya, H. (2001) *India as a Multicultural Federation: Asian Values, Democracy and Decentralization (in Comparison with Swiss Federalism),* Fribourg: Helbing and Lichtenhahn.

Bhattacharyya, H. (2002) *Making Local Democracy Work in India,* New Delhi: Vedams.

Bibliography

Bhattacharyya, H. (2005) 'Federalism and regionalism in India: institutional strategies and political accommodation of identity', Heidelberg Papers in South Asian and Comparative Politics, Working Paper No. 27, http://www.hpsacp.uni-hd.de> (accessed 11 January 2011).

Bhattacharyya, H. (2009) 'Globalization and Indian federalism: re-assertions of states' rights' in H. Lofgren and P. Sarangi (eds) *The Politics and Culture of Globalization: India and Australia*, New Delhi: Social Science Press.

Bhattacharyya, H. (2010) *Federalism in Asia: India, Pakistan and Malaysia*, London and New York: Routledge.

Bhaumik, S. K. and Chakrabarty, M. (2006) *Earnings inequality in India: Has the rise of case and religion based politics in India had an impact?*, Institute for the Study of Labor, IZA Discussion Paper, 2008, http://www.iza.org (accessed 4 July 2010).

Bijukumar, V. (2006) *Reinventing the Congress*, New Delhi: Rawat Publications.

Bradsher, K. (2005) 'Alert to gains by China, India is making energy deals', *New York Times*, 17 January: 56.

Brass, P. (1977) 'Party systems and government stability in the Indian states', *American Political Science Review*, 71: 1384–405.

Brass, P. (1989) 'Pluralism, regionalism and decentralizing tendencies in contemporary Indian politics', in A. J. Wilson and D. Dalton (eds) *The States of South Asia: The Problems of National Integration*, London: Hurst.

Brass, P. (1994) *The Politics of India Since Independence*, 2nd edn, Cambridge: Cambridge University Press.

Brass, P. (1999) 'Secularism out of its place', in V. Das, D. Gupta and P. Uberoi (eds) *Tradition, Pluralism and Identity*, New Delhi: Sage.

Brass, P. (2006) 'Indian secularism in practice', *Indian Journal of Secularism*, 9:115–32.

Brass, P. (2010) 'Introduction' in P. Brass (ed.) *Routledge Handbook of Indian Politics: India, Pakistan, Bangladesh, Sri Lanka, and Nepal*, Oxford: Routledge.

Brown, J., Mukherji, V. and Wu, K. (2008) 'The energy race between China and India: institutions and potential opportunities for cooperation', in Emirates Centre for Strategic Studies and Research, *China, India & the United States: competition for energy resources*, Abu Dhabi, United Arab Emirates: Emirates Centre for Strategic Studies and Research.

Budge, I., Ezrow, L. and McDonald, M. (2010) 'Ideology, party factionalism and policy change: an integrated dynamic theory', *British Journal of Political Science*, 40: 781–804.

Bunsha, D. (2006) 'Killing zeal', *Frontline*, 6–19 May.

Burgess, S. F. (2009) 'India and South Asia: towards a benign hegemony' in H. V. Pant (ed.) *Indian Foreign Policy in a Unipolar World*, New Delhi: Routledge.

Candland, C. (1997) 'Congress decline and party pluralism in India', *Journal of International Affairs*, 51: 19–35.

Cartwright, J. (2009) 'India's regional and international support for democracy: rhetoric or reality?', *Asian Survey*, 49: 403–28.

Chakravarti, D. (2006) *Forging Power: Coalition Politics*, New Delhi: Oxford University Press.

Chand, A. (1985) *Congress Party Politics and New Challenges: A Survey of Indian National Congress from A.O. Hume to Rajiv Gandhi*, Delhi: UDH Publishers.

Chandra, K. (1999) 'The ethnification of the party system in Uttar Pradesh and its consequences', in R. Roy and P. Wallace (eds) *Indian Politics and the 1998 Election*, New Delhi: Sage Publications.

Chandra, K. (2000) 'The transformation of ethnic politics in India: the decline of Congress and the rise of the Bahujan Samaj Party in Hoshiarpur', *Journal of Asian Studies*, 59: 26–61.

Chandra, K. (2007) *Why Ethnic Parties Succeed in India: Patronage and Ethnic Head Counts in India*, Cambridge: Cambridge University Press.
Chengappa, R. (2000) *Weapons of Peace: The Secret Story of India's Quest to be a Nuclear Power*, New Delhi: HarperCollins India.
Chhibber, P. (2009) 'Are national elections any more than aggregations of state-level verdicts?', *Economic and Political Weekly*, 40: 58–63.
Chidambaram, P. (2009) 'Towards a radical restructuring of national security', *Deccan Herald*, 23 December, http://www.deccanherald.com/content/43125/towards-radical-restructuring-national-security.html (accessed 16 June 2010).
Chiriyankandath, J. and Wyatt, A. (2005) 'The NDA and Indian foreign policy', in K. Adeney and L. Sáez (eds) *Coalition Politics and Hindu Nationalism*, London: Routledge.
Chopra, S. K. (2000) *Energy Policy for India: Towards Sustainable Energy Security in India in the 21st century*, New Delhi: Oxford University Press.
CNN. (2008) 'Source: U.S. warned India about possible Mumbai attack', *CNN*, 2 December, http://edition.cnn.com/2008/WORLD/asiapcf/12/01/india.attacks2/index.html (accessed 16 June 2010).
Colclough, C. and De, A. (2010) 'The impact of aid on education policy in India', Research Consortium on Educational Policy and Outcomes, *Working Paper No. 27*, Cambridge, UK: RECOUP, University of Cambridge, http://recoup.educ.cam.ac.uk/publications/WP27-CC_AD.pdf (accessed 1 July 2010).
Coll, S. (2009) 'The back channel', *New Yorker*, 2 March, http://www.newyorker.com/reporting/2009/03/02/090302fa_fact_coll (accessed 28 February 2010).
CSDS. (1996) 'Hindu–CPPS opinion poll, Jan 25th 1993', *India Today*, 31 August: 41.
CSDS/Lokniti. (2004) 'How India voted – verdict 2004', *The Hindu*, 20 May.
Daily News and Analysis. (2006) 'Manmohan Singh sees foreign hand behind Mumbai blasts', 14 July, http://www.dnaindia.com/mumbai/report_manmohan-singh-sees-foreign-hand-behind-mumbai-blasts (accessed 15 January 2011)
Das Gupta, J. (2001) 'India's federal design and multicultural national construction', in A. Kohli (ed.) *The Success of India's Democracy*, Cambridge: Cambridge University Press.
Department of Atomic Energy. (2007) *Nuclear Energy and Societal Development*, Mumbai: Department of Atomic Energy.
Dhavan, R. (2008) *Reserved! How Parliament Debated Reservations:1995–2007*, Delhi: Rupa.
DiJohn, J. (2007) 'Albert Hirschman's Exit-voice Framework and its relevance to problems of public education performance in Latin America', *Oxford Development Studies*, 35(3), 295–327.
DMK. (2009) *DMK Manifesto*, http://www.dmk.in/e2009/emfesto09.pdf (accessed 6 January 2011).
Dodd, L. (1974) 'Party-coalitions in multiparty parliaments: a game-theoretic analysis, *American Political Science Review*, 68: 1093–117
Dodd, L. (1976) *Coalitions in Parliamentary Government*, Princeton, NJ: Princeton University Press.
Drèze, J. and Goyal, A. (2003) 'Future of mid-day meals', *MPRA Paper No. 17386*, http://mpra.ub.uni-muenchen.de/17386/ (accessed 10 November 2009).
Dua, B. (1979) 'Presidential rule in India: a study in crisis politics', *Asian Survey*, 19: 611–26.
Dua, B. (1985) 'Federalism or patrimonialism: the making and unmaking of chief ministers in India', *Asia Survey*, 25: 793–804.

Dua, B. and Singh, M. P. (eds) (2003) *Indian Federalism in the New Millennium*, New Delhi: Manohar.

Duflo, E. (2004) 'Scaling up and evaluation', *Annual World Bank Conference on Development Economics 2004*, The World Bank, http://econ–www.mit.edu/files/766 (accessed 2 July 2010).

Duverger, M. (1951) *Political Parties*, London: Methuen.

Echeverri-Gent, J. (1993) *The State and the Poor: Public Policy and Political Development in India and the United States*, Berkeley, CA: University of California Press.

Emmott, B. (2008) *Rivals: How the Struggle between China, India and Japan will Shape our Next Decade*, London: Allen Lane/Penguin.

External Affairs Minister Mr. Pranab Mukherjee's Suo Motu statement in Parliament (2009) 'Follow up to Mumbai terrorist attack', 13 February, http://www.indianembassy.org/prdetail529/external-affairs-minister-mr.-pranab-mukherjee%27s-suo-motu-statement-in-parliament-on-andquot%3Bfollow-up-to-mumbai-terroris--attackandquot%3B (accessed 15 January 2011)

Ezrow, L. (2005) 'Are moderate parties rewarded in multiparty systems? A pooled analysis of Western European elections, 1984–1998', *European Journal of Political Research*, 44: 881–98.

Ezrow, L. (2008) 'On the inverse relationship between votes and proximity for niche parties', *European Journal of Political Research*, 47: 206–20.

Fair, C. (2009) 'India and the US: embracing a new paradigm', in H. V. Pant (ed.) *Indian Foreign Policy in a Unipolar World*, New Delhi: Routledge.

Fennell, S. (2006) 'Future policy choices for the education sector in Asia', paper presented at the Asia 2015 conference on promoting growth, ending poverty, London, March 2006.

Fennell, S. (2007) 'Tilting at windmills: public private partnerships in Indian education today', Research Consortium on Educational Policy and Outcomes, *Working Paper No. 5*, Cambridge, UK: RECOUP, University of Cambridge, http://recoup.educ.cam.ac.uk/publications/WP5–SF_PPPs.pdf (accessed 1 July 2010).

Fennell, S. (2010) *Rules, Rubrics and Riches: The Relationship Between Law, Institutions and International Development*, Abingdon and New York: Routledge.

Franda, M. (1962) 'The organizational development of India's Congress party', *Pacific Affairs*, 35: 248–60.

Fraser, N. and Honneth, A. (2003) *Redistribution or Recognition? A Philosophical Exchange*, New York: Verso.

Fravel, M. T. (2008) *Strong Borders, Secure Nation: Cooperation and Conflict in China's Territorial Disputes*, Princeton, NJ: Princeton University Press.

Galanter, M. (1984) *Competing Equalities, Law and the Backward Classes in India*, Delhi: Oxford University Press.

Galligan, B. (2009) 'Comparative federalism', in R. A. W. Rhodes *et al.* (eds) *The Oxford Handbook of Political Institutions*, Oxford: Oxford University Press.

Ganesh, K. N. (2005) 'National curriculum framework 2005: a note', *Social Scientist*, 33: 47–54.

Gehlot, N. S. (ed.) (1991) *The Congress Party in India: Policies, Culture, Performance*, New Delhi: Deep & Deep.

Gill, P. P. S. (2001) 'SGPC colleges are "minority institutions"', *The Tribune*, 29 May.

Government of India. (1988) *Commission on Centre State Relations* (Sarkaria Commission Report), 2 vols, New Delhi: Government of India Press.

Government of India. (2001) *Recommendations of the Groups of Ministers on Reforming the National Security System*, New Delhi: Government of India Press.

Government of India. (2002) *National Commission to Review the Working of the Constitution*, New Delhi: Secretary of the Government of India, http://lawmin.nic.in/ncrwc/finalreport.htm (accessed 19 December 2009).

Government of India. (2004) *National Common Minimum Programme of the Government of India*, http://pmindia.nic.in/cmp.pdf (accessed 12 July 2010).

Government of India. (2005) *The Millennium Development Goals Country Report, 2005*, New Delhi: Government of India Press.

Government of India. (2007) *Report of the National Commission for Religious and Linguistic Minorities*, http://minorityaffairs.gov.in/newsite/ncrlm/volume-1.pdf (accessed 17 December 2010).

Government of India. (2010) *Commission on Centre–State Relations* (Punchi Commission), 7 vols, New Delhi: Government of India.

Government of India, Ministry of Defence. (2009) 'Antony announces comprehensive plan to tackle threat from sea Indian Navy to be the nodal authority for maritime security Navy to raise a new specialised force "Sagar Prahari Bal"', 28 February, http://pib.nic.in/newsite/erelease.aspx?relid=48167 (accessed 15 January 2011).

Government of India, Ministry of Minority Affairs website. (2010) http://minorityaffairs.gov.in/newsite/main/FAQ_Ministry.pdf (accessed 22 December 2010).

Guhan, S. (1995) 'Federalism and the new political economy of India', in B. Arora and D. Verney (eds) *Multiple Identities in a Single State: Indian Federalism in Comparative Perspective*, New Delhi: Konark Publishers.

Guruswamy, M. and Singh, Z. D. (2009) *India–China Relations: The Border Issue and Beyond*, New Delhi: Viva Books/Observer Research Foundation.

Habib, I. (2005) 'How to evade real issues and make room for obscurantism', *Social Scientist*, 33: 3–12.

Hasan, Z. (2009) 'Muslim deprivation and debate on equality', *Seminar*, 602: 34–7.

Heath, O. (2005) 'Party systems, political cleavages and electoral volatility in India: state-wise analysis 1998–1999', *Electoral Studies* 24 (2) 177–99.

Imam, J. M. (1970) *Lok Sabha debates*, 14 May: 298–99.

India Energy Forum. (2004) *Integrated Energy Policy for India*, New Delhi: India Energy Forum.

India News Online. (2000) 'India–China exchange of border maps: look-ups in ties', *India News Online*, 27, http://news.indiamart.com/news-analysis/india-china-exchange-6602.html (accessed 2 March 2010).

India Today (2010) 'Sonia bats for Muslim reservation timeframe', 23 May.

Indian Express (2009) 'Arjun may not find a place; SP, RJD talk outside support', 19 May.

Indian Express (2009) 'Reservation in pvt sector no answer for the future: Khurshid', 4 July.

Indian Express (2010) 'Chidambaram, Khurshid strike different note on reservation', 31 March.

Indian Express (2010) 'At minority meet, PC says quota is best way forward', 1 April.

Indian Express (2010) 'Govt pushing for reservation in pvt sector', 24 May.

Indian Express (2010) 'Need for consensus on reservation for Muslims, says PM', 9 July.

Indian National Congress. (2004) *Manifesto 2004*, http://www.congress.org.in/manifesto-2004.php (accessed 12 July 2010).

Indo–Asian News Service. (2009) 'Pakistan epicenter of terrorism: Congress', 24 April, http://www.thaindian.com/newsportal/politics/pakistan-epicenter-of-terrorism-congress_100184156.html (accessed 15 January 2011).

International Energy Agency. (2006) *World Economic Outlook*, Paris: International Energy Agency.

Bibliography

International Energy Agency. (2007) *World Economic Outlook*, Paris: International Energy Agency.

International Institute for Strategic Studies (IISS). (2004) 'India's troubled northeast: insurgency and crime', *Strategic Comments*, 10.

International Institute for Strategic Studies (IISS). (2006a) 'Terror in India: Mumbai bombings', *Strategic Comments*, 12.

International Institute for Strategic Studies (IISS). (2006b) 'Countering Naxalite violence in India: policy confusion', *Strategic Comments*, 12.

International Institute for Strategic Studies (IISS). (2008) 'Terror in Mumbai: attacks raise intelligence, security and political questions', *Strategic Comments*, 14.

International Institute for Strategic Studies (IISS). (2009) 'Islamic extremism in India: rise of home-grown terrorism', *Strategic Comments*, 15.

International Institute for Strategic Studies (IISS). (2010) 'South and Central Asia', in *The Military Balance 2010*, Routledge: London.

International Publication and Information Services. (2005) *Overview of Power Sector in India 2005*, New Delhi: International Publication and Information Services.

Jaffrelot, C. (2000) 'The rise of the Other Backward Classes in the Hindi belt', *Journal of Asian Studies*, 59, 86–108.

Jaffrelot, C. (2003) *India's Silent Revolution*, London: C. Hurst & Co.

Jain, L. C. (ed.) (2005) *Decentralization and Local Governance*, New Delhi: Orient Longman.

Jayaraman, R. (2008) *The Impact of School Lunches on Enrolment: Evidence from an Exogenous Policy Change in India*, http://www.client.norc.org/jole/SOLEweb/9001.pdf (accessed 20 March 2010).

Jenkins, R. (1999) *Democratic Politics and Economic Reform in India*, Cambridge: Cambridge University Press.

Jenkins, R. (2003) 'How federalism influences India's domestic politics of WTO engagement: (and is itself affected in the process)', *Asian Survey*, 43: 598–621.

Jha, P. et al. (2008) *Public Provisioning for Elementary Education*, New Delhi: Sage.

Jha, S. N. and Mathur, P. C. (eds) (1999) *Decentralization and Local Politics*, New Delhi: Sage Publications.

Johari, J. C. (2006) *Indian National Congress Since Independence*, New Delhi: Lotus Press.

John, L. (2009) 'Wada Na Todo Abhiyan', *Outlook* (June): 16.

Joshi, A. (2009) 'Indian army to deploy more troops along Arunachal border. *Hindustan Times*, 12 November, http://www.hindustantimes.com/special-news-report/HindiChinigreatgame/Indian-Army-to-deploy-more-troops-along-Arunachal-border/Article3-475434.aspx (accessed 27 February 2010).

Kabir, Humayun (1968) *Minorities in a Democracy*, Calcutta: K. L. Mukhopadhyay.

Kalicki, J. and Goldwyn, D. (2005) 'Energy, security, and foreign policy', in J. Kalicki and D. Goldwyn (eds) *Energy and Security: Toward a New Foreign Policy Strategy*, Baltimore, MD: Johns Hopkins University Press.

Kapila, S. (2004) 'India's benchmarks for peace dialogue with Pakistan', South Asian Analysis Group, Paper 1133, http://www.southasiaanalysis.org/%5Cpapers12%5Cpaper1133.html (accessed 27 February 2010).

Karan, Jajati. (2009) 'Kandhamal riots forced BJD to snap ties with BJP', 19 March, http://ibnlive.in.com/news/kandhamal-riots-forced-bjd-to-snap-ties-with-bjp/88069-37.html (accessed 26 May 2011).

Karnad, B. (2002) *Nuclear Weapons and Indian Security: The Realist Foundations of Strategy*, New Delhi: Macmillan.

Karnad, B. (2008) *India's Nuclear Policy*, Westport, CT: Praeger Security International.

Kavalski, E. (2008) 'Venus and the porcupine: assessing the European Union–India strategic partnership', *South Asian Survey*, 15: 63–81.
Khan, J. A. (2005) *India's Energy Security and the Arabian Gulf: Oil and Gas Markets in Decontrolled Regimes*, New Delhi: Arise Publishers.
Khera, R. (2005) 'India's Right to Food Campaign', *Just Change*, October.
Khera, R., Samson, M. and De, A. (2009) 'Incentives that work', *The Hindu*, 10 May.
Khwaja, A. I., Andrabi, T., Das, T. and Zajonc, T. (2006) 'Religious school enrollment in Pakistan: a look at the data', *Comparative Education Review*, 50: 446–77.
King, A. (1975) 'Overload: problems of governing in the 1970s', *Political Studies*, 23: 283–96.
King et al. (1997) 'Columbia's targeted voucher scheme: features, coverage, participation, impact evaluation of educational reforms', No. 3, Development Education Research Group, World Bank.
Klare, M. (2008) *Rising Powers, Shrinking Planet: The New Geopolitics of Energy*, New York: Henry Holt.
Kochanek, S. (1969) *The Congress Party of India: The Dynamics of One-Party Democracy*, Princeton, NJ: Princeton University Press.
Kothari, R. (1964) 'The Congress "system" in India', *Asian Survey*, 4: 1161–73.
Kothari, R. (1974) 'The Congress system revisited: a decennial review', *Asian Survey*, 14: 1035–54.
Kuhn, T. (1962) *The Structure of Scientific Revolutions*, Chicago, IL: University of Chicago Press.
Kumar, K. (2004) 'Quality of education at the beginning of the 21st century: lessons from India', *Background Paper for the Education for All Global Monitoring Report 2005, The Quality Imperative*, Paris: UNESCO.
Kumar, K. (2007) 'EFA and the quality debate: perspective from India's National Curricular Framework, 2005', CREATE Lecture, London International Development Centre, 5.
Kumaraswamy, P. R. (2007) 'India's energy cooperation with China: the slippery side', *China Report*, 43: 349–52.
Kundu, A. (2005) 'The NDA and national security', in K. Adeney and L. Sáez (eds) *Coalition Politics and Hindu Nationalism*, London: Routledge.
Kurian, K. M. and Varugheese P. N. (eds) (1981) *Centre–State Relations in India*, New Delhi: Orient Longman.
Ladwig, W. C. (2007/8) 'A cold start for hot wars? The Indian army's new limited war doctrine', *International Security*, 32: 158–90.
Li, N. (2009) 'The evolution of China's naval strategy and capabilities: from "near coast" and "near seas" to "far seas"', *Asian Security*, 5: 144–69.
Lijphart, A. (1984) 'Measures of cabinet durability: a conceptual and empirical evaluation', *Comparative Political Studies*, 17: 265–79.
McGregor, R., Johnson, J. and Hoyos, C. (2006) 'China and India forge an alliance on oil with an aim of ending "mindless rivalry"', *Financial Times*, 13 January: 1.
Madan, T. (2006) *The Brookings Foreign Policy Studies Energy Security Series: India*, Washington, DC: The Brookings Institution.
Madan, T. N. (1987) 'Secularism in its place', *Journal of Asian Studies*, 46: 747–59.
Mahajan, G. (2010) 'Religion, community and development', in G. Mahajan and S. S. Jodhka (eds) *Religion, Communities and Development: Changing Contours of Politics and Policy in India*, New Delhi: Routledge.
Mahajan, G. and S. S. Jodhka (2009) *Religion, Democracy and Governance: Spaces for the Marginalised in Contemporary India*, Birmingham: Religions and Development Research Programme.

Majeed, A. (ed.) (2009) *Federal Power Sharing: Accommodating Indian Diversity*, New Delhi: Manak Publications.

Malakar, S. N. (ed.) (2006) *India's Energy Security in the Gulf*, Delhi: Academic Excellence.

Malik, J. M. (2009) 'As China rises, India stirs', in H. Pant (ed.) *Indian Foreign Policy in a Unipolar World*, New Delhi: Routledge.

Manoj, C. G. (2009) 'Cong won because we pushed NREGA: CPM', *Financial Express*, 20 May, http://www.financialexpress.com/news/cong-won-because-we-pushed-nrega-cpm/462575/ (accessed 24 June 2010).

Manor, J. (1994) 'Introduction', in J. Manor (ed.) *Nehru to the Nineties: The Changing Office of Prime Minister in India*, London: Hurst/Penguin.

Manor, J. (1995) 'The political sustainability of economic liberalization in India', in R. Cassen and V. Joshi (eds) *India: The Future of Economic Reform*, Delhi: Oxford University Press.

Manor, J. (1998) 'Making federalism work', *Journal of Democracy*, 9: 21–35.

Manor, J. (2001) 'Centre–state relations in India', in A. Kohli (ed.) *The Success of India's Democracy*, Cambridge: Cambridge University Press.

Manor, J. (2010) 'The Congress party and the "great transformation"', in S. Ruparelia *et al.* (eds) *Understanding India's New Political Economy, A Great Transformation?*, London: Routledge.

Martin, W., Imai, R. and Steeg, H. (1996) *Maintaining Energy Security in a Global Context*, New York: Trilateral Commission.

Mendelsohn, O. (1978) 'The collapse of the Indian National Congress', *Pacific Affairs*, 51: 41–66.

Miller, D. (1999) *Principles of Social Justice*, Cambridge, MA: Harvard University Press.

Ministry of Home Affairs, Government of India. (2004) 'Annual report of the Ministry of Home Affairs 2003–04', New Delhi: Government of India, http://www.mha.nic.in/pdfs/ar0304-Eng.pdf (accessed 16 June 2010).

Ministry of Home Affairs, Government of India. (2009) 'Annual report of the Ministry of Home Affairs 2008–09', New Delhi: Government of India, http://www.mha.nic.in/pdfs/AR(E)0809.pdf (accessed 16 June 2010).

Ministry of Human Resource Development, Government of India. (2004) *Resolution on the Reconstitution of the CABE*, New Delhi: Government of India Press.

Ministry of Human Resource Development, Government of India. (2005a) *CABE Committee on Regulatory Mechanisms for Textbooks and Parallel Textbooks Taught in Schools Outside the Government System*, New Delhi: Government of India Press.

Ministry of Human Resource Development, Government of India. (2005b) *Report of the CABE Committee on Girls' Education and the Common School System*, New Delhi: Government of India Press.

Ministry of Human Resource Development, Government of India. (2005c) *Report of the CABE Committee on Universalization of Secondary Education*, New Delhi: Government of India Press.

Ministry of Human Resource Development, Department of Secondary Higher Education, Government of India. (2005d) *Report of the Central Advisory Board of Education (CABE) Committee on Autonomy of Higher Education Institutions*, New Delhi: Government of India Press.

Ministry of Human Resource Development, Government of India. (2005e) *Report of the Central Advisory Board of Education (CABE) Committee on Free and Compulsory Education Bill and Other Issues Relating to Elementary Education*, New Delhi: Government of India Press.

Ministry of Labour and Employment, Government of India. (2010a) *Rashtriya Swasthya Bima Yojna*, New Delhi: Government of India, http://www.rsby.in/Overview.aspx (accessed 24 June 2010).

Ministry of Labour and Employment, Government of India. (2010b) 'National summary', *Rashtriya Swasthya Bima Yojna*, New Delhi: Government of India, http://www.rsby.in/Overview.aspx (accessed 24 June 2010).

Ministry of Law, Justice and Company Affairs, Department of Legal Affairs, Government of India. (2002) 'Report of the national commission to review the working of the constitution', New Delhi: Secretary of the Government of India, http://lawmin.nic.in/ncrwc/finalreport.htm (accessed 19 December 2009).

Ministry of Minority Affairs, Government of India. (2007) *Report of the National Commission for Religious and Linguistic Minorities* (Misra report), 2 vols, New Delhi: Government of India, http://minorityaffairs.gov.in/sites/upload_files/moma/files/pdfs/volume-1.pdf (accessed 12 December 2010).

Ministry of Minority Affairs, Government of India. (2008a) *Equal Opportunity Commission: What, Why and How? Report by the Expert Group to Examine and Determine the Structure and Functions of an Equal Opportunity Commission* (Menon report), http://minorityaffairs.gov.in/newsite/reports/eoc_wwh/eoc_wwh.pdf (accessed 10 December 2010).

Ministry of Minority Affairs, Government of India. (2008b) *Report of the Expert Group on Diversity Index* (Kundu report), http://minorityaffairs.gov.in/newsite/reports/di_expgrp/di_expgrp.pdf (accessed 24 June 2010).

Ministry of Minority Affairs, Government of India. (2009) *Annual Report 2009–2010*, http://minorityaffairs.gov.in/sites/upload_files/moma/files/pdfs/ar0910h.pdf (accessed 26 May 2011).

Ministry of Minority Affairs, Government of India. (2010) *Frequently Asked Questions Related to the Ministry*, New Delhi: Government of India, http://minorityaffairs.gov.in/newsite/main/FAQ_Ministry.pdf (accessed 11 June 2010).

Ministry of Power, Government of India. (2005) *National Electricity Policy*, New Delhi: Ministry of Power.

Ministry of Power, Government of India. (2006) *Tariff Policy*, New Delhi: Ministry of Power.

Ministry of Power, Government of India. (2006) *Rural Electrification Policy*, New Delhi: Ministry of Power.

Ministry of Rural Development, Government of India. (2010) *The Mahatma Gandhi National Rural Employment Guarantee Act 2005*, New Delhi: Government of India, http://www.nrega.nic.in/netnrega/home.aspx (accessed 24 June 2010).

Ministry of Welfare, Government of India. (1986) *Sixth Annual Report of the Minorities' Commission (for the period 1 April 1983 to 31 March 1984)*, New Delhi: Government of India.

Mistry, D. (2006) 'Diplomacy, domestic politics, and the U.S.–India nuclear agreement', *Asian Survey*, 46: 675–98.

Mitra, S. K. (1980) 'A theory of government instability in parliamentary systems', *Comparative Political Studies*, 13: 235–63.

Mitra, S. K. (2001) 'Making local government work: local elites, panchayati raj and governance in India', in A. Kohli (ed.) *The Success of India's Democracy*, Cambridge: Cambridge University Press.

Mitra, S. K. (2005) 'The NDA and the politics of "minorities" in India', in K. Adeney and L. Sáez (eds) *Coalition Politics and Hindu Nationalism*, London: Routledge, 77–96.

Mooij, J. (2007) 'Is there an Indian policy process?: an investigation into two social processes', *Social Policy and Administration*, 4: 323–38.

Morris-Jones, W. H. (1967) 'The Indian Congress party: a dilemma of dominance', *Modern Asian Studies* 1: 109–13.

Morris-Jones, W. H. (1987) *The Government and Politics of India*, Cambridgeshire: Eothen Press.

Mortished, C. (2008) 'Why the Doha round of talks finally died', *Times Online*, 30 July, http://business.timesonline.co.uk/tol/business/columnists/article4425744.ece (accessed 3 March 2010).

Muni, S. D. (2009) *Indian Foreign Policy: The Democracy Dimension*, Delhi: Foundation Books.

Muni, S. D. and Pant, G. (2005) *India's Search for Energy Security*, New Delhi: Rupa.

Nadkarni, V. (2010) *Strategic Partnerships in Asia: Balance Without Alliances*, Abingdon: Routledge.

Nanda, M. (2004) 'Postmodernism, Hindu nationalism and "vedic science"', *Frontline*, 9 January: 10.

Narang, V. (2009) 'Pride and prejudice and Prithvis: strategic weapons behavior in South Asia' in S. D. Sagan (ed.) *Inside Nuclear South Asia*, Stanford, CA: Stanford University Press.

Nayar, B. R. (1992) 'The politics of economic restructuring in India: the paradox of state strength and policy weakness', *Commonwealth and Comparative Politics*, 30: 22–56.

Nikolenyi, C. (1998) 'The new Indian party system: what kind of a model?', *Party Politics*, 4: 367–80.

Noorani, A. G. (1990) 'Indira Gandhi and Indian Muslims', *Economic and Political Weekly*, 25: 2417–20.

Noronha, L. and Sundarshan, A. (eds) (2009) *India's Energy Security*, London: Routledge.

Nussbaum, M. (2008) 'Affirmative action and the goals of higher education', paper presented at Conference on Affirmative Action in Higher Education in India, the United States and South Africa, New Delhi, 19–21 March.

Obinger, H., Castles, F. G. and Leibfried, S. (eds) (2005) *Federalism and the Welfare State: New World and European Experience*, Cambridge: Cambridge University Press.

Pachauri, R. K. (1977) *Energy and Economic Development in India*, New York: Praeger Publishers.

Pachauri, R. K. and Mehrotra, P. (2004) 'Sustainability of India's natural resources: Vision 2020', in Planning Commission, *India Vision 2020: The Report*, Report of the committee on India's Vision 2020, New Delhi: Academic Foundation.

Pai, S. (1996) 'Transformation of the Indian party system: the 1996 Lok Sabha elections', *Asian Survey*, 36: 1170–83.

Pant, G. (2008) *India: The Energy Security Player*, New Delhi: Pearson Longman.

Pant, H. (2009) 'India and the Middle East: a re-assessment of priorities?' in H. V. Pant (ed.) *Indian Foreign Policy in a Unipolar World*, New Delhi: Routledge.

Pathan, B. (2002) 'Modi ties hands of cops who put their foot down', *Indian Express*, New Delhi, 26 March: 1.

Perkovich, G. (2000) *India's Nuclear Bomb: The Impact on Global Proliferation*, New Delhi: Oxford University Press.

Phillips, A. (1995) *The Politics of Presence*, Oxford: Clarendon Press.

Phillips, A. (2004) 'Defending equality of outcome', *Journal of Political Philosophy*, 12 (1): 1–19.

Planning Commission, Government of India. (2000) *Hydrocarbon Vision 2025*, New Delhi: Planning Commission.

Planning Commission, Government of India. (2002) *The Tenth Five Year Plan*, 3 vols, New Delhi: Planning Commission.

Planning Commission, Government of India. (2004) *India Vision 2020: The Report*, Report of the committee on India Vision 2020, New Delhi: Academic Foundation.
Planning Commission, Government of India. (2006) *Integrated Energy Policy*, New Delhi: Planning Commission.
Planning Commission, Government of India. (2007) *The Eleventh Five Year Plan*, 3 vols, New Delhi: Planning Commission.
Press Information Bureau, Ministry of Rural Development, Government of India. (2009) http://pibmumbai.gov.in/scripts/detail.asp?releaseId=E2009FR37 (accessed 9 November 2009).
Prime Minister's High Level Committee. (2006) *Social, Economic and Educational Status of the Muslim Community of India* (Sachar Committee report), New Delhi: Cabinet Secretariat, Government of India. http://www.minorityaffairs.gov.in/sites/upload_files/moma/files/pdfs/sachar_ comm.pdf (accessed 10 April 2010)
Pritchett, L. and Pande, V. (2006) 'Making primary education work for India's poor: a proposal for effective decentralisation', *Social Development Department, South Asia Series, No. 95*, June, World Bank, http://siteresources.worldbank.org/PSGLP/Resources/PritchettPande.pdf (accessed 1 July 2010).
Punchi, M. M. (2008) *The Introductory to Questionnaires* (Punchi Commission), New Delhi: Government of India
Raghavan, E. and Manor, J. (2009) *Broadening and Deepening Democracy: Political Innovation in Karnataka*, New Delhi and London: Routledge.
Raina, V. (2008) 'Right to education', *Seminar*, 593: 87–91.
Raja Mohan, C. (2003) *Crossing the Rubicon: The Shaping of India's Foreign Policy*, New Delhi: Penguin India.
Raja Mohan, C. (2006) *Impossible Allies: Nuclear India, United States, and Global Order*, New Delhi: India Research Press.
Raja Mohan C. (2008) 'Balancing interests and values: India's struggle with democracy promotion', in A. T. J. Lennon and A. Kozlowski (eds) *Global Powers in the 21st century: Strategies and Relations*, Washington, DC: CSIS and MIT Press.
Rajlakshmi, T. K. (2011) 'Left in the cold', *Frontline* 28 (1–14 January):1.
Ramachandran, V. (2004) *Gender and Social Equity in Primary Education: Hierarchies of Access*, New Delhi: Sage.
Ramakrishnan, V. (2011) 'Under siege', *Frontline* 28 (1–14 January): 1.
Ramana, M. V. (2006) *Nuclear Power in India: Failed Past, Dubious Future*, Washington, DC: Nonproliferation Education Policy Center.
Rao, G. and Singh, N. (2005) *The Political Economy of Indian Federalism*, Delhi: Oxford University Press.
Rao, N (2005) 'Social justice and empowerment of the weaker sections and gender rights', in K. Adeney and L. Sáez (eds) *Coalition Politics and Hindu Nationalism*, London: Routledge, 116–35.
Rastogi, A. (2008) 'The infrastructure sector in India, 2007', in 3i Network, *India Infrastructure Report 2008*, New Delhi: Oxford University Press.
Rawls, J. (1971) *A Theory of Justice*, Cambridge, MA: The Belknap Press of Harvard University Press.
Reddy, B. M. (2006) 'Islamabad keen on Manmohan visit', *The Hindu*, 6 January, http://www.hindu.com/2006/01/06/stories/2006010604381400.htm (accessed 27 February 2010).
Rediff News (2006) 'Muslims "lagging behind" other groups: Sachar panel', 17 November, http://www.rediff.com/cms/print.jsp?docpath=//news/2006/nov/17sachar.htm.
Rediff News (2009) 'Chidambaram speaks on terrorism, insurgency, police reforms', *Rediff News*, 14 September, http://news.rediff.com/report/2009/sep/14/

chidambaram-speaks-on-terrorism-insurgency-police-reforms.htm (accessed 16 June 2010).
Riker, W. (1962) *The Theory of Political Coalitions*, New Haven, CT: Yale University Press.
Robinson, R. (2007) 'Indian Muslims: the varied dimension of marginality', *Economic and Political Weekly*, 42: 839–43.
Roy, M. S. (2007) 'India's energy security: an overview', in J. Singh (ed.) *Oil and Gas in India's Security*, New Delhi: Institute for Defence Studies and Analyses.
Roy, R. and Wallace, P. (ed.) (2007) *India's 2004 Elections*, New Delhi: Sage.
Rudolph, L. I. and Rudolph, S. H. (2001) 'Redoing the constitutional design: from an interventionist states to a regulatory state in India', in A. Kohli (ed.) *The Success of India's Democracy*, Cambridge: Cambridge University Press.
Rudolph, S. H. and Rudolph, L. I. (1980) 'The centrist future of Indian politics', *Asian Survey*, 20: 575–94.
Rudolph, S. H. and Rudolph, L. I. (1987) *In Pursuit of Lakhsmi*, Chicago, IL: University of Chicago Press.
Russell, P. H. (2005) 'The future of Europe in an era of federalism', in S. Orion, M. Zagar and V. Mastny (eds) *The Changing Face of Federalism: Institutional Reconfiguration in Europe from East to West*, Manchester: Manchester University Press.
Sadgopal, A. (2005a) 'A compilation of notes on the common school system', presented at the Meeting of the Central Advisory Board of Education on 14–15 July, New Delhi.
Sadgopal, A. (2005b) 'On the pedagogy of writing a national curricular framework: some reflections from an insider', *Social Scientist*, 3: 23–36.
Sáez, L. (1999) 'India's economic liberalization, interjurisdictional competition, and development', *Contemporary South Asia*, 8: 323–45.
Sáez, L. (2002) *Federalism Without a Centre*, New Delhi: Sage Publications.
Sáez, L. (2007a) 'U.S. policy and energy security in South Asia: economic prospects and strategic implications', *Asian Survey*, 47: 657–78.
Sáez, L. (2007b) *EU–India Nuclear Energy Co-Operation: Prospects and Challenges*, ENCARI Briefing Paper No. 7, Brussels: European Commission.
Sáez, L. (2007c) 'The United Kingdom, the European Union, and South Asia's energy security', House of Commons, Foreign Affairs Committee, *Fourth Report of Session 2006–2007*, London: House of Commons: Ev 157–62.
Sáez, L. (2009) 'The political economy of financial services reform in India: explaining variations in political opposition and barriers to entry', *Journal of Asian Studies*, 68: 1–26.
Sáez, L. and Vipradas, M. (2006) *Barriers and Opportunities for EU–India Renewable Energy Collaboration*, ENCARI Briefing Paper No. 3, Brussels: European Commission.
Samson, M., Noronha, C. and De, A. (2008) 'Towards more benefit from Delhi's midday meal scheme', in R. Baru (ed.) *School Health Services in India*, Sage, New Delhi.
Sanghvi, V. (1994) 'The RAW truth: why don't the security agencies hire Muslims?', *Sunday*, 27 March–2 April.
Sanghvi, V. (ed.) (2009) *26/11: The Attack on Mumbai*, New Delhi: Penguin.
Sarangapani, P. (2003) *Constructing School Knowledge: An Ethnography of Learning in an Indian Village*, New Delhi: Sage.
Schaffer, H. R. (2009) *The Limits of Influence: America's Role in Kashmir*, Washington, DC: Brookings Institution Press.
Schaffer, T. (2009) *India and the United States in the 21st Century: Reinventing Partnership*, Washington, DC: The CSIS Press.
Setalvad, Teesta. (2002) 'When guardians betray', in Varadarajan, Siddharth (ed.) *Gujarat: The Making of a Tragedy*, New Delhi: Penguin, 177–213.

Seth, D. L. (2009) 'Minority politics: the shifting terms of policy discourse', *Seminar*, 602: 15–19.
Seth, D. L. (2010) 'Political communalisation of religions and the crisis of secularism', in G. Mahajan and S. S. Jodhka (eds) *Religion, Communities and Development: Changing Contours of Politics and Policy in India*, New Delhi: Routledge.
Shariff, A. (1995) 'Socio-economic and demographic differentials between Hindus and Muslims in India', *Economic and Political Weekly*, 30: 2947–53.
Shahabuddin, S. (2007) 'Sachar and Mishra reports', http://www.syedshahabuddin.com/sachar_mishra_reports.html (accessed 26 May 2011).
Sharma, R. (2004) *Sonia Versus Vajpayee*, New Delhi: Deep and Deep Publications.
Shrivastava, M. (2008) 'South Africa in the contemporary international economy: India's competitor or ally?', *South Asian Survey*, 15: 121–42.
Singh, G. (2000) *Ethnic Conflict in India: A Case-Study of Punjab*, Basingstoke: Macmillan.
Singh, G. (2004) 'State and religious diversity: reflections on post-1947 India', *Totalitarian Movements and Political Religions*, 5: 205–25.
Singh, G. (2005) 'Managing anti-corruption rhetoric: the National Democratic Alliance, transparency and corruption', in K. Adeney and L. Sáez (eds) *Coalition Politics and Hindu Nationalism*, London: Routledge, 136–52.
Singh, J. (ed.) (2007) *Oil and Gas in India's Security*, New Delhi: Institute for Defence Studies and Analyses.
Singh, J. (2009) *I Accuse...: The Anti Sikh Violence of 1984*, New Delhi: Viking.
Singh, M. P. (1992) 'The dilemma of the new Indian party system: to govern or not to govern?', *Asian Survey*, 32: 303–17.
Singh, S. (2008) 'India–China relations: perceptions, problems, potential', *South Asian Survey*, 15: 83–98.
Sinha, A. (2005) *The Regional Roots of Developmental Politics in India: A Divided Leviathan*, Bloomington, IN: Indiana University Press.
Skinner, Q. (1988) 'Some problems in the analysis of political thought and action', in Tully, James (ed.) *Meaning and Context: Quentin Skinner and his Critics*, Cambridge: Polity Press, 97–118.
Skinner, Q. (2002) *Visions of Politics, Volume I Regarding Method*, Cambridge: Cambridge University Press.
Smith, D. E. (1967) *India as a Secular State*, Princeton, NJ: Princeton University Press.
Smith, T. (1973) 'The policy implementation process', *Policy Sciences*, 4: 197–209.
South Asian Human Rights Documentation Centre (2008) 'Anti-conversion laws: challenges to secularism and fundamental rights', *Economic and Political Weekly*, 43: 63–73.
Sridharan, E. (2003) 'Coalitions and party strategies in India's parliamentary federation', *Publius*, 33(4): 135–52.
Sridharan, K. (2006) 'Explaining the phenomenon of change in Indian foreign policy under the National Democratic Alliance government', *Contemporary South Asia*, 15: 75–91.
Stewart, F. and Brown, G. (2009) Fragile States. CRISE Working Paper No. 51, January.
Strom, K. (1985) 'Party goals and government performance in parliamentary democracies', *American Political Science Review*, 71: 738–54.
Strom, K. (1988) 'Contending models of cabinet stability', *American Political Science Review*, 82: 923–30.
Subrahmanyam, K. (2009) 'How to resolve Kashmir', *Times of India*, 26 February.
Swami, P. (2008) 'ISI engineered Kabul Embassy bombing: NYT', *The Hindu*, 2 August, http://www.thehindu.com/2008/08/02/stories/2008080255181200.htm (accessed 16 June 2010).

Bibliography

Talbott, S. (2006) *Engaging India: Diplomacy, Democracy and the Bomb*. Washington, DC: Brookings Institution Press.

Tandon, Aditi and Ashok Tuteja (2009) 'Babri report leak throws parliament into tumult: table the report now, demands angry opposition', *The Tribune*, 24 November.

Taylor, M. and Herman, V. (1971) 'Party systems and government stability', *American Political Science Review*, 65: 28–37.

TERI. (2002) *Defining an Integrated Energy Strategy for India: Ensuring Security, Efficiency & Sustainability*, New Delhi: TERI.

TERI. (2008) *Energy Data Directory & Yearbook 2007*, New Delhi: TERI.

Tha Indian. (2009) 'Navy to head Indian maritime security', *Tha Indian*, 28 February, http://www.thaindian.com/newsportal/uncategorized/navy-to-head-indian-maritime-security-antony_100160910.html (accessed 16 June 2010).

The Economist (2008) 'The power and the glory: a special report on energy', *The Economist*, 1–27 June: 22–5.

The Hindu. (2006) 'Minorities must have first claim on resources: Manmohan Singh', *The Hindu*, 19 December, http://www.hindu.com/2006/12/10/stories/2006121003651000.htm (accessed 13 September 2009).

The Tribune (2007) 'Anti-communal violence Bill under fire', 17 June.

Thomas Issac, T. M. and Chakraborty, P. (2008) 'Intergovernmental transfers: disquieting trends and the thirteenth finance commission', *Economic and Political Weekly*, 43: 86–92.

Tilak, J. (2009) 'Universalizing elementary education: a review of progress, policies and problems', in P. Rustagi (ed.) *Concerns, Conflicts, and Cohesions: Universalization of Elementary Education in India*, New Delhi: Oxford University Press.

Times of India. (2006) 'BJP, RSS, flay PM's remarks on minorities', *Times of India*, 9 December, http://timesofindia.indiatimes.com/articleshow/754456.cms (accessed 13 September 2009).

Times of India. (2010) 'Special law can bring rioters to book: experts', 24 August.

Tinbergen, J. (1967) *Development Planning*, London: World University Library.

UNESCO. (2008a) *Global Monitoring Report: Education For All: Will We Make It?*, Oxford and New York: Oxford University Press.

UNESCO. (2008b) *UNESCO Institute for Statistics*, http://www.uis.unesco.org/profiles/EN/EDU/countryProfile_en.aspx?code=3560 (accessed 10 February 2010)

United States Commission on International Religious Freedom. (2010) *Annual Report*, http://www.uscirf.gov/images/annual%20report%202010.pdf (accessed 23 December 2010).

UPA. (2004) *National Common Minimum Programme of the Government of India*, http://www.pmindia.nic.in/cmp.pdf (accessed 5 May 2011).

UPA. (2008) *UPA Government: Report to the People 2004–2008*, http://pmindia.nic.in/upa_en_2004-08.pdf (accessed 23 December 2010).

Upadhyaya, P. C. (1992) 'The politics of Indian secularism', *Modern Asian Studies*, 26:4, 815–53.

US Department of Energy. (various years) *International Energy Outlook*, Washington, DC: US Department of Energy.

Vanderbok, W. (1990) 'Critical elections, contained volatility and the Indian electorate', *Modern Asian Studies*, 24: 173–94.

Varadarajan, S. (2010) 'Assessing the NSA II: it's strategic culture that counts', *The Hindu*, 22 January, http://svaradarajan.blogspot.com/2010/01/asessing-nsa-ii-its-strategic-culture.html (accessed 16 June 2010).

Varshney, A. (1999) 'Mass politics or elite politics? India's economic reforms in comparative perspective' in Sachs, J., Varshney, A. and Bajpai, N. (eds) *India in the Era of Economic Reforms*, 222–58.

Waldman, A. (2005) 'Mile by mile, India paves a smoother road to its future', *New York Times*, 4 December: 33.
Warrick, J. (2009) 'Secret India–Pakistan talks cited', *Washington Post*, 22 February, http://www.washingtonpost.com/wp-dyn/content/article/2009/02/21/AR2009022101714.html (accessed 27 February 2010).
Watts, R. (1966) *New Federations: Experiments in the New Commonwealth*, Oxford: Clarendon Press.
Watts, R. (1999) *Comparing Federal Systems*, 2nd edn, Ontario: McGill University Press.
Watts, R. (2008) *Comparing Federal Systems*, Ontario: Queens McGill University Press.
Wax, E. (2009) 'India's Muslims see bias in housing', *Washington Post*, 19 April.
Weiner, M. (1990) *The Child and the State in India: Child Labor and Education Policy in Comparative Perspective*, Princeton, NJ: Princeton University Press.
Weisskopf, T. (2004) *Affirmative Action in the United States and India: A Comparative Perspective*, New York: Routledge.
Wilkinson, S. (2004) *Votes and Violence: Electoral Competition and Ethnic Riots*, New York: Cambridge University Press, 2004.
Wilkinson, S. (2005) 'Elections in India: behind the Congress comeback', *Journal of Democracy*, 16: 153–67.
Wilkinson, S. (2010) 'Making India's army "modern"', unpublished draft paper.
Wolff, J. (1998) 'Fairness, respect and egalitarian ethos', *Philosophy and Public Affairs*, 27 (2): 97–122.
Wonacott, P. (2009) 'Downturn heightens China–India tension on trade', *Wall Street Journal Asia*, 20 March, http://online.wsj.com/article/SB123749113639187441.htm (accessed 27 February 2010).
Wu, Y. and Zhou, Z. (2006) 'Changing bilateral trade between China and India', *Journal of Asian Economics*, 17: 509–18.
Xu, X. (2008) 'China, India and the United States: competition for petroleum resources and prospects for cooperation', in Emirates Centre for Strategic Studies and Research, *China, India & the United States: Competition for Energy Resources*, Abu Dhabi, United Arab Emirates: Emirates Centre for Strategic Studies and Research: 259–77.
Yadav, Y. and Palshikar, S. (2009a) 'Revisiting "third electoral system": mapping electoral trends in India, 2004–2009', in S. Shastri, K. C. Suri and Y. Yadav (eds) *Electoral Politics in Indian States: Lok Sabha Elections in 2004 and Beyond*, Delhi: Oxford University Press.
Yadav, Y. and Palshikar, S. (2009b) 'Between fortuna and virtu: explaining the Congress' ambiguous victory in 2009', *Economic and Political Weekly* 44: 33–46.
Young, I. M. (1990) *Justice and the Politics of Difference*, Princeton, NJ: Princeton University Press.

Index

Aam Bima Yojana scheme 15
Abhinav Bharat (AB) 137
Advani L.K. 71, 132
Afghanistan 26, 132, 134, 146
Africa 100, 102, 111
Aiyar, Mani Shankar 126
Amendments to the Constitution 34–5, 44–6, 55, 88–9, 93–4
Andhra Pradesh 38, 44, 75–7, 146
anti-conversion legislation 64
anti-discrimination 56, 61–2, 71–8, 87–8 See reservations
anti-terrorism 10, 131–48; attacks on India; 131, 134–8, 135–6t10.1; international cooperation on 103, 145–6; legislation 133, 141 ; reform of security institutions 141–5; role of Pakistan 104, 131, 133, 140–41; strategy on 138–9. See Mumbai attacks, Naxalites
Antony, A.K. 134, 139, 144
Arunachal Pradesh 111–12
Assam 31, 36, 68, 139

Babri Masjid mosque 69, 71; and Liberhan Commission 63, 71, 150
backward groups 86–7
Backward States 31, 36, 38, 81
Bahujan Samaj 5, 18
Bajrang Dal 70–71
Bangladesh; relations with 101–102, 135, 139, 146
Bharatiya Janata Party (BJP): and anti-terrorism, 141; attitude to minorities 18, 61–2, 69, 76, 78–9; differences with Congress Party 7–8, 18–23, 55; electoral competition, 2 4–5, 7–8, 18–23, 55; and federalism 37–8, and foreign policy 99–100, 111, 132; and minorities 18, 61–2, 69, 76, 78–9 and

secularism10, 55–6, 58, 90–5; and violence 63, 67–8, 70–1
Bhutan 135, 139
Bhutto, Benazir 107
Bihar 5, 25, 28, 31, 38, 68–9
Biju Janata Dal (BJD) 71
Border Security Forces 32

caste 65–6, 69, 73–9, 81–3, 86–95, 151–2
Central Advisory Board for Education (CABE) 45–51
Central Asia; relations with 100,111, 138
Central Bureau of Investigation 63
Central Educational Institutions (Reservations in Admission) Bill 2006 88
Christians 73; and discrimination 60, 62, 84; violence against, 63, 70, 150
Central Government Border Area Development Fund 37
centre-state relations (see federalism)
Chhattisgarh 23, 25, 38, 64, 137; Naxalites in 146–7
Chidambaram, P. 71, 134, 143, 148
China; relations with 10, 100–102, 107–12, 126–9, 151
clientelism, see post-clientelism
climate change 100, 110, 113, 117
coalitions: theory of 1–2, 6, 9–10; Indian experience of 37, 149; differences between UPA and NDA 37–8, 79–80, 94, 99–112, 129, 151
coastal security 132, 139, 143–5, 148
Common Minimum Programme (CMP): 8, 150–51; and anti-poverty measures 17; and anti-discrimination 81–2, 94; and anti-terrorism 132–4, 141 and education 39–44, 50–51; and energy policy 113–17; and federalism 30–31; and foreign policy 100–102; and language

policy 32, 38; and *Panchayati*, 35; and secularism 55, 57–9
communal violence 62–4, 68–71, 79
Communist Party of India (Marxist) (CPI (M)) 4, 30, 100
Congress Party: and elections 5, 79; and foreign policy 100–101; organisational decay of, 18, 153; and secularism 69, 80, and anti-discrimination 85–95, 152; and UPA, 2, 5–6, 39
corruption 1, 69, 134, 149, 153

Dalit parties 5, 56, 58, 152
de-saffronisation, 39, 44, 46, 57–9
Dravida Munnetra Khazagam (DMK) 4, 5, 30–32, 38

East Asia: relations with 102, 107, 108–9
economic liberalisation, 13, 15, 79, 87, 101, 151; and federalism 26–9, 33–8
education 8, 17, 39–52, 149–51; and CMP 8, 39–40, 44; curriculum reform 46–47; evaluation of record 40–4, 48–51; financial provisions 40–4, 49; institutional changes 45, 47; and minorities 57, 59–62, 72–6, 78–84; Midday Meals Scheme (MDM) 41–3, 49; right to education 43–4; personnel changes 45, 48; and *Sarva Shiksa Abhiyan (*SSA) 8, 41–4, 49 (see de-saffronisation)
energy 113–30: Common Minimum Programme 117; cooperation with China 126, 128; cooperation with US 124–8; energy legislation 119–20; energy policy: 121–9; energy security 10, 113–4, 117–19; energy sources 116; energy use projections 114–15, 125–6; India Energy Forum Report 2004 122–3; Iran-Pakistan-India Pipeline 127; role of private sector 117, 127–8; rural electrification 113, 120–1; subsidies 124; sustainability 10, 113, 122–3, 130
equality of opportunity, see anti-discrimination
European Union: relations with 101–2,114

federalism: 23, 27–38, 150–51
foreign policy, 9–10, 79, 99–112; and CMP 101. See US, China, Pakistan
Foreign Direct Investment 28
Forest Rights Act 2006 17–8

Gandhi, Indira 14, 27, 68, 72, 152
Gandhi, M.K. 66

Gandhi, Rajiv 14, 87
Gandhi, Rajmohan 87
Gandhi, Sonia 6, 14, 18, 84, 151
Gandhi, Rahul 13
Goa 4, 68
GoM Report on National Security 132, 142–4
Gram Sabha 35
Gujarat 7, 144–5; riots in 8, 9, 62–4, 68, 70–1, 150; terrorist attacks in 105, 136t10.1, 137

Haryana 13–14
Himachal Pradesh 4, 25, 69
Hindu: attacks by extremists131, 135–7, 151; attacks on 63, 68, 105, 135–6t10.1; nationalism 1, 56, 151–2
Hindutva 38, 56–8, 65–7, 151

Indian Council for Social Science Research (ICSSR) 58
Indian Jihadis, 10, 131, 134, 137–9
Indian Mujahideen (IM) 134, 137, 139
Indian National Congress, see Congress Party
Integrated Child Development Services (ICDS) 8, 39
Intelligence 10, 103, 132–4, 139, 142–5 146–7
Iran: relations with 101, 104, 127
Iran-Pakistan-India gas pipeline (IPI) 127
Iraq 101–2

Jaish-e-Mohamed (JeM) 132
Jammu and Kashmir 10, 31–2, 105, 131, 138; talks with Pakistan on 100, 105–6, 110, 135
Janata Dal coalition 9, 79–80, 83, 85–7, 91–5
Jharkhand 4, 24–5, 38, 147
Joshi, Murli Manohar, 58

Kargil crisis 36, 105, 132
Karnataka 4, 22–3, 25, 28, 57, 68, 70, 75
Kashmir, see Jammu and Kashmir
Kasuri, Khurshid 106
Kerala 4, 25, 57, 68, 76, 83
Kundu Committee on Diversity Index, 61, 82

Lashkar-e-Taiba (LeT) 132–4, 177–8, 140–41
Latin America: relations with 100, 102, 111
Left Front 29–30

Language policy 30–2, 38, 74
Local Government reform (see *Panchayati*)
Lok Jan Shakti Party (LJNSP) 2, 79

Madhya Pradesh 22–3, 25, 29, 38, 77
Maharastra 137
Mandal Commission report on backward classes 9, 152 ; debates on 79, 83–9, 91–3; implementation of 56, 65, 82–3
Manipur 139
Mayawati 79
Menon Committee on Equal Opportunities 61
Millenium Development Goals (MDG) 39, 42
Ministry for Human Resource Development (MHRD) 45–6, 58, 60
Ministry of Defence 37, 103
Ministry of Minority Affairs (MoMA) 60–61, 73, 75, 84–5
Ministry of Personnel, Public Grievances and Pensions 62, 84
Ministry of Power 119, 123
minorities see Christians, Muslims
Mishra Commission on religious and linguistic minorities 62, 150
Mizoram 4
Modi, Narendra 63, 70–1
Mukherjee, Pranab 101, 103, 106, 134
Mumbai: 2006 attacks 131, 137, 140; 2008 attacks 6, 10, 70, 131, 137, 148, 139–40,   Pakistani role in 100, 107, 111, 140–1; political response to 70, 100, 107, 111,127, 151; security changes in aftermath of 141–3
Musharraf, Perwez 105-7, 110, 132
Muslims: as backward group 57, 60–1, 65, 73–7; and reservations 62, 72, 75–6 83–4; status of 9, 56, 69–70, 72, 77–8; violence against 9, 68; violence by 70, 136, 137; voting behaviour of 65, 68, 70

Nagaland 139
Narasimha Rao, P.V. 15, 35, 69, 71, 99–101, 105, 108
Narayanan, M.K. 134, 142
Narayanan, K.R. 107
National Association for the Fundamental Right to Education 44
National Commission for Minority Educational Institutions 60
National Council for Educational Research and Training (NCERT) 47
National Curriculum Framework 47, 58

National Democratic Alliance (NDA): comparisons with UPA 9–10, 27, 35–8, 40, 85; elections 2, 4, 19–20; federalism 8; foreign policy 10, 39, 99–102, 105–112, 118–21; saffronisation 39, 44, 51, 57–8; secularism 8, 55, 58, 79; security 132–2; social justice 91–6
National Election Study 7, 13, 19–20
National Investigative Agency 10, 141–2, 148
National Rural Employment Guarantee Scheme (NREGS) 17, 19, 22–3, 35, 82
National Rural Health Mission 15, 19
Naxalites 10, 30, 131, 133, 135, 146–8
Nehru, Jaharlawal: and anti-discrimination 71, 76, 85–6, 89; and diplomacy 99; legacy 149–151; and secularism 55–6, 65–6
Nepal: relations with 101–2
North-Eastern states 31–2, 131, 133, 135, 138–9

Operation Bluestar 63
Operation Sadbhavana 32, 36–7
Orissa 25, 63–4, 70–71, 137, 147, 150
Other Backward Classes (OBC) 56–8, 81–3, 87–94, 151–2

Pachauri, R.K. 117, 123
Pakistan, relations with, 10, 100–2, 104–7, 110–12, 132–4, 139–41, 151 ; See Mumbai: attacks
Panchayati 33–6
Patil, Shivraj 133
Patnaik, Naveen 71
patronage democracy 18–9
policy implementation 6, 75, 151
policy style 151–2
polling data, see National Election Study
post-clientelism 7, 24–5, 152–3
Prime Minister (see Singh, Dr. Manmohan)
Public Study Group (PSG) 47, 49
Punchhi Commission on centre-state relations 33–4
Punjab 13–4, 25, 63
Rajasthan 4, 22–3
Raje, Vasundhara 94
Rashtriya Jagran Manch (RJM) 137, 139
Rashtriya Janata Dal (RJD) 2, 5
Rashtriya Sama Vikas Yogna (RSVY) 36
Rashtriya Swashtya Bima Yojana programme 15
Rashtriya Swayamsevak Sangh (RSS) 70, 78

Religious minorities: see Christians, Muslims
Report to the People 32-3
Research and Analysis Wing 134
reservations 9; and CMP 81-2; Constituent Assembly debates on 85-8, 93; evolution of Congress view 79-81, 83-91, 152; and social justice 61-2; religiously-based 65-6, 72, 74-9, 83-4
Right to Information Act 2005 17
Roy, Arjun 36

Sachar Committee 9, 61, 65, 71-5, 77-8, 84
saffronisation, see de-saffronisation
Samajwadi Party 2
Sangh Parivar 71
Sarkaria Commission on centre-state relations 27, 31
Sarvadarma sabha 56
Scheduled Castes and Tribes (SC/ST) 18, 56, 81-3, 93-4
Secularism 6-7, 53-95; CMP 57-8, evaluation of UPA record, 62-7, 79-80, 150, 151; theories of 55-7. See Nehru
security, see anti-terrorism
Shahabuddin, Syed 72, 76
Sharif, Nawaz 105
Shiv Sena 79
Sikhs 60, 62-3, 68, 71, 73, 150
Sikkim 108
Sikkim Democratic Front, 2
Singh, Arjun 88-9, 94
Singh, Jaswant 102, 107
Singh, Kalyan 71
Singh, Manmohan Dr: anti-Christian riots 70; anti-Sikh riots 63; backward areas 36; corruption, 149; economic liberaliser 14-5, 101; energy 119, 122, 124-5 foreign policy, 101, 104; Gujarat massacres 66; Iran 104; minorities 78, 90; national security 133-4; Naxalites 146; Pakistan 106, 110, 140; policy style 110-12, 151-2; reservations 84; social democrat 14-15; terrorism 135, 140 United States 102-4, 124-5
Singh, Mulayam 71
Singh, V.P. 91-2, 94
social democracy 7, 14-5, 81, 152-3
Solanki, Sunil 70
South Asian Association for Regional Cooperation (SAARC) 102, 109, 129, 132, 145-6
South East Asia; relations with 102-3, 129
Sri Lanka 101-2
Students Islamic Movement of India (SIMI) 77, 137

Tamil Nadu 30-31, 68
Tamils 30-2, 38, 101-2
Telengana 38
Telugu Desam Party 4
terrorism, see anti-terrorism
Trade talks 100, 102, 110
TRS 38
tsunami relief operations 103
Tytler, Jadish 63, 71

United States Commission on International Religious Freedom 63-4
United States of America; intelligence cooperation 146; nuclear deal with 6, 30, 103-4, 110-12, 124-7; relations with 10, 99-105, 110-12
Universities Grants Commission (UGC) 58-9
Uttar Pradesh 5, 18, 25, 29, 38, 71, 73, 77
Uttarakhand 4, 25, 38

Vajpayee, A.B 100, 105-8, 132
Vishwa Hindu Parishad (VHP) 70

Wada Na Todo Abhiyan 19
West Asia relations with 101-2
West Bengal 25, 29-31, 147
Women, and CMP 81; legislation 17, 83, 94; and reservations 81, 83, 94, 151

Yadav, Yogendra 19, 21, 23